Unraveling the
Complexities of
Social Life

Unraveling the Complexities of Social Life

A Festschrift in Honor of Robert B. Zajonc

Edited by
John A. Bargh and
Deborah K. Apsley

DECADE
of BEHAVIOR

American Psychological Association
Washington, DC

Published by
American Psychological Association
750 First Street, NE
Washington, DC 20002

150
Un 7

Copies may be ordered from
APA Order Department
P.O. Box 92984
Washington, DC 20090-2984

In the U.K., Europe, Africa, and the Middle East, copies may be ordered from
American Psychological Association
3 Henrietta Street
Covent Garden, London
WC2E 8LU England

Typeset in Berkeley Book by Automated Graphic Systems, Inc., White Plains, MD

Printer: Automated Graphic Systems, Inc., White Plains, MD
Cover Designer: Naylor Design, Washington, DC
Technical/Production Editors: Eleanor Inskip and Emily Welsh

The opinions and statements published are the responsibility of the authors, and such opinions and statements do not necessarily represent the policies of the APA.

Library of Congress Cataloging-in-Publication Data
Unraveling the complexities of social life : a festschrift in honor of Robert B. Zajonc / editors, John A. Bargh, Deborah K. Apsley.
    p. cm.
    Includes bibliographical references and index.
    ISBN 1-55798-692-4 (cloth : alk. paper)
    1. Psychology—Congresses. 2. Social psychology—Congresses. I. Zajonc, Robert B. (Robert Boleslaw), 1923- II. Bargh, John A. III. Apsley, Deborah K.
BF121 .U57   2000
150—dc21   00-033178

British Library Cataloguing-in-Publication Data
A CIP record is available from the British Library.

Printed in the United States of America
First Edition

APA Science Volumes

Attribution and Social Interaction: The Legacy of Edward E. Jones

Best Methods for the Analysis of Change: Recent Advances, Unanswered Questions, Future Directions

Cardiovascular Reactivity to Psychological Stress and Disease

The Challenge in Mathematics and Science Education: Psychology's Response

Changing Employment Relations: Behavioral and Social Perspectives

Children Exposed to Marital Violence: Theory, Research, and Applied Issues

Cognition: Conceptual and Methodological Issues

Cognitive Bases of Musical Communication

Cognitive Dissonance: Progress on a Pivotal Theory in Social Psychology

Conceptualization and Measurement of Organism–Environment Interaction

Converging Operations in the Study of Visual Selective Attention

Creative Thought: An Investigation of Conceptual Structures and Processes

Developmental Psychoacoustics

Diversity in Work Teams: Research Paradigms for a Changing Workplace

Emotion and Culture: Empirical Studies of Mutual Influence

Emotion, Disclosure, and Health

Evolving Explanations of Development: Ecological Approaches to Organism–Environment Systems

Examining Lives in Context: Perspectives on the Ecology of Human Development

Global Prospects for Education: Development, Culture, and Schooling

Hostility, Coping, and Health

Measuring Patient Changes in Mood, Anxiety, and Personality Disorders: Toward a Core Battery

Occasion Setting: Associative Learning and Cognition in Animals

Organ Donation and Transplantation: Psychological and Behavioral Factors

Origins and Development of Schizophrenia: Advances in Experimental Psychopathology

The Perception of Structure

Perspectives on Socially Shared Cognition

Psychological Testing of Hispanics

Psychology of Women's Health: Progress and Challenges in Research and Application

Researching Community Psychology: Issues of Theory and Methods

The Rising Curve: Long-Term Gains in IQ and Related Measures

Sexism and Stereotypes in Modern Society: The Gender Science of Janet Taylor Spence

Sleep and Cognition

Sleep Onset: Normal and Abnormal Processes

Stereotype Accuracy: Toward Appreciating Group Differences

Stereotyped Movements: Brain and Behavior Relationships

Studying Lives Through Time: Personality and Development

The Suggestibility of Children's Recollections: Implications for Eyewitness Testimony

Taste, Experience, and Feeding: Development and Learning

Temperament: Individual Differences at the Interface of Biology and Behavior

Through the Looking Glass: Issues of Psychological Well-Being in Captive Nonhuman Primates

Uniting Psychology and Biology: Integrative Perspectives on Human Development

Viewing Psychology as a Whole: The Integrative Science of William N. Dember

APA Decade of Behavior Volumes

Computational Modeling of Behavior in Organizations: The Third Scientific Discipline

Unraveling the Complexities of Social Life: A Festschrift in Honor of Robert B. Zajonc

Contents

Contributors   ix

Foreword   xi

Preface   xiii

About Robert B. Zajonc   xv

CHAPTER 1   Introduction
             John A. Bargh and Deborah K. Apsley   3

CHAPTER 2   Seek Out the Magician: Contrarian Tricks of Mere Simplicity
             Make Affect Appear and Disappear From Social Psychology
             Susan T. Fiske   11

PART 1: THE ANTI-MEDIATIONAL STANCE

CHAPTER 3   The Psychology of the Mere
             John A. Bargh   25

CHAPTER 4   Feeling Without Thinking: Affective Primacy and the
             Nonconscious Processing of Emotion
             Sheila T. Murphy   39

CHAPTER 5   Relational Schema Activation: Does Bob Zajonc Ever Scowl at You
             From the Back of Your Mind?
             Mark W. Baldwin   55

PART 2: AFFECT AND COGNITION

CHAPTER 6   The Nature of Pleasure
             Nico H. Frijda   71

CHAPTER 7   The Affect System and Racial Prejudice
             John T. Cacioppo and Gary G. Berntson   95

CHAPTER 8   How and When Preferences Influence Inferences: A Motivated
             Hypothesis-Testing Framework
             Yaacov Trope and Melissa J. Ferguson   111

PART 3: PERSONAL AGENCY

CHAPTER 9   Human Infancy and the Beginnings of Human Competence
Jerome Bruner   133

CHAPTER 10   Control Preferences
Janusz Grzelak   141

CHAPTER 11   Monitoring Adaptation to Social Change: Research at the Institute
for Social Studies
Grazyna Wieczorkowska and Eugene Burnstein   155

CONCLUSIONS

CHAPTER 12   The Art of Bob Zajonc and the Communicative Basis of Prejudice
Claude M. Steele   175

APPENDIX: The Publications of Robert B. Zajonc   187

Author Index   197
Subject Index   203
About the Editors   209

Contributors

Deborah K. Apsley, BS, School of Information, University of Michigan, Ann Arbor

Mark W. Baldwin, PhD, Department of Psychology, McGill University, Montreal, Quebec, Canada

John A. Bargh, PhD, Department of Psychology, New York University

Gary G. Berntson, PhD, Department of Psychology, Ohio State University, Columbus

Jerome Bruner, PhD, School of Law and Department of Psychology, New York University

Eugene Burnstein, PhD, Institute for Social Research and Department of Psychology, University of Michigan, Ann Arbor

John T. Cacioppo, PhD, Department of Psychology, University of Chicago

Melissa J. Ferguson, MA, Department of Psychology, New York University

Susan T. Fiske, PhD, Department of Psychology, University of Massachusetts, Amherst

Nico H. Frijda, PhD, Department of Psychology, Free University of Amsterdam, The Netherlands

Janusz Grzelak, PhD, Department of Psychology, University of Warsaw, Warsaw, Poland

Sheila T. Murphy, PhD, Annenberg School of Communication and Department of Psychology, University of Southern California, Los Angeles

Claude M. Steele, PhD, Department of Psychology, Stanford University

Yaacov Trope, PhD, Department of Psychology, New York University

Grazyna Wieczorkowska, PhD, Institute for Social Science and Department of Psychology, University of Warsaw, Warsaw, Poland

From left to right—Back Row: Sheila T. Murphy, Tory Higgins, John T. Cacioppo, John A. Bargh, Yaacov Trope, and Mark W. Baldwin. *Front Row*: Nico H. Frijda, Susan T. Fiske, Hazel Markus, Robert B. Zajonc, Janusz Grzelak, Jerome Bruner, Deborah K. Apsley.

Foreword

In early 1988, the APA Science Directorate began its sponsorship of what has become an exceptionally successful activity in support of psychological science—the APA Scientific Conferences program. This program has showcased some of the most important topics in psychological science, and the conference participants have included many leading figures in the field.

As we enter a new century, it seems fitting that we begin with a new face on this book series—that of the Decade of Behavior (DoB). The DoB is a major interdisciplinary initiative designed to promote the contributions of the behavioral and social sciences to address some of our most important societal challenges and will occur from 2000 to 2010. Although a major effort of the initiative will be related to informing the public about the contributions of these fields, other activities will be put into place to reach fellow scientists. Hence, the series that was the "APA Science Series" will be continued as the "Decade of Behavior Series." This represents one element in APA's efforts to promote the Decade of Behavior initiative as one of the partner organizations.

Please note the Decade of Behavior logo on the inside jacket flap, as well as on the title page. We expect this logo will become a familiar sight over the next few years. For additional information about the DoB, please visit http://www.decadeofbehavior.org.

As part of the sponsorship agreement with APA, conference organizers commit themselves not only to the conference itself, but also to editing a scholarly volume that results from the meeting. This book is such a volume. Over the course of the past 12 years, we have partnered with 44 universities to sponsor 57 conferences on a wide variety of topics of interest to psychological scientists. The APA Science Directorate looks forward to continuing this program and to sponsoring other conferences in the years ahead.

We are very pleased that this important contribution to the literature was supported in part by the Scientific Conferences program. Congratulations to the editors and contributors on their sterling effort.

Richard McCarthy, PhD
Executive Director for Science

Virginia E. Holt
Assistant Executive Director for Science

Preface

Festschrifts are typically given in the 70th year of great scholars who have dramatically influenced their field during their career. Often they are seen as "retirement parties" and so have a "looking backward" or reminiscent quality to them. This may be why it took us 5 years after Robert Zajonc's 70th birthday to finally convince him to allow us to hold a *Festschrift* in his honor. Bob has not retired and shows no signs of ever doing so. At his insistence, and with our own enthusiastic commitment as editors, the contributions to the *Festschrift* would not be backward-looking reminiscences but state-of-the-art analyses of contemporary psychological research problems. The resulting chapters in this volume are, indeed, as much forward-looking and prospective as they are informed by the theoretical and empirical advances of the past and present. And as the authors of those chapters make clear, many of the most important past and present influences on their thinking and research agenda are attributable to Dr. Zajonc.

The *Festschrift* conference itself, held May 15 and 16, 1998, in Ann Arbor, Michigan, drew an audience of hundreds from near and far. We could not have organized and held that conference were it not for the generous joint financial and administrative support of the American Psychological Association (APA) Science Directorate and the University of Michigan—specifically Sophia Birdas and William Howell at APA, and Patricia Gurin (chair of the Psychology Department), James Jackson (director of the Research Center for Group Dynamics), and Earl Lewis (dean of the Rackham Graduate School) at the University of Michigan. The intellectual atmosphere was electric, and many in the audience participated as well with questions and discussion after each presentation. It was a family atmosphere in more ways than one—not only did many of Bob's former graduate students and colleagues attend, so did his far-flung family, and it made for a weekend that all of us who attended will never forget and will always treasure.

About Robert B. Zajonc

Robert B. Zajonc was born in Lodz, Poland, in 1923. After World War II, he attended the Sorbonne in Paris and then came to the United States in 1948—directly to Ann Arbor, Michigan, where he completed his undergraduate and graduate work at the University of Michigan's Research Center for Group Dynamics (RCGD). Dr. Zajonc's mentor at the RCGD was Dorwin (Doc) Cartwright. After receiving his PhD in 1955, and for the next 40 years, Dr. Zajonc was on the faculty of the University of Michigan and was also affiliated with the RCGD and the Institute of Social Research, serving as directors of both. In 1994 Dr. Zajonc moved to Stanford University, where he is professor of psychology.

Dr. Zajonc's research spans a number of theoretical problems, such as the nature of the relationship between cognition and communication, the effect of the presence of others on one's performance, emotional influences including unconscious effects, the emergence of preferences, the aggregate pattern of intellectual performance scores as they are influenced by changing family configurations, and the nature and causes of genocide. The Appendix contains a complete list of his books, journal articles, and chapters.

Dr. Zajonc's career is distinguished by many awards, including the Distinguished Scientific Contribution Award from the American Psychological Association (APA) in 1978, the Distinguished Scientist Award from the Society for Experimental Social Psychology, Doctorates Honoris Causa from the University of Leuven and the University of Warsaw, and the American Association for the Advancement of Science Research Prize (shared with G. Markus) in 1975 for his work on birth order and intellectual development. His curriculum vitae also includes many major service contributions to the field—for 8 years he was the associate editor of the *Journal of Abnormal and Social Psychology;* he is a past president of Division 1 (General Psychology) of the APA and a past president of the Society for Experimental Social Psychology; he has served on the APA Board of Scientific Affairs; and he was a member of the National Academy of Sciences mission to the then Soviet Union in 1976. He was also instrumental in founding the Institute for Social Studies at the University of Warsaw.

Unraveling the Complexities of Social Life

CHAPTER 1

Introduction

John A. Bargh
Deborah K. Apsley

S ocial psychology, Robert Zajonc often reminds us (e.g., Zajonc, 1980a), has always been cognitive; has always been about affective experience such as feelings, goals, and desires; and has always been about the self. In fact, it was this focus on internal experiences such as feelings and beliefs, and the "about-self-ness," that gave social psychology its natural concern with internal psychological processes mediating between the outside environment and a person's behavioral or other responses to that environment—while the rest of experimental psychology, in the time of behaviorism, was in denial as to the importance and even reality of these internal mediating processes. The "cognitive revolution" against behaviorism in the 1960s did not occur in social psychology because there was no need for it. Concern with internal cognitive processes had begun long before: in works in the 1930s by Louis Thurstone, Rensis Likert, and others on measuring a person's internal attitudes (literally, how the individual *feels* about different people and things); the New Look research begun by Jerome Bruner and Leo Postman in the mid-1940s on the effects of internal motivational and need states on perception of objects; Leon Festinger's focus on internal processes and standards of comparing oneself with other people, as well as his theory of cognitive dissonance about the relations between cognitive beliefs and the motivational states that inconsistent relations put in motion; and of course Kurt Lewin's ideas of the life space and the "psychological situation" and how it, and not the actual external situation, drove human behavior and other responses to that situation.

Kurt Lewin founded the Research Center for Group Dynamics, which had recently moved to the University of Michigan from the Massachusetts Institute of Technology when Bob Zajonc arrived in 1948. Zajonc had been a refugee during the Second World War, and afterwards he landed in Paris to study at the Sorbonne. He arrived in Ann Arbor and began his studies with Dorwin ("Doc") Cartwright, who was one of Lewin's proteges along with Leon Festinger, Harold Kelley, Stanley Schachter, Harold Gerard, and many other famous, historically important social psychologists.

It was in this heady milieu that Zajonc learned how to think about social psychological issues at a time when how exactly one *should* think about them was largely uncharted territory (see, e.g., the interesting and entertaining account of that early era in Gilbert, 1998). Even among such innovators, Zajonc made his own mark with a 1955 dissertation on "Cognitive Tuning in Communication." This work, demonstrating how people organize information in memory differently depending on whether they are communicating the information to another person or are the recipient of it, was a generation ahead of its time. It was not until 1981 that Tory Higgins reintroduced and expanded on the idea in his model of the "communication game," which became an influential model in human communications theory and research. Beyond the core idea that an individual's communicative purpose within a social interaction would influence the individual's mental organization of the relevant information, another major contribution of this work—startling as it was done in 1955, before any of the early shots of the cognitive revolution in experimental psychology had been fired—was the highly sophisticated methodology Zajonc developed with which to objectively measure the organization of a person's knowledge about a certain subject matter: a way to measure its complexity and its internal organization. It was a dramatic and sudden leap because Zajonc did not measure, as was standard practice at the time, single attitudes of liking or disliking, or single opinions or beliefs, but rather the entire internal structure of complicated knowledge representations.

And Now for Something Completely Different . . .

But Zajonc was to show very early on that he was not a single-minded proponent of one and only one meta-theory. His next major contribution was to solve the very old, puzzling problem of social facilitation effects—not with a cognitive explanation, but, contrarian that he is (see Fiske, chap. 2, this volume), with principles of Hullian drive theory (of all things at the time! Was he not aware that there was a cognitive revolution going on against those behaviorist models?). If there was a research topic that is the core issue in social psychology, in fact which distinguishes social psychology from other branches of psychology, it is the question of how the presence of others affects psychological processes and behavior. How does merely being in the presence of other people change (or not) how people think and behave?

The long-standing conundrum within social facilitation research was that some studies had shown that the presence of others improved task performance and an about equal number of studies had shown that the presence of others hurt task performance. Zajonc (1965) elegantly argued in the journal *Science* that Hull's "Habit × Drive" principle could account for the whole messy literature: That is, the presence of others increased a person's arousal or drive level, and this made the dominant response more likely in that situation. For the studies in which facilitating effects of the presence of others had been observed, the task was relatively easy (meaning that the dominant response of the person was the correct response); for the other studies in which the audience had hindered performance, the task had been novel or difficult (so that the dominant response of the person was the incorrect one). Zajonc had again launched another social psychological research ship, one that would sail productively in the field for the next 20 years.

In 1968, two more landmark papers were published: the first-ever chapter in the *Handbook of Social Psychology* on cognitive theories, and the monograph in the *Journal of Personality and Social Psychology* on the "mere-exposure effect" (Zajonc, 1968a, 1968b). This latter idea—that attitudes (preferences) can be formed based merely on the frequency with which one encounters the object of the attitude, with frequency increasing liking—was the beginning of Zajonc's career-long interest in the development and operation of affective processes outside of the person's knowledge and awareness. In many ways, this article could be considered the seminal one for the now burgeoning research in social psychology (and elsewhere) into nonconscious influences. The ensuing debate over whether conscious deliberations did or did not mediate the mere-exposure effect (see Birnbaum & Mellers, 1979a, 1979b; Moreland & Zajonc, 1979) led Zajonc and his colleagues to demonstrate the effect occurred even with subliminal presentations of the novel stimuli (e.g., Kunst-Wilson & Zajonc, 1980), such that the experimental participants never saw, and later could not recognize, the very stimuli they reported liking as a function of how many times it had been presented.

In 1980 Zajonc expanded on the general idea of nonconscious preference formation in his classic and highly cited *American Psychologist* article, "Feeling and Thinking: Preferences Need No Inferences" (Zajonc, 1980b). The subliminal presentation technique and the important breakthrough that social judgments such as preference judgments did not have to be produced only through conscious reasoning processes influenced the research careers of several of the authors in this volume— Mark Baldwin, John Bargh, and Sheila Murphy, directly—and it should be noted that the historical roots of both the method and the theoretical breakthrough are in the 1940s and 1950s "New Look" research on perception founded by another contributor to this volume, Jerome Bruner.

When the "Feeling and Thinking" paper was published, no neuroanatomical or neurophysiological evidence existed to support Zajonc's hypothesis that emotion and cognition, although in virtually continuous interaction, are in fact separate systems, and that the affective system often commands temporal primacy. The evidence is now in clear agreement with Zajonc's 20-year-old conjectures.

Zajonc has continued his research on unconscious emotional determinants and influences throughout the 1980s and 1990s, and it remains a theme of his research today (see Murphy, chap. 4, this volume). But there were other major contributions: the work with Greg Markus on modeling intellectual development on the basis of birth order and family size (e.g., Zajonc & Markus, 1975), which led to predictions about the rise and fall of children's test performance (e.g., the Scholastic Aptitude Test [SAT]) over the years, and his 1982 analysis of cooperation and competition tendencies in the overarching framework of interdependence (see Grzelak, chap. 10, this volume). As there is no chapter in this volume dealing specifically with the birth order and intelligence work, and also perhaps because one of us worked on that project during his first 2 years of graduate school, a few sentences here about it are in order.

First, like most of Zajonc's major research statements, his *Psychological Review* article on birth order and intellectual performance was a tour de force (Zajonc & Markus, 1975) and it sparked a great deal of subsequent research. But more important, it was a serious attempt to understand and also explain the disturbing and worrisome decline in SAT scores in the United States that had been going on for 20 years or more. Unlike all the popular explanations of the time—television, permissiveness, even fluoride in the water system—Zajonc boldly predicted in a 1976 *Science* article that the decline would stop (around 1980), and then, in fact, reverse course so that scores would increase every year. And 20 years later (Zajonc & Mullally, 1997), Zajonc was able to present the actual SAT scores for that period and show that this is exactly what had happened.

About the Book

The chapters in this volume are organized around three central themes in Zajonc's research. What is more, Susan Fiske and Claude Steele provide us with bookends for them. Fiske (chap. 2) introduces the reader to Zajonc's theory and research by placing it in historical context and by tracing its subsequent influence on the field. But she also introduces the reader to Zajonc as a scientist, and how he thinks, through an insightful analysis of his particular choices of research problems over time.

Part 1 of the volume concerns the legacy of Zajonc's "antimediational" stance concerning the role of deliberate, conscious reasoning processes in important social psychological phenomena. That is, in his work on the *mere-exposure effect* of repeated experience of an attitude object (e.g., a new song on the radio) on the favorability of one's attitude toward it, and the *mere presence* of another person as a determinant of social facilitation effects on performance, Zajonc pushed a phenomenon to its unconditional limits. It needed only or *merely* something to happen in the environment to happen inside the person's head; no mediating cognitive transformation of the event or deliberate, conscious thought or evaluation of the event was needed.

The authors of the chapters in Part 1 have all been deeply influenced by this approach to research. In chapter 3, John Bargh relates how this approach of questioning and testing the necessity of intervening conscious processes has long guided his own research on "automatic" or nonconscious determinants of social judgment, motivation, and behavior. Next, Sheila Murphy (chap. 4) similarly relates her ongoing research program with Zajonc on nonconscious affective reactions to stimuli. And in chapter 5, Mark Baldwin describes a study he performed while visiting at the University of Michigan in the 1980s on the importance of significant others in one's life as evaluation standards—a study in which Zajonc had a starring role as a subliminal stimulus. The studies discussed by these three researchers attest to the varied and pervasive ways that one's affective experience, self-esteem, and even social behavior occur outside of (and not mediated by) one's conscious, intentional control.

The second main theme concerns the nature of affect and its interplay with cognitive processes. One enduring research question that has dominated the recent study of both social psychology (attitude and impression formation) and emotion psychology is that of the relation between affect and cognition, between feeling and thinking. Zajonc's 1980 *American Psychologist* essay (see Zajonc, 1980b) on that topic set the agenda for that research. By questioning the strongly held assumption that deliberations precede and mediate evaluations—that thinking generates feelings—Zajonc posed a challenge to dominant models in many areas of psychology.

The three chapters in Part 2 of the book focus on this question. In chapter 6, Nico Frijda provides a trenchant essay on the nature of pleasure, dissecting the meaning of the term in several languages and in doing so illuminating a concept that is rather dry and impoverished in English. He focuses in particular on Zajonc's idea that feelings can be unconscious, and he considers what that means for the nature of the concept of feelings itself. Next, in chapter 7, John Cacioppo and Gary Berntson describe the remarkable advances in the neuropsychological understanding of the separate affective processing system that Zajonc proposed 20 years ago; their chapter makes clear that what was a controversial and provocative proposal then is a well-established scientific fact today. Yaacov Trope and Melissa Ferguson then focus, in chapter 8, on one important corollary of Zajonc's (1980b) position that affect often precedes cognition: how one's initial and immediate preferences in many ways guide the ostensibly objective and impartial inferential processes that follow.

The final section of the book deals with another side of Zajonc that seems to contradict his "antimediational" tendency mentioned earlier, namely, his writings on the role of personal agency. In these, there is an emphasis on personal control, cognitive manipulation and transformation of one's world (e.g., the 1985 *Handbook of Social Psychology* chapter on "The Cognitive Perspective in Social Psychology"; see Markus & Zajonc, 1985), and goal striving in the face of adversity. Three chapters share the focus on personal agency. The first of these, chapter 9, is Jerome Bruner's historical summary of the exploratory and agentic behavior of infants, as opposed to the earlier view that they were only rather passive recipients of stimulation. Next, Janusz Grzelak (see chap. 10) describes his own and related research on an individual's preferences for control over situations and interpersonal outcomes, the conflict between these goals and the group interest, and the bases for the resolution of this conflict. Finally, Grazyna Wieczorkowska and Eugene Burnstein (see chap. 11) analyze how individuals adapt psychologically to sudden and massive sociopolitical change in a society, as occurred in Eastern Europe over the past decade. They argue that what is most important to successful adaptation when the group's goal is blocked by powerful political forces or by other circumstances is the perception that there are alternative routes to attaining the group goal. In this chapter, Wieczorkowska and Burnstein also relate the critical role played by Zajonc in the establishment of the Institute for Social Studies (ISS) in Warsaw, modeled after the Institute for Social Research (ISR) at the University of Michigan. (It is interesting to note, while on the topic of personal agency, that the founding and purpose of ISS were very similar to Kurt Lewin's founding of the Research Center for Group Dynamics, now part of ISR—that is, a focus on important societal problems and what can be done to better understand and ultimately ameliorate them.)

Claude Steele concludes the book in chapter 12 by providing an account of Zajonc's research career from the vantage point of a close and long-time colleague. He brings together many of the seemingly disparate strands of Zajonc's research career, its major themes—most important, Zajonc's early work on cognitive tuning in communication—and applies them to his own research program on the nature and resolution of prejudice. We have included an Appendix that chronicles Zajonc's career by presenting citations to his five books and more than 100 journal articles and chapters.

A Preference for Simplicity

The many and differing ways that Zajonc continues to influence generations of social psychologists is one theme that weaves itself through the book. As seen especially in the opening and concluding chapters by Susan Fiske and by Claude Steele, some of these influences were in the way he approaches a scientific problem: taking a "contrarian" attitude toward the dominant assumptions of the field, for example, forcing the rest of us to defend them logically and empirically instead of allowing us to hold them complacently and nonskeptically.

Another of Zajonc's hallmarks is to take complex, even irritatingly perplexing problems and find the surprisingly simple, basic explanations underlying them. It is remarkable how often, and consistently, Zajonc manages to find the simple and elegant solution in the midst of confusion and disorder. Several of the present authors emphasize, however, that these solutions did not appear casually or magically out of whole cloth, but emerged only after a sustained period of intense, focused Zajoncian consideration of the problem. (As a famous professional golfer remarked a few years ago, "Golf is simple. You hit the ball into the hole. [Pause.] I didn't say it was *easy*, I said it was simple!")

But there are apparent contradictions here too: how someone who championed the important role of mediating cognitive processes in social psychology and who had in fact provided one of the first studies of an interpersonal influence on cognitive structure in his 1955 dissertation could then, just 10 years later, propose a galvanizing neobehaviorist approach to social facilitation effects. And then take the side, for years in the debate that followed, that social facilitation effects did *not* involve the mental transformation of the situation into an evaluative one (as his opponents argued, that the effect on arousal and behavior was mediated by a person's worries about how others think of the person).

In many ways, Zajonc's 1965 *Science* article proposing his model of social facilitation was, relative to the evaluation apprehension alternative, quite analogous to Daryl Bem's 1965 article arguing for a behavioristic reinterpretation of cognitive dissonance effects. Both took a contrarian stance, very much against the cognitive *Zeitgeist* of the mid-1960s, saying "not so fast" to those positing cognitive processes mediating between the external situation on the one hand, and one's behavior and beliefs about it on the other. And indeed, internal contradiction or not, Zajonc's skepticism toward the necessity of conscious deliberative mediation of social psychological phenomena is another stamp he has put on contemporary psychology.

References

Birnbaum, M. H., & Mellers, B. A. (1979a). One-mediator model of exposure effects is still viable. *Journal of Personality and Social Psychology, 37,* 1090–1096.

Birnbaum, M. H., & Mellers, B. A. (1979b). Stimulus recognition may mediate exposure effects. *Journal of Personality and Social Psychology, 37,* 391–394.

Gilbert, D. T. (1998). Ordinary personology. In D. T. Gilbert, S. T. Fiske, & G. Lindzey (Eds.), *Handbook of social psychology* (4th ed., pp. 89–150). Boston: McGraw-Hill.

Higgins, E. T. (1981). The "communication game": Implications or social cognition and persuasion. In E. T. Higgins, C. P. Herman, & M. P. Zanna (Eds.), *Social cognition: The Ontario symposium* (Vol. 1, pp. 343–392). Hillsdale, NJ: Erlbaum.

Kunst-Wilson, W. R., & Zajonc, R. B. (1980). Affective discrimination of stimuli that cannot be recognized. *Science, 207,* 557–558.

Markus, H., & Zajonc, R. B. (1985). The cognitive perspective in social psychology. In G. Lindzey & E. Aronson (Eds.), *Handbook of social psychology* (3rd ed., Vol. 1, pp. 137–230). New York: Random House.

Moreland, R. L., & Zajonc, R. B. (1979). Exposure effects may not depend on stimulus recognition. *Journal of Personality and Social Psychology, 37,* 1085–1089.

Zajonc, R. B. (1955). *Cognitive tuning in communication.* Unpublished doctoral dissertation, University of Michigan.

Zajonc, R. B. (1965). Social facilitation. *Science, 149,* 269–274.

Zajonc, R. B., (1968a). Cognitive theories in social psychology. In G. Lindzey & E. Aronson (Eds.), *Handbook of social psychology* (2nd ed., pp. 319–411). New York: Random House.

Zajonc, R. B. (1968b). Attitudinal effects of mere exposure. *Journal of Personality and Social Psychology*, Monograph Supplement, 9, 1–27.

Zajonc, R. B. (1976). Family configuration and intelligence. *Science, 192*, 227–236.

Zajonc, R. B. (1980a). Cognition and social cognition: A historical perspective. In L. Festinger (Ed.), *Retrospections on social psychology* (pp. 180–204). New York: Oxford University Press.

Zajonc, R. B. (1980b). Feeling and thinking: Preferences need no inferences. *American Psychologist, 35*, 151–175.

Zajonc, R. B. (1982). Altruism, envy, competitiveness, and the common good. In V. Derlega & Grzelak (Eds.), *Cooperation and helping behavior: Theories and research* (pp. 417–437). New York: Academic Press.

Zajonc, R. B., & Markus, G. B. (1975). Birth order and intellectual development. *Psychological Review, 82*, 74–88.

Zajonc, R. B., & Mullally, P. R. (1997). Birth order: Reconciling conflicting effects. *American Psychologist, 52*, 685–699.

CHAPTER 2

Seek Out the Magician: Contrarian Tricks of Mere Simplicity Make Affect Appear and Disappear From Social Psychology

Susan T. Fiske

> People like to make sense of their world, but they
> also seek out the magician to be entertained by
> incongruity. (Zajonc, 1960a, p. 380)

The science of Zajonc possesses a magic that mesmerizes his audiences again and again, compelling them to try his tricks in their home laboratories. His work fascinates social psychologists (and wider audiences) by two brilliant lifelong techniques: a contrarian approach and mere simplicity. In the pursuit of these two strategies, Zajonc has, with a flourish, made affect appear and disappear from the stage of social psychology. Social psychologists have historically leaned toward a relative emphasis on the affective or the cognitive side of social phenomena over the 20th century, and Zajonc has pointed the way most times, his influence owing to his two hallmarks.

First, the contrarian strategy: Normally an investment strategy that entails putting money into stocks that oppose the conventional wisdom, a contrarian approach likewise profits both magic and science. In each arena, investing virtuosity where others are not currently looking simultaneously innovates and impresses the audience. Robert Zajonc dislikes too much agreement, too much consensus, because they make for dull conversation. His work always aims to go where others are not. Although he starts out alone, the others soon follow, and then he again seeks more deserted venues. An overview of his major contributions reveals a brilliant new idea about every 5 years, just when his previous work starts to attract a crowd. He follows each idea with convincing arguments and data, but his contrarian approach keeps each project surprising anew.

In addition, his work follows "mere" simplicity as a rule. As other contributors to this volume will note, parsimony pervades Zajonc's most inspired insights. Each idea he has brought to the field can be summarized in a sentence, and not a very complicated sentence: Simplicity constitutes its brilliance. Zajonc explains that his work has been

> concerned with the four-letter word "mere." I happen to have used this seemingly innocent word on two separate occasions and on both found it became a source of mild controversy. There must be some well-founded psychoanalytic interpretation of my vulnerability to this four-letter word, and, most certainly it is rooted in the deep and unsavory unconscious—as is true of course with all four-letter words. On a level more accessible to introspection (which we all know to be but a source of self-deception), my use of this word had probably something to do with a compulsion to simplify things—based, self-deceptively, on the famous hope that they indeed *can* be simplified. But one who simplifies runs the risk of *over*simplifying, and in our field, as in others, whereas the first is sublime, the second is sinful. And I must have sinned. (Zajonc, 1980a, pp. 35–36)

He goes on to describe two kinds of social psychologists, those who believe the world is "above all enormously complex" and

> then there are those . . . who aren't awestricken, and perhaps not even much moved, by the complexity of the social world. In fact we really don't know whether the "real" social world is or isn't complex. We do believe, however, that whatever its ultimate complexity (a question to be decided perhaps by metaphysicians), scientific statements about it need not be complex. On the contrary, if at all possible they should be simple. Given that real life is miserably complex, why should we complicate it further by duplicating its complexity in our journals and books? (Zajonc, 1980a, pp. 35–36)

The dazzling combination of the unexpected contrarian and the mere simplicity appears most clearly in the coming and going of affect social psychology, shifts with Zajonc at their leading edge. Examining affect and cognition in the spirit of these two themes, this chapter will provide historical perspective on Zajonc's work, specifics elaborated in the chapters that follow. Viewing the pageant of social psychology from the back of the theater, this chapter takes the contrarian view that cognition did not suddenly overwhelm affect, that there was no social cognitive revolution, contrary to the popular view. Instead, each of Zajonc's mere simplicities have refocused in turn on affect or cognition.

A Contrarian View of the (Social) Cognitive Revolution

The standard view holds that the social cognitive revolution, mimicking the nearby cognitive revolution, wiped affect off the social psychological itinerary (see Fiske & Taylor, 1991, for one such account). But a closer examination suggests that social psychology has always preserved cognition (Zajonc, 1980b), in the sense that it has always harbored a safe haven for mentalistic concepts and variables, even when the rest of the field was at sea in a behaviorist boat. Beliefs and stereotypes, both heavily cognitive, have constituted mainstays of social psychology from its beginnings.

Moreover, even a weaker version of this argument, that the balance between cognition and affect has, since the 1970s, favored cognition, may not stay afloat. As a first approximation, we[1] searched PsycINFO abstracts for the frequency of (a) "social" plus "affect" (also plus "emotion" and "feelings," but the results are similar) and compared them with the frequency of (b) "social" plus "cogniti*" (with the asterisk presumably including both "cognition" and "cognitive"). To be conservative, we subtracted out "cognitive dissonance," as that might artificially inflate the prerevolutionary frequencies of "cogniti*"; cognitive dissonance is not typically numbered among the cognitive revolutionaries.

Over the course of Zajonc's career, the relevant historical period, the relative frequency of social cognition and social affect defies conventional wisdom. On the contrary, "affect" dominates "cogniti*" in every 6-year period, except in the 1990s, where they equal each other. As Figure 2.1 indicates, the relative proportion of psychological abstracts mentioning social + cognition does steadily increase, even without cognitive dissonance theory, but no sudden revolution is evident, and perhaps the rough equivalence, from 1984 on, suggests a balance of power, rather than a cognitive coup d'état.

So how has Zajonc influenced the balance between affect and cognition, if not leading a single revolutionary attack, at this strategic macro level? His impact has turned the field's attention to new themes, alternating cognition and affect with more nuanced tactics.

Mere Simplicity Captures the Field's Attention

The major contributions of Robert Zajonc with astonishing regularity attack the dominant perspective with a simple, mere effect that shakes the field's foundations. Five themes in his contributions, discussed in the following sections, capture this pattern of a new phenomenon every 5 or so years.

Cognitive Structure

During the mid-1950s through 1960s, social psychology focused wholeheartedly on dissonance and other consistency theories (for historical perspectives, see Jones, 1998; Taylor, 1998) but neglected to examine carefully the mediating mechanisms themselves. That is, attitudes certainly changed to reduce cognitive inconsistencies, but few investigators examined the actual cognitive structure (Kiesler, Collins, &

---

[1] I am indebted to Stephanie Strebel for obtaining this information.

FIGURE 2.1

The proportion of psychological abstract references to "cognition" and "cognitive" (cog) relative to total "cognition-plus-affect" (cog + aff) references, out of abstracts also using the term "social," from PsycINFO (see text), over the last half-century.

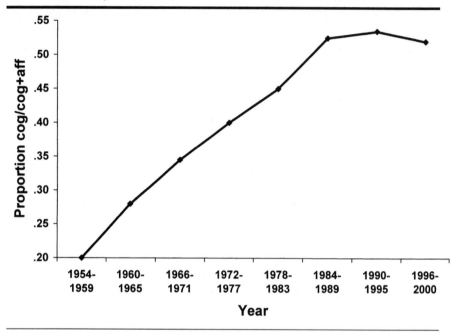

Miller, 1969). Zajonc went beyond consistency to dissect the cognitive structures that undergird consistency and inconsistency. Although, as noted, the field had always been cognitive in some respects, the basic elements or building blocks had not been examined.

In Figure 2.2, the vertical axis makes a time line from the start of 1960, with Zajonc's publications in the first line of cognitive structure work. The cognitive balance and cognitive tuning articles appeared in 1960 (Zajonc, 1960a, 1960b). His 1968 *Handbook of Social Psychology* (2nd ed.) chapter on cognitive theory heralded, as some people would date it, the social cognitive revolution; the 1985 *Handbook of Social Psychology* (3rd ed.) cognitive perspective chapter with Hazel Markus fortified the social cognitive position. Looking at these early publications, one sees that Zajonc said it all, and the rest of us have been busy catching up ever since. A quote from the cognitive tuning article will illustrate:

> The purpose of this study is to examine the nature of cognitive structures that are activated . . . when persons enter into communication with others. . . . Cognitive structures represent organized systems whose nature depends on the various interrelations among their components. (Zajonc, 1960b, p. 159)

FIGURE 2.2

Time lines of five major themes in Robert Zajonc's work, as predating major trends in the field (indicated in shaded type). "Handbook" Field's lag to adopt Zajonc's theme is estimated or extrapolated in the last line of each column.
Handbook = Handbook of Social Psychology.

	Cognitive Structure	Social Motives	Affect & Cognition	Cognitive Intelligence	Group Hostility
1960	cognitive tuning & balance				
1965		social facilitation			
	Handbook: cognitive theory		mere exposure		
1970		cockroaches			
1975	social cognition revolution	day-old chicks		intelligence & family configuration	
		compresence			
1980			preferences need no inferences	validating confluence model	altruism, envy, competition, & common good
			primacy of affect		
1985	Handbook: cognitive perspective		facial efference		
1990			vascular theory		
			nonconscious affect		
1995		social motives redux			
				birth order & SATs	collective violence
			Handbook: emotions		
2000					
Field's lag to adopt	+20	+30	2010 affect & brain-imaging coup +40	2025 social-gene interaction +50	2045 end group violence +60

This quote has aged gracefully. Indeed, the entire cognitive tuning article grapples with issues that social psychologists still struggle to understand. First, Zajonc tackles cognitive structures, or organized subsets of a person's cognitive universe. He defines dimensional values of stimuli (black, animated, or beautiful) as the attributes or elements of a cognitive structure. Each cognitive structure possesses degrees of differentiation, complexity, unity, and organization. When people expect to transmit information to others, as compared with receiving it, their cognitive structures become more differentiated, complex, unified, and organized. Differences between transmitters and receivers decrease when people expect to receive incongruent information, but it was the transmitter–receiver contrast in structure that captured the field's imagination. Nobody else was looking in such detail at cognitive structures. This first battle cry to investigate fine-grained cognitive structures of course then summoned others to rush into the fray, resulting in the active enterprise of social cognition that we now know.

As an assistant professor coming of professional age at a time when cognitive consistency theory was the dominant paradigm, Zajonc dared to say the unsayable. He dared to write, for example,

> Cognitive doctrines . . . lack specification of the conditions under which their predictions will hold. People like to make sense of their world, but they also seek out the magician to be entertained by incongruity. Historically the concept of consistency resembles the concept of vacuum in physics. A useful doctrine for organizing knowledge although full of exceptions and contradictions. (Zajonc, 1960a, p. 380)

Without this chutzpah, the field might never have appreciated his contrarian views.

By about 20 years after Zajonc's 1960 cognitive tuning and cognitive balance articles, the rest of the field undertook the examination of cognitive structure in earnest, debating schemas, prototypes, scripts, as well as consistency and inconsistency in memory, significantly stimulated by his cognitive contributions.

Social Motives

As consistency theories receded from center stage, with them went the interest in social motives such as consistency seeking. The field as a whole was not to return to motivational issues in earnest until recently. But way ahead of the curve, 5 years after the cognitive structure articles, Zajonc (1965) brought us modern research on social facilitation.

> Until the late 1930s, interest in social facilitation was quite active, but . . . it suddenly died. And it is truly regrettable that it died, because the basic questions about social facilitation, . . . which are in effect the basic questions of social psychology, were never solved. It is with these questions that this article is concerned . . . this nearly completely abandoned area of research. (Zajonc, 1965, p. 269)

Again, the contrarian investment. Again, the simple idea—the mere presence of others as a motivator—made elegant by the compelling research that was to support it, including the infamous studies of cockroaches, day-old chicks, and sophomores in the "compresence" of conspecifics. The presence of others, whether audience or co-actors, enhances arousal, which in turn encourages the individual's dominant response (enhancing performance on well-practiced tasks and undermining performance on novels tasks). The rest of the field quickly followed up the revival of social facilitation (and this may be Zajonc's single most-cited article).

Nevertheless, the field neglected Zajonc's focus on specifically *social* motivations that shows so clearly in the social facilitation phenomenon. The more general issue of specifically social motives took the rest of the field nearly 30 years to catch up. Only by the 1990s would we coin the term *motivated tactician* (Fiske & Taylor, 1991), though Showers and Cantor (1985) earlier forecasted the idea of *motivated social cognition*. A full-throated chorus of social motivational effects on cognition did not arise until nearly three decades later (Pittman, 1998; Snyder & Cantor, 1998). If cognitive structures took 20 years to capture the field, and social motives 30 years, the field learning its lessons from Zajonc suggests a decelerating curve.

Affect and Emotion

Following the decelerating curve, the next 5-year plan will probably not hit the field fully for another 10 years, making a 40-year lag. In fewer than 5 years after his first social facilitation article, Zajonc rattled psychology's chain by claiming that *mere* exposure to stimuli alone could induce liking.

> It has been known for some time that social interaction enhances the attitudes of interactors toward each other. . . . But it is not known just what contribution to the relationship between interaction and attitudes is made by *mere* exposure on the one hand, and by the variety of psychologically significant processes that necessarily accompany mere exposure during the course of social interaction, on the other. (Zajonc, 1968, p. 2)

In a brilliant synthesis of linguistic analyses and experimental manipulations, Zajonc showed first that positive affective connotations and positive attitudes correlate with (a) relative word frequency within antonym pairs across four languages; (b) frequency of trait adjectives; (c) frequencies of country and city names; (d) frequencies of scientific occupations; and (e) frequencies of trees, fruits, vegetables, and flowers. Next, he showed that experimental manipulation of exposure frequency increased the positive connotations of nonsense words, Chinese-like characters, and facial photographs. Finally, he argued for the logarithmic shape of the function (bigger differences at small levels of exposure) and its focus on novel stimuli.

At this time and just after, the rest of the field was trudging knee-deep in attribution and social cognition, but Zajonc's contrarian strategy dictated heavily investing in feelings, preferences, affect, and emotion. He had to hammer away at this message, revealing its full implications later in a much cited, much debated 1980 *American Psychologist* article. There, Zajonc (1980b) argued that affective preferences precede and may be independent of various cognitive operations previously presumed to underlie them. Affect and cognition might be separate systems, he suggested. This challenge was followed by a decade's more of arguments for the primacy of affect over cognition (Zajonc, 1984). He also espoused the nonconscious nature of affect (e.g., Murphy & Zajonc, 1993), as well as a noncognitive, physical theory of emotion: Facial efference (expression) alters vascular configurations (i.e., blood flow) to the brain, regulating brain temperature and thereby emotion (Zajonc, 1985, 1994; Zajonc, Murphy, & Inglehart, 1989). Switching earlier allegiances, his next *Handbook of Social Psychology* (4th ed.) chapter (Zajonc, 1998) concentrates fully on emotion, with nary a cognitive perspective.

Given the resistance of the rest of the field to his brain-and-blood theory of emotion, the full development of neural imaging techniques may ultimately facilitate the field's catch-up to Zajonc However, according to our decelerating function, the lag looks to be 40 years or so from the original mere-exposure article, predicting a conversion to his agenda by about 2010. Not an unlikely scenario!

Cognitive Intelligence

Not content with three field-shaking contributions, about 8 years after his article on mere exposure, Zajonc brought us family configurations and intelligence. Having convinced the rest of the field to take affect seriously, he kept his own cognitive options open. While the rest of social psychology had abandoned the intelligence area to genetic psychologists, Zajonc focused on a simple feature of social context: mere family configuration.

> This model . . . [tries] to capture the effects of the immediate intellectual environment on intellectual growth, and to specify how individual differences emerge in the social context of the family. (Zajonc, 1976, p. 227)
>
> [From] a substantial sample of family configurations, examined repeatedly over several years . . . , the relation of environmental variables that it specifies to the total IQ variance in the sample can be measured. . . . It would be of some interest to establish just how much can be assigned to environmental factors when the analysis begins with them. (Zajonc, 1976, p. 235)

Zajonc went on to demonstrate that, along with several other implications of his model:

- smaller families beget better intellectual performance,
- earlier-born children fare better than later-borns when the between-birth gaps are short,
- larger gaps between births enhance performance.

Essentially, the number of intellectual marbles possessed by the parent(s) and any much older siblings are divided among the youngsters, resulting in more abundant or more sparse intellectual environments and ultimately reflected in standardized test performance. The initial article was followed by significant analyses validating the confluence model (Zajonc, 1983) and examining birth order as a predictor of SAT scores (Zajonc & Mullally, 1997).

At the field's decelerating rate of adoption of Zajonc's theories, the lag for this contribution should be about 50 years, landing us in 2025 before we fully appreciate the effects of social environmental factors on intelligence. Some of us fear it may be longer.

Group Hostility

The four best-known of Zajonc's contributions, discussed in the preceding sections, still leave room for surprises. In 1982, Zajonc authored a less-known paper on altruism, envy, competitiveness, and the common good, claiming in part:

> Justice, equity, and fairness are judgmental criteria under the control of social norms. And defying social norms may be costly. So it is in one's self-interest to be just and fair. (p. 436)

While the rest of social psychology abandoned game theory to economists and mourned the death of the group, Zajonc's contrarian strategy focused on social intent as a function of subjective, more than objective, payoffs. Justice and fairness, in the context of social norms, brought Zajonc to group-level analyses. This 1982 chapter until recently might be viewed as a single-shot effort, but recently Zajonc indeed has begun to tackle group-on-group conflict. If this work requires 60 years (on our decelerating curve), then the field will not truly understand group violence until 2045, when it may be too late.

A more optimistic view traces the Zajontific interest in these problems to 1950s and 1960s articles on aggression of a stranger under conformity pressure (Zajonc, 1952), cross-cultural norm conflict (French & Zajonc, 1957; Zajonc & Wahi, 1961), and cooperation, competition, and interpersonal attitudes (Zajonc & Marin, 1967). At this estimate, we might catch up to the group hostility problem somewhat sooner, or so one hopes.

Conclusion

The simple and contrarian magic of Robert Zajonc has molded and will continue to mold the places of affect and cognition in social psychology. The contributors in this volume pay Bob the ultimate tribute of locating their work in his spotlight. Many of us have tried to emulate his example, in our own small sideshows. Expect many more to follow his act, but none of us with the flair of the headliner.

References

Fiske, S. T., & Taylor, S. E. (1991). *Social cognition.* New York: McGraw-Hill.

French, J. R. P., Jr., & Zajonc, R. B. (1957). An experimental study of cross-cultural norm conflict. *Journal of Abnormal Social Psychology, 54,* 218–224.

Jones, E. E. (1998). Major developments in five decades of social psychology. In D. T. Gilbert, S. T. Fiske, & G. Lindzey (Vol. Eds.), *The handbook of social psychology* (4th ed., Vol. 1, pp. 3–57). New York: McGraw-Hill.

Kiesler, C. A., Collins, B. E., & Miller, N. (1969). *Attitude change: A critical analysis of theoretical approaches.* New York: Wiley.

Murphy, S. T., & Zajonc, R. B. (1993). Affect, cognition, and awareness: Affective priming with optimal and suboptimal stimulus exposures. *Journal of Personality and Social Psychology, 64,* 723–739.

Pittman, T. S. (1998). Motivation. In D. T. Gilbert, S. T. Fiske, & G. Lindzey (Vol. Eds.), *The handbook of social psychology* (4th ed., Vol.1, pp. 549–590). New York: McGraw-Hill.

Showers, C., & Cantor, N. (1985). Social cognition: A look at motivated strategies. *Annual Review of Psychology, 36,* 275–305.

Snyder, M., & Cantor, N. (1998). Understanding personality and social behavior: A functionalist strategy. In D. T. Gilbert, S. T. Fiske, & G. Lindzey (Vol. Eds.), *The handbook of social psychology* (4th ed., Vol. 1, pp. 635–679). New York: McGraw-Hill.

Taylor, S. E. (1998). The social being in social psychology. In D. T. Gilbert, S. T. Fiske, & G. Lindzey (Vol. Eds.), *The handbook of social psychology* (4th ed., Vol. 1, pp. 58–95). New York: McGraw-Hill.

Zajonc, R. B. (1952). Aggressive attitudes of the stranger as a function of conformity pressures. *Human Relations, 5,* 205–216.

Zajonc, R. B. (1960a). The concepts of balance, congruity, and dissonance. *Public Opinion Quarterly, 24,* 380–396.

Zajonc, R. B. (1960b). The process of cognitive tuning in communication. *Journal of Abnormal and Social Psychology, 61,* 159–167.

Zajonc, R. B. (1965). Social facilitation. *Science, 149,* 269–274.

Zajonc, R. B. (1968). Attitudinal effects of mere exposure. *Journal of Personality and Social Psychology Monograph Supplement, 9,* 1–27.

Zajonc, R. B. (1976). Family configuration and intelligence. *Science, 192,* 227–236.

Zajonc, R. B. (1980a). Compresence. In P. B. Paulus (Ed.), *Psychology of group influence* (pp. 35–60). Hillsdale, NJ: Erlbaum.

Zajonc, R. B. (1980b). Feeling and thinking: Preferences need no inferences. *American Psychologist, 35,* 151–175.

Zajonc, R. B. (1982). Alturism, envy, competitiveness, and the common good. In V. J. Derlega & J. Grzelak (Eds.), *Cooperation and helping behavior: Theories and research* (pp. 417–437). New York: Academic Press.

Zajonc, R. B. (1983). Validating the confluence model. *Psychological Bulletin, 93*, 457–480.

Zajonc, R. B. (1984). On the primacy of affect. *American Psychologist, 39*, 117–123.

Zajonc, R. B. (1985). Emotion and facial efference: A theory reclaimed. *Science, 228*, 5–21.

Zajonc, R. B. (1994). Emotional expression and temperature modulation. In S. H. M. Van Goozen, N. E. Van De Poll, & J. A. Sergeant (Eds.), *Emotions: Essays on emotion theory* (pp. 3–27). Hillsdale, NJ: Erlbaum.

Zajonc, R. B. (1998). Emotions. In D. T. Gilbert, S. T. Fiske, & G. Lindzey (Vol. Eds.), *The handbook of social psychology* (4th ed., Vol. 1, pp. 591–632). New York: McGraw-Hill.

Zajonc, R. B., & Marin, I. C. (1967). Cooperation, competition, and interpersonal attitudes in small groups. *Psychonomic Science, 7*, 271–272.

Zajonc, R. B., & Mullally, P. R. (1997). Birth order: Reconciling conflicting effects. *American Psychologist, 52*, 685–699.

Zajonc, R. B., Murphy, S. T., & Inglehart, M. (1989). Feeling and facial efference: Implications of the vascular theory of emotion. *Psychological Review, 96*, 395–416.

Zajonc, R. B., & Wahi, N. K. (1961). Conformity and need achievement under cross-cultural change. *Human Relations, 14*, 241–250.

PART 1

The Anti-Mediational Stance

CHAPTER 3

The Psychology of the Mere

John A. Bargh

One hallmark of Robert Zajonc's research career has been his leadership in making mainstream social psychology more cognitive—exemplified by his 1955 dissertation on cognitive tuning (Zajonc, 1960) and his landmark 1968 *Handbook of Social Psychology* chapter, "Cognitive Theories in Social Psychology." At the same time, however, there has been another consistent theme, that of a skeptical stance toward cognitive mediation of basic social psychological phenomena. This "antimediational" theme is exemplified by Zajonc's *mere-presence theory* of social facilitation effects, his *mere-exposure theory* of attitude formation, and his *affect-without-cognition* model of evaluation. How, one might well ask, can one of the founders of modern cognitive social psychology have, simultaneously, such an anti-mediational streak?

To me, this is a puzzle reminiscent of pre-1965 social facilitation research: Some studies find that the presence of others helps one's performance, whereas other studies find that the presence of others hinders performance. It took Bob Zajonc to sort that one out; we might need a Bob Zajonc to sort Bob Zajonc out.

Social Facilitation: Mere Presence

Let us begin with the 1965 synthesis of social facilitation effects in terms of Hullian drive theory, which accounted for why the presence of an audience sometimes helps, and sometimes hurts, performance on a task. Accounts of social facilitation effects by Cottrell (1968), Sanders (1981), and others argued that the presence of observers to a performance either caused distraction of attention or else induced worries about social approval, or "evaluation apprehension," which then as a source of arousal affected performance. Contrary to such mediational accounts, Zajonc argued that no mental transformation of the situation in this way was necessary for the effects to occur—they required only the *mere presence* of the conspecific, or fellow member of the species. In Zajonc's model, the mere presence of another person in the perceived environment increased the drive level of the individual, with effects on performance—both facilitative and deleterious—predicted from Hullian drive theory. (Increased drive levels facilitate habitual or well-learned responses but hinder nonhabitual or novel task performances.)

When I began reading the social psychology journals as an undergraduate in the 1970s, one of the more entertaining back-and-forths of that time was between the cognitive mediation and the mere-presence camps. In response to repeated articles reporting that the presence of an audience increased evaluation apprehension or caused greater distraction of attention (e.g., Sanders, 1981), Zajonc's response was simple, and devastating. He showed the effects in cockroaches. Put a cockroach in a dark box and then turn a light on—the habitual or instinctive response of the cockroach is to run to darkness. But put several other cockroaches in the same box as an "audience" and the subject-cockroach runs even faster (Zajonc, Heingartner, & Herman, 1969). Others (e.g., Rajecki, Kidd, & Ivins, 1976) found social facilitation effects in chickens. It was pretty tough to then argue for the necessity of cognitive mediation of social facilitation effects, given such demonstrations.

Attitude Formation: Mere Exposure

As has been noted by others in this book, Zajonc has never restricted himself to a given methodology or paradigm in attacking a research question. Instead, he goes to whatever discipline and level of analysis would supply the evidence most relevant to the question at hand—whether with population statistics, psychophysiology, subliminal stimulus presentation, or cockroaches. In no single work was this methodological virtuosity more evident than in the 1968 *Journal of Personality and Social Psychology* monograph on the mere-exposure effect in attitude formation. Here one finds experimental studies involving repeated exposures to pseudo-Turkish words such as *Jandara* and *Iktiktaf* or pseudo-Chinese ideograms; an examination of frequency of word use and their positivity of connotation; and the change in word meaning from initially negative to positive over centuries of usage (e.g., *terrific, fantastic*). The approach to research exemplified here was as follows: IF the hypothesis that mere repeated exposure leads to greater attitudinal positivity were true, what else should be true?

The mere-exposure idea was the direct intellectual ancestor of the later "preferences need no inferences" idea of separate affective and cognitive processing systems (see, e.g., Moreland & Zajonc, 1977, 1979). Mediational accounts of the mere-exposure effect ran as follows: The more often a stimulus was presented, the more likely the individual would be to (consciously) recognize it, and the more chances the person would have to intentionally consider and form an attitude about it. Repeated exposure also might give the individual some motivational reasons for the positivity effect (e.g., "Well, as long as it seems this thing is going to be around here all the time, I might as well like it"). The mere-exposure account, on the other hand, held that none of these mediating cognitive or motivational processes were required for the effect on liking.

Again, as with the mere-presence theory of social facilitation, Zajonc and colleagues ruled out the necessity of mediation by demonstrating that the effect of repeated exposure on liking occurred even in the absence of conscious processing of the attitude object. The Moreland–Zajonc studies did this statistically, by showing that the effect of repeated exposure on liking was independent of the effect of repeated exposure on stimulus recognition. Subsequent studies demonstrated it experimentally, eliminating conscious awareness of the repeatedly presented stimulus through subliminal presentation techniques (Kunst-Wilson & Zajonc, 1980; Murphy, chap. 4, this volume; Murphy & Zajonc, 1993; Wilson, 1979).

Conditional Automaticity

I have only recently realized that this same plan of pushing the conditional envelope of an effect characterizes my own research since leaving graduate school at the University of Michigan. About 10 years ago, in the course of reviewing the literature on automatic processes in social psychology (Bargh, 1989), I noticed that different researchers meant very different things by the term *automatic process*. For some, an automatic process was one that a person intended but had practiced so often that it occurred effortlessly and efficiently. A good example is Eliot Smith's research (e.g., Smith & Lerner, 1986) on the proceduralization of social judgment. For others, however, automatic effects were those that occurred immediately and unintentionally. Examples of these effects are the categorization of a behavior in trait terms on perception of the event, as in Higgins's (e.g., 1989) and Wyer and Srull's (e.g., 1989) priming research; stereotype activation on the mere presence of a member of the stereotyped group (e.g., Brewer, 1988; Devine, 1989; Fiske & Neuberg, 1990); and attitude activation on the mere presence of the attitude object, as argued by Fazio (1990) and colleagues. Different strains of automatic processes differed, therefore, in the experimental conditions needed for them to occur.

What struck me the most while writing that review was that often the claims being made about the conditionality of the effect did not match up with the experimental conditions actually used to produce it. On the one hand, for many of the effects in question, claims were being made about their unconditional nature—their *mereness*, if you will—although the experimental paradigm actually contained several potential contributory conditions. Other effects, on the other hand, were claimed to be limited to those times when the person was intending to make social judgments, or ingratiate oneself to a new acquaintance, and so on, without any examination or test of whether the effect was indeed limited to those occasions—that is, whether or not the effect *depended* on having that particular intention or goal in place.

To me, such questions mattered for both an important theoretical reason and an important practical reason. Theoretically, it matters how much of a role conscious choice and strategic guidance play in psychological and behavioral phenomena, so it is worth testing any untested assumption that they play a role. More often than not, as Daryl Bem has repeatedly cautioned us (e.g., 1972), and as Zajonc has shown consistently throughout his research career, one finds that they are not needed after all.

The question of whether important effects depend on a particular intention or goal that they occur, or on the availability of sufficient attentional resources at that moment, also has important practical implications, mainly for the ecological validity or generalizability of laboratory phenomena to the busy "real world." People have a wide variety of purposes and goals to pursue and are not, for example, constantly concerned with forming personality impressions of everyone they encounter. Moreover, these various goals and purposes demand and direct the person's limited attention and thereby make it *un*available for other processes.

In short, it is precisely those mental processes that are goal independent, and that are efficient and not demanding of limited attention, that will tend to occur more often and be constantly important in one's moment-to-moment navigation of the world. Indeed, these chronic, omnipresent nonconscious processes, described in the next section, can be thought of as "psychological gravity" that adheres people, in a natural and effortless way, to their present social environment, while their conscious minds are (as they often are) somewhere in the past or future.

The Automatic Evaluation Effect

The original proposal by Fazio (see Fazio, Sanbonmatsu, Powell, & Kardes, 1986) was that strongly held attitudes could be activated automatically by the *mere presence* of the attitude object in the environment. For these attitudes, then, a stronger and more consistent influence on behavior toward the attitude object would be expected, because the attitude would be more likely to become active "online" at the same time the person was encountering the object.

The basic experimental paradigm used to test for the automaticity of attitude activation was based on Neely's (1977) sequential priming paradigm. In this procedure, an attitude object "prime" (e.g., *puppy*) is presented on a computer screen for a brief interval and is then overwritten by a "target" word (e.g., *beautiful*) to which the participant responds by indicating, as quickly as possible, whether the target is positive or negative in meaning. A key ingredient of this paradigm is the short stimulus onset asynchrony between prime and target (250 ms), which is too short a time for a person to be able to prepare a strategic, intentional response to the target based on the prime word (which generally takes about half a second at least). Thus, to the extent the positivity or negativity of the attitude toward the prime affects responses to the target (which is what Fazio et al., 1986, found), this can only be because that attitude became active immediately, unintentionally, and reflexively merely because of the presence of the name of the attitude object on the screen.

There were several aspects to this basic procedure in addition to just the presence of the (name of the) attitude object. To discover what the participant's attitude was toward the various prime objects, the paradigm required each participant to indicate, just before the test of attitude automaticity, his or her evaluation (good vs. bad) of each of the attitude objects. Thus, the participant had just recently thought about his or her evaluation of each of the potential attitude object primes, and so these evaluations could have been temporarily activated at the time of the later test of their automaticity. Research has shown (e.g., Bargh, Bond, Lombardi, & Tota, 1986) that such temporary activation or "priming" mimics chronic or long-term automatic effects (see Bargh & Chartrand, 2000, for a review). Generalizing this aspect of the paradigm to the "real world" would mean that attitudes only become triggered by the perception of their corresponding object if the person had just previously been thinking about his or her evaluation of the object.

Another potential contributor to the automatic attitude activation effect was that, in the task assessing automaticity, described above, the participants were intentionally and explicitly evaluating the target words as either good or bad. Again, extrapolating this aspect of the paradigm to the nonlaboratory world would mean that the automatic attitude activation effect happens only when people are actively and consciously evaluating things. In short, there were more potential contributory conditions present in the paradigm than just the mere presence of the attitude object.

Accordingly, Shelly Chaiken and I set out to test the necessity of these various theory-irrelevant aspects of the paradigm for the production of the automatic attitude activation effect, by removing them, one at a time, from the paradigm. At each step of the way, we were surprised by what we found (see Bargh, Chaiken, Govender, & Pratto, 1992; Chaiken & Bargh, 1993). Instead of the elimination of the automatic attitude activation effect, the removal of each of these theory-irrelevant aspects actually increased its size and, most importantly, its generality. For example, we first interpolated a 2-day delay between the attitude assessment and automaticity tasks, so that participants no longer had just given conscious thought to their attitudes when their automaticity was measured. What we found was that the effect showed up more strongly and more pervasively than before: Instead of holding for only the person's strongly held attitudes, as Fazio et al. (1986) had found, it held for all of them, even quite weak ones (e.g., such as for *tuna* and *Monday*).

Ultimately, we showed that the effect was truly goal independent, when we substituted a pronunciation task for the target evaluation task (Bargh, Chaiken, Raymond, & Hymes, 1996). Participants were instructed instead to pronounce each target as quickly as they could; no mention was ever made of evaluating anything. But we continued to obtain the automatic attitude activation, or *automatic evaluation*, effect as before. It is clear the effect was goal independent and unintentional.

Recently, we examined the necessity of one last precondition for the automatic evaluation effect—that the individual, at one point in the past, had intentionally formed an evaluation of the object in question, with this evaluation then stored in memory. All previous work on this issue had assumed, more or less implicitly, that what was being activated by the attitude object primes was a previously formed attitude toward them. But what if the effect did not require the existence of a previously consciously made and stored attitude?

The strong version of Zajonc's (1980) argument in the "Feeling and Thinking" article, after all, was that *preferenda* existed to which the affective system reacts. If a prior evaluation of the attitude object was not required—as it was not required for the mere-exposure effect on liking—then the automatic evaluation effect should occur even for novel stimuli, ones that the participants had never encountered before.

Duckworth, Garcia, Bargh, and Chaiken (2000) performed four such experiments, in which novel wordlike sounds or abstract, nonrepresentational pictures were presented to participants as priming stimuli, 250 milliseconds before the target stimulus. In the auditory version of the study, the primes were novel word sounds (e.g., *zabulon, chakaka, bargalu*, based on the structure of Zajonc's 1968 pseudo-Turkish words) intermixed with the names of actual attitude objects (e.g., *puppy, priest, lettuce*). In the visual version of the study, abstract art paintings by Mondrian, Kandinsky, Klee, and Magda Garcia's 8-year-old niece (via Etch a Sketch) were intermixed as primes with pictures of real attitude objects (such as a puppy and a knife). Pretesting on a separate group of participants had provided normative evaluative ratings of these novel stimuli as being generally good or bad.

Even though the priming stimuli were entirely novel to the participants, the automatic evaluation effect was again obtained. Somehow participants were evaluating, without knowing they were doing so and without intending to do so, the novel stimulus objects as either good or bad—and doing so for each object within a quarter of a second of its presentation. The automatic evaluation effect is therefore truly an online *evaluation* effect, in which original evaluations are generated instantly, as opposed to only a perceptual effect, in which evaluations are memory representations activated by the presence of their object in the environment. It would seem that, consistent with the strong version of Zajonc's (1980) *preferenda* hypothesis, people are evaluating everything in their experience immediately, and without knowing they are doing so.

Given the pervasiveness of this evaluative stance people take toward the world, it would be surprising indeed if the initial automatic evaluative response had no "downstream" consequences for judgment, mood, or behavior. And, at least the initial evidence on this question suggests that the initial evaluation of something as good or as bad qualitatively shifts a person's experience of, thinking about, and behavior toward that object in one direction or the other. Moods are affected by the general tone of the automatic evaluations made in one's current environment (Bargh & Chartrand, 1999), social judgments are influenced by them (Ferguson & Bargh, 2000), and behavioral dispositions at the level of muscular readiness to approach or to avoid the object are also automatically put into motion by the evaluative reaction (Chen & Bargh, 1999; Duckworth et al., 2000). The power of the affective system to guide subsequent cognition and behavior is perhaps just beginning to be revealed.

The Chameleon Effect

Scholars from Adam Smith to Charles Darwin, Clark Hull to Jean Piaget, and more recently Albert Bandura (1977), Leonard Berkowitz (1984), and Frank Bernieri (1988) have all remarked on the human (and primate) tendency to mimic and imitate the behavior of others. Two different causal candidates are repeatedly put forth: that mimicry is in the service of ingratiation through demonstrating empathic understanding and rapport with the interaction partner, or that imitation is in the service of vicariously learning one's own future responses to the observed situation. For example, Zajonc, Adelmann, Murphy, and Niedenthal's (1987; see also Murphy, chap. 4, this volume) study of the role of facial expressions in mimicry—that merely creating the same facial expression helped produce the actual emotion felt by the other person, because of the participation of the facial muscles in regulating emotion through regulating blood flow to the brain—also posited mimicry to be in the service of creating empathy in close relationships.

Recently, Tanya Chartrand and I (Chartrand & Bargh, 1999) examined whether such goals are really necessary for mimicry and imitation effects. There is a simpler, more unconditional possibility: that perceiving another person's behavior automatically increases the probability that you yourself will behave that way. William James (1890) called this the *principle of ideomotor action,* that merely thinking about doing something increases the probability that you will do it. This is hypothetically because the perceptual and the actional representations of a given type of behavior are strongly connected, perhaps because they overlap in so many features (Carver, Ganellen, Froming, & Chambers, 1983). Thus, mimicry and imitation may occur because of the automatic expressway between perception and behavior, which naturally, unintentionally, and nonconsciously increases the tendency to behave in the same way as those around you.

If the same essential representation is used in perception as in behavior, then it should be difficult to use that representation for both purposes at the same time. Exactly this finding has been obtained by Muesseler and Hommel (1997). Participants trained on each trial to reproduce key sequences involving left (L) and right (R) keys pressed by their respective index fingers, such as LLRL or RLRL. They were to type this sequence correctly but also as quickly as possible. When they were ready, they began to type the sequence, and as they were typing the second key, a computer display presented a fifth key to press that they were to add at the end of their practiced sequence. This was either the same or the opposite from the key they were hitting with their finger at that moment. As would be expected if the same representation is used in perception as in behavior, participants made more errors if the key they were to perceive was the same as the one they were currently striking than if it was the opposite one. Moreover, Rizzolatti and Arbib (1998) have found that the same area of the pre-motor cortex in macaque monkeys becomes activated when they reach for an object as when they watch an experimenter reach for the object.

In our own experimental demonstrations, we had participants engage in a task with a confederate—namely, giving free-association reactions to a series of photographs—in which attention of both parties was primarily focused on the photographs, and the confederate did not make eye contact with the participant. Thus, there was no affiliation or ingratiation goal operating and the two individuals were strangers, so no social bond existed between them. One confederate touched her face, and a second confederate shook her foot during separate interactions with the participant, and we recorded how much the participant did the same thing. In what we called the *chameleon effect*, the behavior of the participant changed to be similar to that of the current interaction partner.

This natural, unmotivated effect of perception on behavior did indeed produce feelings of empathic understanding in the participants. In Study 2, we studied the reverse causal direction and had the confederate mimic the general body orientation of the participant—the tilt of the body, crossing versus not crossing legs, and so on, to create a "mirror image." At the end of the interaction, the participant rated how smoothly the interaction went and how much he or she liked the interaction partner, and on both measures the ratings for the mirror-image condition were higher than for the control, no-mimicry condition.

We concluded that the automatic effect of perception on behavior is not mediated by any interpersonal goal to bond or empathize with the other person, yet it does have the consequence of producing such bonding and facilitating social interaction. And, to return to Zajonc et al.'s (1987) observation that married couples grow more similar in facial appearance to each other over time, we would concur that it is the repeated sharing of facial expressions that produces this similarity. However, we would suggest that it may be a genuinely *mere* effect of perceiving each other's facial expressions that causes the mimicry and the shared expressions; the motivation to empathize with the partner's reactions not being a necessary precondition for the effect.

Self-Fulfilling Prophecies

The self-fulfilling prophecy effect is the most compelling example we have in social psychology of the impact of perceptual processes on social interaction (see Darley & Fazio, 1980; Jones, 1990). The standard model of such self-fulfilling prophecy, or "behavioral confirmation" effects—according to its major researchers such as Robert Rosenthal, John Darley, Mark Snyder, Lee Jussim, James Hilton, and Steven

Neuberg—is that the stereotype relevant to the social group of the person with whom one is interacting becomes active upon perceiving that person and is the basis for consciously held expectancies about that person's likely qualities and behaviors. These expectancies are said to then guide one's own behavior toward the person in a way that actually causes those behaviors to occur, thus confirming the stereotype.

But the perception–behavior link described above leads to a different possibility: that conscious expectancies are not needed as a mediator of such effects. Instead, perhaps the stereotype activated in the course of perceiving the minority group member increases the probability of the perceiver himself or herself automatically and unintentionally behaving in line with the activated content of the stereotype; this causes the stereotyped group member to respond in kind, thus producing behavioral confirmation of the stereotype through entirely nonconscious means.

Let us take it one step at a time. Bargh, Chen, and Burrows (1996, Experiment 2) primed the stereotype about the elderly in some participants by exposing them in an ostensible language test to stimuli related to that stereotype (e.g., *gray, Florida, conservative*) but not to stimuli semantically related to slowness or weakness, which are also components of the stereotype. After they finished the task, participants were thanked and told that the experiment was over. When they left the experimental room and headed for the elevator to leave the building, backs to us, we timed how long it took them to walk down the hall. Elderly stereotype-primed participants walked more slowly than did control participants. Dijksterhuis, Bargh, and Miedema (2000) recently replicated this effect for the "poor memory" aspect of the elderly stereotype: Elderly-primed college students recalled 40% fewer of the objects in the room they were just in, when given a surprise recall test, compared with control participants (see also Dijksterhuis & van Knippenberg, 1998).

Mark Chen and I (see Chen & Bargh, 1997) took the effect one step further. We primed the African American stereotype by subliminally flashing photographs of young, Black male faces to some participants in the course of a distractor frequency-estimation task. Other participants were presented subliminally with faces of young White men. Participants (who were all White) then interacted through headphones and microphones with another participant who had not received any priming, and we recorded their interaction in separate audio channels. Interactants played the game of "Password" in which one was given a word to try to get the partner to guess, using clues but not the word itself.

We turned these recordings over to judges who were not aware of the experimental hypotheses and had them rate each person for hostility. Our hypothesis was that the activation of the African American stereotype, which contains the trait *hostile*, would cause the first participant to behave toward his or her partner with greater hostility, and this would cause the partner to behave with increased hostility in return. The first participant would then consider his or her partner to be more hostile than would control participants considering their partners. Our results confirmed all of these hypotheses. Without having any awareness of the source of the influence, those in whom the stereotype was automatically activated by the subliminally presented African American faces behaved in line with that stereotype and produced by this behavior the greater hostility in their partner. The self-fulfilling prophecy effect, in other words, was produced entirely through nonconscious means.

Conclusion

More often than not, and across a variety of different psychological phenomena, testing the widely held assumption that an effect is mediated by conscious thought processes, such as deliberation and choice, reveals that the participation of conscious deliberation is not necessary. In Zajonc's research, it was not needed to produce social facilitation effects of the presence of another person on task performance, and in the mere-exposure research it was not needed to produce effects of repeated exposure of an attitude object on greater liking for that object. For very adaptive and functional reasons having to do mainly with the unreliability and limitations of deliberate, conscious processing (see Bargh & Chartrand, 1999; Baumeister, Bratslavsky, Muraven, & Tice, 1998), all of these basic and important effects require only the mere presence of their relevant social objects in the environment.

As Holland (1998) pointed out, it does not take very many simple, basic processes to produce complexity of great magnitude. In his example, the game of chess has only 12 rules but they are sufficient to produce an infinity of different, complex games. The difficulty in understanding something as complex as social behavior is to discover those basic, simple mechanisms in the chaos of the apparent complexity. This is the hallmark of Zajonc's many contributions to the social sciences as well as his lesson to us: When confronted by confusion, seek out the profound simplicities.

References

Bandura, A. (1977). *Social learning theory*. Englewood Cliffs, NJ: Prentice Hall.

Bargh, J. A. (1989). Conditional automaticity: Varieties of automatic influence in social perception and cognition. In J. S. Uleman & J. A. Bargh (Eds.), *Unintended thought* (pp. 3–51). New York: Guilford Press.

Bargh, J. A., Bond, R. N., Lombardi, W. J., & Tota, M. E. (1986). The additive nature of chronic and temporary sources of construct accessibility. *Journal of Personality and Social Psychology, 50*, 869–878.

Bargh, J. A., Chaiken, S., Govender, R., & Pratto, F. (1992). The generality of the automatic attitude activation effect. *Journal of Personality and Social Psychology, 62*, 893–912.

Bargh, J. A., Chaiken, S., Raymond, P., & Hymes, C. (1996). The automatic evaluation effect: Unconditionally automatic attitude activation with a pronunciation task. *Journal of Experimental Social Psychology, 32*, 185–210.

Bargh, J. A., & Chartrand, T. L. (1999). The unbearable automaticity of being. *American Psychologist, 54,* 462–479.

Bargh, J. A., & Chartrand, T. L. (2000). A practical guide to priming and automaticity research. In H. Reis & C. Judd (Eds.) *Handbook of research methods in social psychology,* (pp. 253–285). New York: Cambridge University Press.

Bargh, J. A., Chen, M., & Burrows, L. (1996). Automaticity of social behavior: Direct effects of trait construct and stereotype activation on action. *Journal of Personality and Social Psychology, 71,* 230–244.

Baumeister, R. F., Bratslavsky, E., Muraven, M., & Tice, D. M. (1998). Ego depletion: Is the active self a limited resource? *Journal of Personality and Social Psychology, 74,* 1252–1265.

Bem, D. J. (1972). Self-perception theory. In L. Berkowitz (Ed.), *Advances in experimental social psychology* (Vol. 6, pp. 1–62). New York: Academic Press.

Berkowitz, L. (1984). Some effects of thoughts on anti- and prosocial influences of media events: A cognitive–neoassociation analysis. *Psychological Bulletin, 95,* 410–427.

Bernieri, F. J. (1988). Coordinated movement and rapport in teacher–student interactions. *Journal of Nonverbal Behavior, 12,* 120–138.

Brewer, M. B. (1988). A dual process model of impression formation. In T. K. Srull & R. S. Wyer, Jr. (Eds.), *Advances in social cognition* (Vol. 1, pp. 1–36). Hillsdale, NJ: Erlbaum.

Carver, C. S., Ganellen, R. J., Froming, W. J., & Chambers, W. (1983). Modeling: An analysis in terms of category accessibility. *Journal of Experimental Social Psychology, 19,* 403–421.

Chaiken, S., & Bargh, J. A. (1993). Occurrence versus moderation of automatic attitude activation: Reply to Fazio. *Journal of Personality and Social Psychology, 64,* 759–764.

Chartrand, T. L., & Bargh, J. A. (1999). The chameleon effect: The perception–behavior link and social interaction. *Journal of Personality and Social Psychology, 76,* 893–910.

Chen, M., & Bargh, J. A. (1997). Nonconscious behavioral confirmation processes: The self-fulfilling consequences of automatic stereotype activation. *Journal of Experimental Social Psychology, 33,* 541–560.

Chen, M., & Bargh, J. A. (1999). Nonconscious avoidance and approach behavioral consequences of the automatic evaluation effect. *Personality and Social Psychology Bulletin, 25,* 215–224.

Cottrell, N. B. (1968). Performance in the presence of other human beings: Mere presence, audience, and affiliation effects. In E. C. Summel, R. A. Hoppe, & B. A. Milton (Eds.), *Social facilitation and imitative behavior* (pp. 91–110). Boston: Allyn & Bacon.

Darley, J. M., & Fazio, R. (1980). Expectancy confirmation processes arising in the social interaction sequence. *American Psychologist, 35,* 867–881.

Devine, P. G. (1989). Stereotypes and prejudice: Their automatic and controlled components. *Journal of Personality and Social Psychology, 56,* 680–690.

Dijksterhuis, A., Bargh, J. A., & Miedema, J. (2000). Of men and mackerels: Attention and automatic behavior. In H. Bless & J. P. Forgas (Eds.), *Subjective experience in social cognition and behavior.* Philadelphia: Psychology Press.

Dijksterhuis, A., & van Knippenberg, A. (1998). The relation between perception and behavior or how to win a game of Trivial Pursuit. *Journal of Personality and Social Psychology*, 74, 865–877.

Duckworth, K., Garcia, M., Bargh, J. A., & Chaiken, S. (2000). *Preferences need no attitudes: The automatic evaluation of novel stimuli*. Manuscript under review, New York University.

Fazio, R. H. (1990). Multiple processes by which attitudes guide behavior: The MODE model as an integrative framework. In M. P. Zanna (Ed.), *Advances in experimental social psychology* (Vol. 23, pp. 75–109). San Diego, CA: Academic Press.

Fazio, R. H., Sanbonmatsu, D. M., Powell, M. C., & Kardes, F. R. (1986). On the automatic activation of attitudes. *Journal of Personality and Social Psychology, 50*, 229–238.

Ferguson, M. J., & Bargh, J. A. (2000). *The impact of automatic evaluation on construct accessibility and social judgment*. Manuscript under review. New York University.

Fiske, S. T., & Neuberg, S. E. (1990). A continuum of impression formation, from category-based to individuating processes: Influences of information and motivation on attention and interpretation. In M. P. Zanna (Ed.), *Advances in experimental social psychology* (Vol. 23, pp. 1–74). San Diego, CA: Academic Press.

Higgins, E. T. (1989). Knowledge accessibility and activation: Subjectivity and suffering from unconscious sources. In J. S. Uleman & J. A. Bargh (Eds.), *Unintended thought* (pp. 75–123). New York: Guilford Press.

Holland, J. H. (1998). *Emergence: From chaos to order*. Reading, MA: Addison-Wesley.

James, W. (1890). *The principles of psychology* (Vol. 2). New York: Holt.

Jones, E. E. (1990). *Interpersonal perception*. New York: Freeman.

Kunst-Wilson, W. R., & Zajonc, R. B. (1980). Affective discrimination of stimuli that cannot be recognized. *Science, 207*, 557–558.

Moreland, R. L., & Zajonc, R. B. (1977). Is stimulus recognition a necessary condition for the occurrence of exposure effects? *Journal of Personality and Social Psychology, 35*, 191–199.

Moreland, R. L., & Zajonc, R. B. (1979). Exposure effects may not depend on stimulus recognition. *Journal of Personality and Social Psychology, 37*, 1085–1089.

Murphy, S. T., & Zajonc, R. B. (1993). Affect, cognition and awareness: Affective priming with suboptimal and optimal stimulus. *Journal of Personality and Social Psychology, 64*, 723–739.

Muesseler, J., & Hommel, B. (1997). Blindness to response-compatible stimuli. *Journal of Experimental Psychology: Human Perception and Performance, 23*, 861–872.

Neely, J. H. (1977). Semantic priming and retrieval from lexical memory: Roles of inhibitionless spreading activation and limited-capacity attention. *Journal of Experimental Psychology: General, 106*, 226–254.

Rajecki, D. W., Kidd, R. F., & Ivins, B. (1976). Social facilitation in chickens: A different level of analysis. *Journal of Experimental Social Psychology, 12*, 233–246.

Rizzolatti, G., & Arbib, M. A. (1998). Language within our grasp. *Trends in Neuroscience, 21*, 188–194.

Sanders, G. S. (1981). Driven by distraction: An integrative review of social facilitation theory and research. *Journal of Experimental Social Psychology, 17,* 227–251.

Smith, E. R., & Lerner, M. (1986). Development of automatism of social judgments. *Journal of Personality and Social Psychology, 37,* 2240–2252.

Wilson, W. R. (1979). Feeling more than we can know: Exposure effects without learning. *Journal of Personality and Social Psychology, 33,* 811–821.

Wyer, R. S., Jr., & Srull, T. K. (1989). *Memory and cognition in its social context.* Hillsdale, NJ: Erlbaum.

Zajonc, R. B. (1960). The process of cognitive tuning in communication. *Journal of Abnormal and Social Psychology, 61,* 159–167.

Zajonc, R. B. (1968a). Attitudinal effects of mere exposure. *Journal of Personality and Social Psychology* (Monograph Suppl.), *9,* 1–27.

Zajonc, R. B. (1968b). Cognitive theories in social psychology. In G. Lindzey & E. Aronson (Eds.), *Handbook of social psychology,* (2nd ed., pp. 319–411). New York: Random House

Zajonc, R. B. (1980). Feeling and thinking: Preferences need no inferences. *American Psychologist, 35,* 151–175.

Zajonc, R. B., Adelman, P. K., Murphy, S. T., & Niedenthal, P. M. (1987). Convergence in the physical appearance of spouses. *Motivation and Emotion, 11,* 335–346.

Zajonc, R. B., Heingartner, A., & Herman, E. M. (1969). Social enhancement and impairment of performance in the cockroach. *Journal of Personality and Social Psychology, 13,* 83–92.

CHAPTER 4

Feeling Without Thinking: Affective Primacy and the Nonconscious Processing of Emotion

Sheila T. Murphy

I n 1980, as a freshman at the University of Michigan, I walked into an undergraduate honors class in psychology. During the very first meeting of the class, the professor did two things: First, he corrected the pronunciation of his name—noting that it was Zajonc, which rhymes with *science*. Second, he distributed a draft of a paper he was working on titled "Feeling and Thinking: Preferences Need No Inferences." In reading the manuscript, I became entranced. I distinctly remember thinking that this paper contained some of the most insightful and provocative ideas I had ever read.

The paper proposed that perhaps the simple emotional or affective qualities of stimuli, such as good/bad, are processed extremely quickly and efficiently without extensive perceptual and cognitive processing. It further argued that some sort of primitive positive/negative affective reaction may occur very early on in the information-processing chain, even prior to the sorts of cognitive operations such as categorization that are commonly assumed to be the basis of these affective reactions. In other words, affect may be primary.

From a theoretical perspective, the notion of affective primacy was nothing short of heresy. The current consensus was clear: Affect was postcognitive, elicited only after considerable cognitive processing. Zajonc (1980) summarized this position as follows:

> An affective reaction, such as liking, disliking, preference, evaluation, or the experience of pleasure or displeasure, is based on a prior cognitive process in which a variety of content discriminations are made and features are identified, examined for their value, and weighted for their contributions. Once this analytic task has been completed, a computation of the components can generate an overall affective judgment. (p. 151)

As depicted in Figure 4.1, if affect was incorporated in information-processing models at all, it tended to be begrudgingly appended to the end of the process, almost as an afterthought.

FIGURE 4.1

Typical information-processing model of affect. Reprinted with permission from Zajonc, 1980.

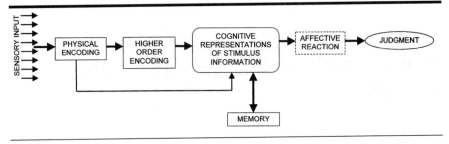

In his "Feeling and Thinking" article, Zajonc contested this temporal order. He asserted that the notion that people go through life in a rational manner, objectively weighing the pros and cons of various alternatives prior to taking a position as suggested by extant information-processing models, might be little more than wishful thinking. Instead, he argued that the affective qualities of stimuli such as good/bad, like/dislike, or approach/avoid might be processed extremely quickly and efficiently and, consequently, could be among the very first reactions of an organism to its environment. But moving affect to the front of the information-processing chain as Zajonc was proposing drastically alters one's conception of human behavior. Within an affective primacy framework, individuals gather information about various alternatives, not to make more informed choices, but to corroborate their initial preferences and desires. For example, an individual seeks out favorable statistics on gas mileage and resale value to justify purchasing the very car he or she coveted in the first place. Thus, from an affective primacy perspective, man is not so much a rational being as a rationalizing one.

The notion of affective primacy struck me as true. But if true, there were at least two issues left unresolved. First, the evidence presented in "Feeling and Thinking" drew heavily on the mere-exposure phenomenon in which liking increases as a function of repeated exposures, even when stimuli are presented at exposures so brief that they cannot be consciously recognized (Moreland & Zajonc, 1979). But while suggestive, the mere-exposure effect does not directly test the notion that affective reactions enjoy a privileged position in the information-processing chain, perhaps preceding even rudimentary cognitive processes such as recognition and categorization. The second unresolved issue involved the precise mechanism that would allow for such an early affective reaction. In other words, what mechanism would permit an individual to affectively evaluate an object even prior to knowing what the object is? This question harkens back to the perceptual defense studies of the New Look in which participants seemed to take longer to recognize "dirty words" such as *Kotex, penis,* and so on (see Erdelyi, 1974, for a review). The theoretical explanation offered for this slower response time was that some unspecified part of the brain was protecting participants from these potentially threatening words. Critics of perceptual defense pointed out that this was tantamount to proposing that humans have a homunculus or "little man" in their heads who, in essence, previews content and acts as an internal censor by attempting to shield them from perceiving anything sordid.

Over the past 18 years, Bob Zajonc and I have attempted to address the issues of whether affect is, indeed, primary in the information-processing chain and, if so, what mechanisms might make this possible. In the remainder of this chapter, I briefly sketch some of the ways Zajonc, I, and our collaborators have approached these questions. I have included some of the highlights of our endeavors and some of our less well-known unpublished efforts that may prove even more illuminating. My hope is that our 20-year search for evidence of affective primacy will provide a unique insight into how expansive and inventive a methodologist Robert Zajonc truly is for those who have never had the privilege of collaborating with him.

The Role of Nonverbal Channels in the Production and Transmission of Emotion

In "Feeling and Thinking," Zajonc (1980) proposed that the communication of affect relies heavily on nonverbal channels and that perhaps an affective reaction such as approach/avoid is

> not always transformed into semantic content but is instead often encoded in, for example, visceral or muscular symbols, we would expect information contained in feelings to be acquired, organized, categorized, represented, and retrieved somewhat differently than information having direct verbal referents. . . . In light of these intuitions, it is not unreasonable to speculate that the processing of affect is closer to the acquisition and retention of motor skills than of word lists. (p. 158)

Following this logic, Zajonc noted that the term typically used to describe a preference or opinion, namely *attitude*, had as its origin the literal "arrangement of the parts of a body or figure" (Webster's Ninth Collegiate Dictionary, 1983). Clearly, this was more than mere coincidence. We set out to determine if there was a correlation between the literal meaning of attitude, namely, the physical leaning toward or away from a stimulus, and its more figurative or psychological meaning. To do so, Zajonc had what, at first blush, appeared to be an ingenious idea. We would place bathroom scales under each of the four legs of a chair and monitor how individuals redistributed their weight when presented with various positive and negative stimuli. We would then correlate these physical movements with participants' self-reported attitudes.

The logistical flaw in our design did not become apparent until I had the apparatus assembled in the lab. Simply put, bathroom scales are designed to be read from above. This meant that the only way someone could simultaneously read all four scales was to locate himself or herself physically underneath the chair. Unfortunately, when participants discovered me lying in wait beneath their chair they tended to sit abnormally still, thus defeating the purpose of the study. I attempted to salvage the study by making my presence under the chair covert by enshrouding the entire chair with a blanket. Unfortunately, this meant that I was crouched beneath a chair for up to 45 minutes at a time in pitch darkness trying to simultaneously read four bathroom scales with a flashlight. Needless to say, you will not find this study gracing the pages of the *Journal of Personality and Social Psychology*.

Convergence in the Physical Appearance of Spouses

Shortly thereafter, Zajonc decided to restrict his focus of attention from movement of the entire body to movement of the face. More specifically, he became fixated on the fact that the face seems to have a disproportionate number of muscles. He contended that these facial muscles must have evolved to serve some purpose, and went on to speculate that perhaps the function they serve is the production and transmission of emotion (Zajonc, 1985). One evening at a cocktail party, Robert Zajonc, Paula Niedenthal, Pam Adelmann, and I became embroiled in a discussion of the implications of this position. For instance, wouldn't two people who interact frequently tend to involuntarily mimic each other's expressions and consequently build and atrophy the same muscles? In other words, wouldn't couples who interact on a daily basis grow to look more alike over time?

To test whether or not couples do, in fact, increase in resemblance to one another over time, we gathered photographs of married couples from roughly the same age cohort who had recently celebrated their 25th wedding anniversary. We asked each couple to provide individual photographs of themselves from the year prior to their wedding (Time 1) and current photos (Time 2), as well as answer some questions about their relationship. Participants were then presented with various arrays of photographs and were asked to rank order the probability that a given woman was married to each of six men and vice versa. Our participants were, in fact, better able to match spouses at Time 2 after 25 years of marriage, supporting the conjecture that couples may indeed grow to look more alike over time (Zajonc, Adelmann, Murphy, & Niedenthal, 1987).[1] It is interesting to note that couples

---

[1] Andy Warhol once observed that everyone at some point in their lives will have 15 minutes of fame. I often lie in bed at night and worry that I expended my 15 minutes on this study. After our findings became public, we were hounded by every major talk show and tabloid. My personal favorite was a summary of our findings in that bastion of fine journalism, *STAR* magazine, where our results were juxtaposed between "DOG DRIVES TRUCK" and "WOMAN GIVES SELF CESAREAN WITH CAN OPENER."

who spent more time together were not only more likely to resemble one another but also self-reported a higher level of marital satisfaction.

The Vascular Theory of Emotional Efference

I suspect that one reason that our finding that couples grow to look more alike over time was embraced by the popular press was that it confirmed something that many already believed to be true. Related research involving the Vascular Theory of Emotional Efference (VTEE) did not enjoy similar critical acclaim, I believe, in part because it actively contradicted the common wisdom. The VTEE reexamined William James's contention that emotional expression is not merely a passive signal but that facial movement—which we referred to as *emotional efference*—might be capable of both producing and proceeding subjective feeling. In short, while it is undoubtedly the case that we smile because we are happy, the VTEE proposed that it may also be possible that we are happy because we smile. By reversing the temporal order of the emotional sequence, the vascular theory provided a potential mechanism whereby affect or emotion could influence judgments with very little cognitive mediation.

This line of research was also inspired by a book Zajonc had unearthed written in 1907 by an obscure French physician named Israel Waynbaum. Waynbaum speculated that the reason that the face has more than its fair share of muscles is that facial gestures in general, and emotional expressions in particular, have regulatory and restorative functions for the vascular system of the head. Although some of Waynbaum's assumptions, which were based on conceptions of physiology at the turn of the century, were clearly in error, Zajonc maintained that at least one central tenet may still be true:

> Facial action may alter the temperature of blood entering the brain by interfering with or facilitating the cooling process. These changes, in turn, may have subjective consequences through the release and synthesis of various neurotransmitters. (Zajonc, Murphy, & McIntosh, 1993, p. 212)

But how might one go about testing the relationship of facial movement, blood flow, temperature, and emotional state? Previous researchers had brought individuals into their lab, asked them to smile, and then proceeded to interrogate them about their subjective state. Not only is such an approach rife with demand characteristics, in and of itself such data would not provide a direct test of the relationship between brain temperature and affective state.

Never one to be constrained by traditional methodologies or logistical considerations, Zajonc convinced the U.S. military to sell us a used thermographic camera. This thermographic camera could detect and record heat changes as small as a fraction of a degree from a considerable distance. All we had to do was lure participants into the lab, induce them to make facial movements consistent with emotional expressions, and monitor changes in their facial temperature and mood. And this is precisely what we did. In one such study, under the guise of conducting a study in phonetics, individuals were instructed to repeat various vowel sounds—*ah, e, i, o, a, u,* and *ü*—20 times each at approximately 3-s intervals. We were particularly interested in the vowels *e*, which forces the face into an approximation of a smile; the sound *ah*, which mimics delight; and the vowels *u* and *ü*, which produce facial expressions similar to those seen in anger and disgust.

As can be noted in Figures 4.2a and 4.2b (reprinted from Zajonc, Murphy, & Inglehart, 1989), the vowel sounds *u* and *ü* were associated with a significant increase in forehead temperature as well as a significantly more negative subjective state as predicted by VTEE. Of course, one could argue that individuals were in a negative mood following the *ü* sound simply because it was relatively unfamiliar. To eliminate this alternative explanation, Zajonc, Marita Inglehart, and I subsequently replicated this finding using only native German speakers, for whom the *ü* sound was quite familiar.

Bolstered by these and similar results, Zajonc began to search for the precise mechanism whereby the blood flow to the brain is heated and cooled. He focused on a structure known as the cavernous sinus, which appears to act much like the radiator of a car by diffusing heat and thus keeping the brain relatively cool. Zajonc conjectured that if the cavernous sinus does, in fact, operate like a radiator to diffuse heat, it must do so, in part, by taking advantage of its proximity to the nasal cavity. In other words, breathing through the nose must help cool the brain. Such a mechanism would account for a range of phenomena, including why people feel so miserable when they have sinus congestion to why Lamaze and Yoga reduce pain.

All things being equal, then, people should prefer to breathe through their nose as opposed to their mouth. This line of reasoning gave rise to Project SNORT. Along with Steve Emerick from the University of Michigan Dental School, Zajonc devised an astronautlike apparatus that could be put over an individual's head and sealed to make it airtight. Air could then be pumped out of the helmetlike chamber, and one could calibrate precisely how much effort the participant expended struggling for oxygen through a small tube that had been placed in their nostril.[2] Our findings were conclusive: Individuals found not breathing in general and not breathing through the nasal passages in particular to be aversive. This provided further support for the role of the cavernous sinus in the regulation of emotion.

---

[2] As you may well imagine, we had difficulty recruiting individuals to participate in this study. Steve Emerick, who was actually running participants for us at the Dental School, soon determined that I was an "almost 100% nasal breather," which means I rarely, if ever, breathe through my mouth and, moreover, that I had exceptional lung capacity, making me a perfect candidate for SNORT. During the course of the next several months, I voluntarily allowed myself to be systematically suffocated a total of 23 times in the name of science.

(a) Changes in forehead temperature (in Celsius) for vowel phonemes.
(b) Pleasantness ratings (from 1 = bad to 7 = good) of vowel phonemes. From
"Feeling and Facial Efference: Implications of the Vascular Theory of Emotion,"
by R. B. Zajonc, S. T. Murphy, and M. Inglehart, 1989, Psychological Review,
96, p. 406. Copyright 1989 by the American Psychological Association.
Reprinted with permission.

(a)

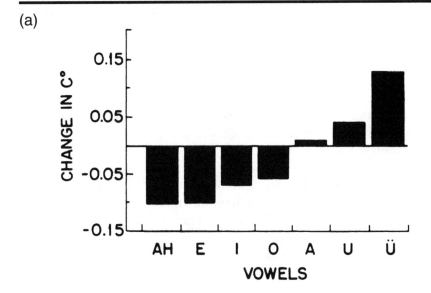

(b)

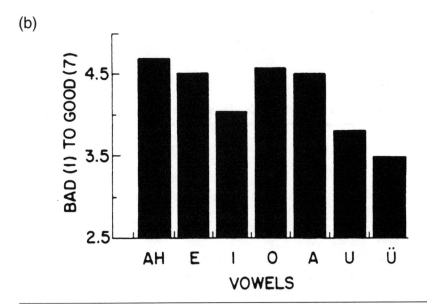

Priming and the Primacy of Affect

In the late 1980s, I began to collect data for my dissertation (part of which was later published as Murphy & Zajonc, 1993), which, in essence, attempted to gather more direct evidence for the affective primacy hypothesis. To test the notion that simple positive and negative emotional reactions can occur even without such basic cognitive processes as conscious identification, I conducted a study in which participants evaluated neutral stimuli (Chinese ideographs) that were preceded by 4-ms suboptimal exposures to positive or negative affective primes: smiling or angry faces. I selected smiling and angry faces as affective primes because I wanted primes that did not necessitate cognitive or semantic processing, as may have been the case with emotionally charged words like those used in the original perceptual defense studies of the New Look.

The cover story for a series of five experiments was that we were interested in snap judgments of novel stimuli. Participants were told that they would be presented with an assortment of Chinese characters which they were to rate on a scale from 1 to 5, on some dimension where 1 = *not at all* and 5 = *quite a bit*. They were then shown slides of 45 target ideographs. Within this series of 45 ideographs, 10 of the target ideographs in each study were shown twice, preceded by opposing primes. For instance, in Study 1, the 10 key Chinese ideographs appeared once primed with positive affect (in other words, preceded by a slide of an individual smiling) and once primed with negative affect (a slide of the same individual scowling). Because participants were unfamiliar with the ideographs, they were unaware that 10 of the 45, in fact, repeated. In each of five studies, ratings of these 10 repeating ideographs served as the dependent measure.

As is evident in Table 4.1, affective primes presented outside of conscious awareness had a significant influence on perceptions of the 10 repeating ideographs.

TABLE 4.1

Summary of Suboptimal Priming Conditions in Murphy and Zajonc (1993).

STUDY	SUBOPTIMAL PRIME	JUDGMENT OF TARGET IDEOGRAPH	STATISTICAL SIGNIFICANCE
1	Smiling and angry faces	Liking of ideographs	Yes
2	Smiling and angry faces	Is object represented by ideograph good or bad	Yes
3	Symmetrical and asymmetrical shapes	Symmetry of ideograph	No
4	Big and small shapes	Size of object represented	No
5	Male and female faces	Masculinity/femininity of object represented	No

For instance, in Study 1, the same target stimuli were rated significantly higher in likability when preceded by positive suboptimal primes (smiling faces) than when preceded by negative suboptimal primes (angry faces of the same individuals). Study 2 replicated this procedure of presenting affective suboptimal primes at 4-ms durations immediately prior to the target ideographs but now asked participants whether they thought the ideographs represented something good or bad. Once again, these affective primes presented outside of conscious awareness produced a significant shift in good/bad judgments of the target ideographs.

While the findings of these first two studies confirmed the expectation that emotional stimuli of which we are unaware can color our judgments, they leave unanswered the question of whether nonconscious affect is unique in its ability to sway subsequent judgments. After all, it may be the case that *any* relevant prime, regardless of whether it is emotional in nature or not, is more potent when presented suboptimally. On the other hand, if, as Zajonc's Primacy of Affect Hypothesis suggests, affective information is processed faster and more efficiently than other types of information, then we would expect very weak or nonexistent effects at the suboptimal level for simple affectively bland primes.

To test whether nonconscious affect was indeed unique in its ability to sway subsequent judgments, I conducted a series of replications using a variety of priming stimuli and judgments. For example, in Study 3, which again ostensibly dealt with judgments of novel stimuli, participants were presented with symmetrical and asymmetrical shapes as primes and were asked to rate the symmetry of the actual target ideographs. Participants in Study 4 were asked to rate the same 45 ideographs with respect to the size of the object each represented, where a 1 implied that a particular ideograph represented a relatively small object and a 5 implied that the ideograph represented a relatively large object. (The ideographs themselves were all roughly equal in size.) And finally, to eliminate the possibility that faces represent some sort of unique, socially significant stimuli to which our emotional reactions are "hard-wired" (Ekman, 1972), Study 5 used male and female faces as primes but asked participants whether each target ideograph represented a masculine object or a feminine object.

In summary, affective priming, using positive and negative facial expressions as primes, produced effects under very brief suboptimal exposures, whereas primes varying on such dimensions as size, symmetry, and gender did not. Affective information, therefore, at least within the constraints of this series of experiments, seemed to be processed earlier than equally simple information that was not affective in nature. These data, then, corroborated Zajonc's contention that emotional reactions can occur with minimal stimulation and they can therefore precede and alter subsequent cognitions.

Neurological Evidence for the Primacy of Affect

But how is it that we are somehow able to assess the emotional significance of stimuli presented at exposures so brief that they are not available to conscious awareness? How can individuals like or dislike something even before knowing what it is? It is on precisely these points that the physiological literature may be the most illuminating. Until fairly recently, the common wisdom has been that after registering stimuli, the sensory apparatus sends signals to the thalamus which, in turn, relays them to the sensory areas of the neocortex for integration and the analysis of meaning. This view is consistent with a strict cognitive appraisal view such as that espoused by Lazarus (1982, 1984) and others which would require all emotional reactions to be mediated by neocortical activity.

On the basis of Zajonc's concept of affective primacy, however, LeDoux and his colleagues have located a direct pathway between the thalamus and the amygdala that is just one synapse long (LeDoux, 1994, 1995). This direct access from the thalamus to the amygdala allows the amygdala to respond faster to a stimulus event than the hippocampus, which is separated from the thalamus by several synapses. According to LeDoux, the amygdala can respond to a stimulus as much as 40 ms faster. If LeDoux is correct, this neuroanatomical architecture would then allow for an affective evaluation even prior to conscious awareness. Thus, although the question is far from resolved, there is at least one plausible neurological account of how affective reactions can be rapidly initiated on the basis of crude stimulus properties prior to and perhaps independent of more complex stimulus appraisals.

The Additivity of Nonconscious Affect

In 1990, I accepted an assistant professor position at the Annenberg School for Communication at the University of Southern California (USC). This did not, however, mark the end of my collaboration with Zajonc. For the past several years, he and I have had the distinct pleasure of working with Jennifer Monahan, who was my graduate student at USC and is currently an assistant professor at the University of Georgia. Our first joint collaboration was published in 1995 (Murphy, Monahan, & Zajonc, 1995) and addressed the issue of whether affect generated from a source of which one is unaware may be distinct from affect whose source is known.

To examine this issue, we ran four parallel studies in which participants were first shown a series of 72 Chinese ideographs. Of these 72, 24 were filler ideographs, each of which was shown only once and was not included in the subsequent priming/evaluation phase. For the remaining 48 exposures, we attempted to generate differential levels of liking among the ideographs by varying frequency of presentation. More specifically, 12 key ideographs were presented only once, whereas 12 others appeared three times.

Following this initial exposure phase, participants were asked to indicate how much they liked and whether they recognized each of 48 ideographs—24 of which were completely novel (zero exposure), 12 of which they had been exposed to once previously (single exposure), and 12 others which had been presented three times previously (multiple exposure). During this subsequent evaluation phase, the ideographs were preceded by a positive affective prime (a smiling face), a negative affective prime (an angry face), or no prime. Each of the four studies, therefore, included an initial exposure phase followed by an priming/evaluation phase. The four studies differed, however, in that the exposure duration in both the initial mere-exposure phase and the subsequent priming/evaluation phase was orthogonally varied such that both were either at optimal 1-s exposures, both were at suboptimal 4-ms exposures, or one was presented at an optimal exposure duration whereas the other was presented suboptimally.

Our results suggest that when two sources of affect are unavailable to conscious awareness, the affect generated from one source (repeated exposures) may be able to combine with nonconscious affect generated from a second unrelated source (suboptimal priming of smiling and angry faces). Indeed, positive suboptimal priming roughly added a constant, whereas negative suboptimal priming subtracted a constant from the positive affect induced through repeated exposures. It is interesting that this effect occurred regardless of whether the ideographs in the initial exposure phase were presented suboptimally for 4 ms or optimally for 1 s. Table 4.2 summarizes the change in liking scores on a 5-point scale from a baseline control (no previous exposures, no affective primes) for those ideographs preceded by three prior repetitions and a positive affective prime as a function of the exposure duration.

As evident in Table 4.2, whereas affective priming only produced effects suboptimally, the growth in preference associated with repeated exposures proceeded regardless of the stimulus duration in the initial exposure phase. This finding highlights the inadequacy of relying solely on exposure duration as an indicator of subjective awareness. During debriefing, participants in the optimal priming conditions reported being suspicious of the smiling and angry faces presented immediately prior to the ideographs they were asked to judge. In contrast, under conditions involving optimally repeated exposures, participants—although aware of the repetition as revealed in their elevated recognition rate—did not attribute any sinister

TABLE 4.2

Increase in Liking Ratings Following Three Prior Exposures and Positive Affective Prime as a Function of Exposure Duration.

Exposure duration of positive affective prime during subsequent evaluation phase	EXPOSURE DURATION OF IDEOGRAPH IN INITIAL EXPOSURE PHASE	
	SUBOPTIMAL (4 MS)	**OPTIMAL (1 S)**
Suboptimal	0.94_b	1.09_b
Optimal	0.39_a	0.31_a

Note. Table entries that share the same letter subscript are not significantly different from one another.

intent to the repetition. In fact, when requested during debriefing to speculate as to what impact multiple repetitions may have had on their ratings, the majority of respondents predicted that repetition would lead to boredom and decreased liking.[3] We concluded that it was this lack of awareness regarding the actual source of the affect, namely, that repeated exposures results in increased liking, that allowed the affect generated to remain diffuse. In contrast, when a source of affect is obvious and readily available to conscious awareness—as was clearly the case with the optimally presented smiling and angry facial primes—it becomes dedicated and, consequently, is no longer able to merge with affect from other unrelated sources.[4]

The Mere-Exposure Effect: Dedicated or Diffuse?

But these 1995 results contain an intriguing paradox. There have been more than 200 empirical demonstrations of the mere-exposure phenomenon whereby as long as one starts out feeling at least neutral toward an object, repeated exposures tend to increase liking for that specific object (for reviews, see Bornstein, 1989; Harrison, 1977). Typically, these studies take the following form: There is an initial exposure phase in which an individual is presented with an array of stimuli, some of which are shown only once whereas others are included multiple times. This initial exposure phase is followed by an evaluation phase during which individuals are exposed to a range of stimuli including both "old" or previously presented stimuli and "new" or novel stimuli and are asked both how much they like each item and whether they recognize it from the initial exposure phase. The classic result is that the greater the number of repetitions in the initial exposure phase the more participants report liking a particular stimuli. For example, an item that was shown 25 times is typically favored over one that is shown 5 times, which, in turn, is preferred to a completely novel item. Recognition, in contrast, is generally unrelated to liking. The finding that liking increases as a function of prior exposure has been shown to hold regardless of whether the stimuli are presented at levels above or below conscious awareness (Moreland & Zajonc, 1979).

In Murphy et al. (1995), we stated that nonconscious affect whose source is unknown is diffuse and able to spill over or attach itself to even unrelated stimuli. Furthermore, we present data demonstrating that by and large people are unaware of the relationship between repeated exposure and liking. Which brings us to the paradox: Is the affect generated by repeated exposures outside of conscious awareness

---

[3]A study by Snell, Gibbs, and Varey (1995) likewise demonstrated that people do not believe that repeated exposure alone could increase liking.

[4]This is somewhat analogous to Schwarz and Clore's (1983) finding that the weather has a profound effect on all manner of seemingly unconnected judgments until its influence is pointed out, at which point individuals are able to discount its impact.

dedicated to the specific stimuli involved, or is it nonconscious and therefore diffuse and capable of coloring other unrelated objects and events?

To answer this question, we recently ran a study in which participants were randomly assigned to one of three initial exposure conditions: They were presented suboptimally for 4 ms with five repetitions of 5 stimuli (i.e., Chinese ideographs or random polygons), they were suboptimally presented with 25 different stimuli, or they were assigned to a no-exposure control condition. Following this initial suboptimal exposure phase, they were asked to indicate how much they liked each of 15 stimuli on a scale ranging from 1 to 5, where 1 = *not at all* and 5 = *quite a bit*. There were three distinct types of stimuli included in this evaluation phase: 5 "old" or previously shown stimuli, 5 new but structurally similar stimuli ("novel similar"), and 5 stimuli that were both new and structurally dissimilar to those presented in the initial exposure phase ("novel different").

If one looks within each exposure condition in Figure 4.3, one can readily see that these results are consistent with those of prior studies in that there is a direct relation between number of prior exposures and preference. This suggests that the mere-exposure effect is due, at least in part, to affect that is dedicated to the specific generating stimuli. But looking across the exposure conditions reveals a second, somewhat unexpected, trend. Although prior repeated exposure does, in fact, increase liking of the *specific* "old" stimuli presented, repeated exposures also appears to increase ratings of novel stimuli as well.

FIGURE 4.3

Liking ratings as a function of number of prior exposures and stimulus type (Monahan, Murphy, & Zajonc, in press).

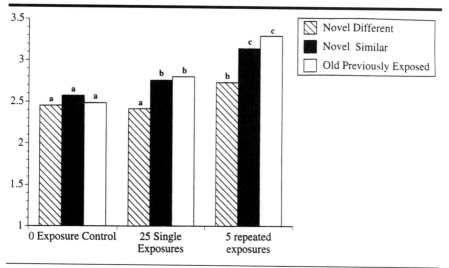

One could argue that this is simply an "anchoring artifact" whereby higher ratings of "old" stimuli produce an overall inflation of liking ratings across stimuli. However, although such an explanation might account for the higher ratings across all stimuli shown, it does not explain why participants in the multiple exposure condition (who were presented with five repetitions of five stimuli) also reported themselves to be in a significantly better mood on multiple measures than their counterparts in the other two exposure conditions (25 single exposures and the zero exposure control).

Thus, it appears that repetition of even seemingly innocuous stimuli such as Chinese ideographs and random polygons may be sufficient to temporarily enhance an individual's affective state. This elevation in mood might, in turn, influence subsequent evaluations of both the specific stimuli that elicited the positive affect as well as other stimuli in the immediate environment. Such a process would predict that previously presented or "old" stimuli should receive the greatest boost in ratings, similar but novel stimuli the second highest boost, and novel and dissimilar objects the least. This is precisely the pattern we found. While we are still exploring the implications of these findings, it seems quite possible that repeated exposures may generate positive affect that is in part dedicated to the specific stimuli and partly diffuse and thus able to "spill over" and influence a range of judgments including one's own subjective state.

Conclusion

It is rare that one can point to a single article or even a single theory as having a profound impact on the direction of a field. But one need only contrast the frequency with which the words *affect* and *emotion* appear in the psychological literature in the years preceding and following 1980 to underscore how Zajonc's notion that perhaps the simple emotional or affective qualities of stimuli, such as good/bad, are processed extremely quickly and efficiently without extensive perceptual and cognitive processing has indelibly altered models of information processing. Affect is no longer an unwanted appendage but is now understood to play an early and integral part in how individuals interact in their world.

In closing, I would like to provide one final piece of evidence for Zajonc's theory of affective primacy. In preparing this chapter, I recently reread his "Feeling and Thinking" article. I remain more convinced than ever that this work contains some of the most insightful and provocative ideas I have ever read.

References

Bornstein, R. F. (1989). Exposure and affect: Overview and meta-analysis of research, 1968–1987. *Psychological Bulletin, 106*, 265–289.

Ekman, P. (1972). Universals and cultural differences in the facial expression of emotion. In J. Cole (Ed.), *Nebraska symposium of motivation, 1971* (Vol. 19, pp. 207–283). Lincoln: University of Nebraska Press.

Erdelyi, M. H. (1974). A new look at the New Look: Perceptual defense and vigilance. *Psychological Review, 81,* 1–25.

Harrison, A. A. (1977). Mere exposure. In L. Berkowitz (Ed.), *Advances in experimental social psychology* (Vol. 10, pp. 39–83). San Diego, CA: Academic Press.

Lazarus, R. S. (1982). Thoughts on the relationship between emotion and cognition. *American Psychologist, 37,* 1019–1024.

Lazarus, R. S. (1984). On the primacy of cognition. *American Psychologist, 37,* 124–129.

LeDoux, J. E. (1994). Emotion, memory and the brain. *Scientific American, 270*(6), 50–57.

LeDoux, J. E. (1995). Emotion: Clues from the brain. *Annual Review of Psychology, 46,* 209–235.

Monahan, J. L., Murphy, S. T., & Zajonc, R. B. (In press). Mere exposure: Specific, general and diffuse effects. *Psychological Science.*

Moreland, R. L., & Zajonc, R. B. (1979). Exposure effects may not depend on stimulus recognition. *Journal of Personality and Social Psychology, 37,* 1085–1089.

Murphy, S. T., Monahan, J., & Zajonc, R. B. (1995). Additivity of nonconscious affect: The combined effects of priming and exposure. *Journal of Personality and Social Psychology, 69,* 589–602.

Murphy, S. T., & Zajonc, R. B. (1993). Affect, cognition, and awareness: Affective priming with suboptimal and optimal stimulus. *Journal of Personality and Social Psychology, 64,* 723–739.

Schwarz, N., & Clore, G. L. (1983). Mood, misattribution, and judgments of well-being: Informative and directive functions of affective states. *Journal of Personality and. Social Psychology, 45,* 513–523.

Snell, A., Gibbs, B. J., & Varey, C. (1995). Intuitive hedonics: Consumer beliefs about the dynamics of liking. *Journal of Consumer Psychology, 4,* 33–60.

Waynbaum, I. (1907). La physionomie humaine: Son mechanisme et son role social. [The human face: Its mechanism and social function]. Paris: Alcon.

Webster's Ninth New Collegiate Dictionary. (1983). Springfield, MA: Merriam-Webster.

Zajonc, R. B. (1980). Feeling and thinking: Preferences need no inferences. *American Psychologist, 35,* 151–175.

Zajonc, R. B. (1985). Emotion and facial efference: A theory reclaimed. *Science, 228,* 15–21.

Zajonc, R. B., Adelmann, P. K., Murphy, S. T., & Niedenthal, P. M. (1987). Convergence in the physical appearance of spouses. *Motivation and Emotion, 11,* 335–346.

Zajonc, R. B., Murphy, S. T., & Inglehart, M. (1989). Feelings and facial efference: Implications of the vascular theory of emotion. *Psychological Review, 96,* 395–416.

Zajonc, R. B., Murphy, S. T., & McIntosh, D. N. (1993). Brain temperature and subjective emotional experience. In M. Lewis & J. M. Haviland (Eds.), *The handbook of emotions* (pp. 209–220). New York: Guilford Press.

CHAPTER 5

Relational Schema Activation: Does Bob Zajonc Ever Scowl at You From the Back of Your Mind?

Mark W. Baldwin

I had the good fortune to spend some postdoctoral time at the University of Michigan in 1984. It was an exciting time then. For one thing, being 1984, society was abuzz with talk of George Orwell's Big Brother. At the Institute for Social Research, the halls were abuzz with talk of unconscious processes, self-regulation, social intelligence, motivated cognition, affective processes, and the like. In this chapter, I describe a couple of studies I did at that time, which certainly show the influence of what was going on at the University of Michigan; then I discuss some of my recent work that has grown out of that.

During that time there were a number of people, from different areas of social and personality psychology, who were beginning to study a specific type of cognitive/affective/motivational structure having to do with interpersonal patterns of interaction. Object relations, attachment, and interpersonal theorists of personality, for example, all were interested in the models people form of how they relate to their significant others, and how these models shape their emotions, perceptions, and behaviors in interpersonal interaction (e.g., Horowitz, 1988; Mitchell, 1988; Safran, 1990; Stern, 1985; see also Andersen & Cole, 1990; Fiske, 1992; Planalp, 1985). Self theorists were interested in internalization processes, whereby, for example, experiences of being criticized by a parent or authority figure become stored in a person's memory and later shape self-evaluation and regulation according to demanding standards, producing associated emotional reactions such as low self-esteem and depression (e.g., Ogilvie & Ashmore, 1991).

A number of us felt that to understand these kinds of processes we needed to posit knowledge structures, which some of us have been calling *relational schemas* (see Baldwin, 1992, for a review), that represent regularities in interpersonal interaction and communication. The assumption is that relational schemas consist of some aggregation of information, including episodic memories about past interactions, along with generic representations of both self and other as both are experienced

55

in a given relationship. Self and other are presumably linked together in a self-with-other schema as some people have described it: Central to the notion of relational schemas is the assumption that the critical link between self and other is an interpersonal script or event schema representing the typical interaction patterns occurring in that relationship.

Private Audiences

One of the main issues of interest to me was how cognition regarding the self was shaped by structures relating to communicative contexts. As Zajonc (1960) suggested in his provocative work on cognitive tuning, people's thought processes are often shaped by thoughts of communicating with specific other people having specific traits, knowledge, goals, and so on. While I agree with Zajonc and Adelmann (1987) that this profound principle has not been studied adequately by social psychologists, it has received some attention (e.g., Higgins & Rholes, 1978; Levine, Bogart, & Zdaniuk, 1996). My contribution has been to seek some evidence that this communicative context need not be a function of one's current or immediately anticipated interactions but can be established by the activation of a knowledge structure representing a well-learned interaction pattern. The audience shaping the cognitive tuning of thought, therefore, need not be present in the flesh but can be a completely private audience.

One benefit of formulating a social cognitive model such as this is that it allows one to tie in with the broader social cognitive literature, and therefore to anticipate numerous information-processing consequences of relational schemas. Research has shown that, as with other knowledge structures, attention is drawn to relevant information, interpretation of ambiguous information is biased, memory is enhanced for relevant information, and affective and goal-oriented responses are triggered.

Building on a core idea in the social cognitive literature, I now describe research that involves the activation or priming of relational schemas. The notion here is simply that most people have available to them a range of relational schemas representing different interpersonal patterns—for example, secure, unconditional acceptance by a friend versus critical evaluation by an authority figure—therefore, it should be possible to prime a specific structure and see an impact on perceptions of self and other.

Reactions to Sex

In my early work with John Holmes (ultimately published as Baldwin & Holmes, 1987), we examined the activation of norms and evaluative styles associated with specific relational schemas. In one study, we asked undergraduate women to read a sexually permissive passage from *Cosmopolitan* magazine that described a woman having sex with an attractive man she did not know particularly well. They were asked to rate how enjoyable and exciting they found the passage. Ten minutes earlier, down the hall ostensibly in an unrelated experiment about visual imagination, these women had just spent a few minutes visualizing either friends of theirs from campus or their parents. We hypothesized that when the participants later rated the sexy story, their ratings would be influenced by the particular "private audience" that was in the back of their mind as a result of the visualization prime. As predicted, women who had visualized their parents rated the passage less positively than those who had visualized their (presumably more permissive) friends from campus. During debriefing, one woman in the parent-prime condition apologized for how long it took her to fill out the questionnaire, saying that when she came to the question asking how exciting she felt the story was, she found herself carrying on, in fantasy, a heated discussion with her mother about which number to circle!

Reactions to Failure

In another study (Baldwin & Holmes, 1987, Study 2), we examined the influence of different relational schemas on reactions to failure. We first used a guided visualization procedure to prime male undergraduate students with either a supportive, unconditionally accepting relationship—a friend who "would accept you no matter what"—or a more demanding relationship in which acceptance was conditional or contingent on performing well at things. We then had participants carry out an extremely difficult task, which they performed quite poorly, to see if their style of self-evaluation would be shaped by the earlier prime. As predicted, those who had been primed with a conditional, evaluative relationship felt worse about their failure and were particularly likely to say their failure was due to something about themselves rather than something about the task. As I have argued elsewhere (Baldwin, 1997), people learn the evaluative rules or procedures (e.g., comparison to high standards, internal attribution, and focus on negatives vs. positives) that tend to be applied by different significant others. When a specific relationship later becomes activated in a performance situation, the associated rules become accessible and likely to be applied in self-evaluation.

Unconscious Processes

My assumption was that the effects of relational schemas on self-construal were not the result of deliberate calculation, or even actively taking the role of the other. Rather, I thought an activated audience exerted its influence from the periphery, as in previous discussions of tacit knowledge (Polanyi, 1966; Wegner & Giuliano, 1982). Most of social psychology still emphasized conscious, deliberate thought processes, however, and the field lacked models and methods for addressing such implicit processes.

Then I came to Michigan. It was the early 1980s, and the field was struggling to come to terms with Zajonc's arguments and findings that affective and evaluative processes could be affected by stimuli perceived without awareness (Zajonc, 1980). Other work (e.g., Bargh & Pietromonaco, 1982) was showing the possibility of also triggering social cognitive structures, such as trait categories, using subliminal primes.

Shortly after arriving in Ann Arbor, I was at a departmental social gathering, talking with Sheila Murphy about her emotional priming work with Bob (e.g., Murphy & Zajonc, 1993) and my interest in internalized relationships and self-evaluation. Somewhere along the line it became clear that a salient authority figure—one might even say Big Brother figure—in the department, from the students' point of view, was the director Bob Zajonc. Now, many of us know Bob for the warm, good-humored, generous person he is.[1] For the students, however, it seemed that while he was well loved and certainly respected for his keen intellect, the prospect of him being in the audience while one gave a talk, tuning in that keen intellect on the flaws or shortcomings in one's research, was absolutely terrifying.

So I asked Bob if I could meet with him one morning. I explained my idea for a study to him, and he graciously agreed to pose for some photographs. A few weeks later I was set up in the lab and ran a short experiment with 16 of the graduate students in the department. I asked the students to jot down three of their own research ideas they were working on; then I had them evaluate each on a number of scales asking about originality, quality, and so on—certainly an ego-involving task in this heavily research-oriented program. Before evaluating each idea, though, I had them perform a bogus reaction-time task in which they responded as quickly as possible by pressing a button when they saw a flash of light projected briefly on the wall before them. On the first trial, they saw four exposures of a multicolored design, then they rated the quality of their first idea. This trial served as a kind of pretest of the masking stimulus. On the second trial, unbeknownst to the participants, half of them were given four masked 2-ms exposures of a picture of Bob Zajonc, scowling at them in total disgust (see Figure 5.1).

For the other half of the sample, I originally intended to use a picture of Bob smiling in approval, but he advised me that this probably would still terrify the students! So instead I used a smiling picture of John Ellard, a postdoctoral fellow in the department at the time, as a kind of control condition. After the bogus reaction-time task, participants rated their second idea; then on the final trial they were exposed to the other picture and they rated their third idea. To make a long story short, whereas they rated their ideas an A− in the approval condition, they gave themselves only a C+ after they were exposed to Bob's scowling face (see Figure

---

[1] Indeed, Bob's warmth and generosity were well evidenced by his gracious sharing of some fine Polish vodka with all the attendees at the Festschrift conference.

FIGURE 5.1

The scowling Bob stimulus. From "Priming Relationship Schemas: My Advisor and the Pope Are Watching Me From the Back of My Mind," by M. W. Baldwin, S. E. Carrell, and D. F. Lopez, 1990, Journal of Experimental Social Psychology, 26, 435–454. Copyright 1990 by Academic Press. Reprinted with permission.

5.2). It is worth noting that while this brief-exposure effect might seem remarkable, some of Bob's former students have confirmed that 2 ms was approximately the amount of time it usually took Bob to make a good/bad judgment of their ideas!

There were plenty of possible explanations for these findings, of course. I have not tried to pin down the effect precisely, but I have conducted a couple of follow-up studies. Maybe, for example it was the stark unpleasantness of the *preferenda* (or affect-relevant features; see Zajonc, 1980) in Bob's facial expression that induced a negative mood, rather than anything about Bob or his reputation as an authority figure.[2] If so, then exposure to any scowling face might be expected to have this kind of impact. A year later I was at the University of Waterloo supervising the senior theses of Suzanne Carrell and David Lopez, who are both Catholic. We devised a study in which we asked undergraduate Catholic women to read the sexy passage I mentioned earlier, and later answer some questions about their own morality, self-esteem, anxiety, and so on (see Baldwin, Carrell, & Lopez, 1990). Before they made these self-ratings, though, some of them were subliminally exposed to a picture of Pope John Paul II, scowling in mild disapproval. We found that self-

---

[2]Alternatively, perhaps it was the inherent benevolence of the approving face that actually accounted for most of the effect. I am grateful to John Ellard for alerting me to this possible explanation.

FIGURE 5.2

Idea evaluations as a function of prime and trial. From "Priming Relationship Schemas: My Advisor and the Pope Are Watching Me From the Back of My Mind," by M. W. Baldwin, S. E. Carrell, and D. F. Lopez, 1990, Journal of Experimental Social Psychology, 26, p. 441. Copyright 1990 by Academic Press. Reprinted with permission.

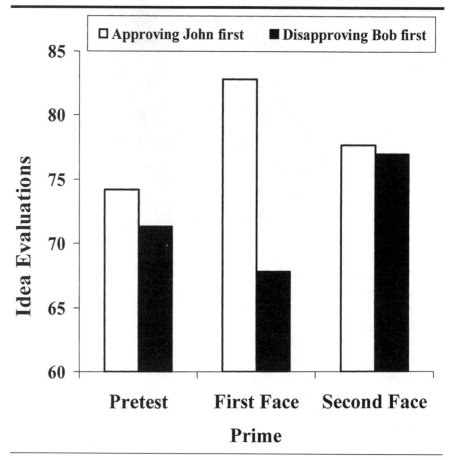

ratings were lower in the group exposed to the picture of the Pope, compared with a no-picture control group. It was not purely a function of facial expression, however. In another condition, participants were shown the scowling face of Bob Zajonc, who was unknown to them: For these participants, ratings were no lower than in the no-picture control condition. And, as another indication that the identity of the scowler matters, women who considered themselves practicing Catholics were partic-ularly likely to show the low ratings in the Pope condition, and especially on items having to do with morality. Thus, the priming was effective to the extent that the stimulus person was significant to the participants in some way.

Still, it seemed possible we were merely tapping into some hardwired response to facial expressions, rather than into any knowledge structures related to social authority or evaluation per se. Also, one anonymous reviewer suggested (with tongue in cheek, I can only assume) that because we had used only the Pope and Bob as stimulus persons, we had no way of knowing whether the effect might only hold when the stimulus person was a Polish man in his 60s. So I did one final study (Baldwin, 1994) in which I asked people for the names of two of their own significant others: one who was relatively approving of them and one who was relatively critical or disapproving of them. Then I presented one of these names subliminally and measured self-evaluative reactions to a failure experience. Again, people were more self-critical in the condition in which a disapproving relationship had been primed.

So the good news—or bad news, depending on how you look at it—is that the effect generalizes beyond scowling pictures of Bob. It seems to matter who the stimulus person is, meaning that face recognition and personal significance are both relevant factors. Moreover, it is possible to produce the same effect with significant others' names rather than pictures. It seems safe to say that any number of different cues can prime relational schemas and influence the way people think about themselves.

Cued Activation

I now leave the issue of subliminal priming and turn to a question I have been interested in more recently, which has to do with the formation of cues or triggers for relational schemas. When you are thinking of quitting work for the day and going out to a party to meet new people, for example, which relational schema is activated: Is it your graduate advisor, leading you to feel that you should stay in and get more work done? Is it your religious leader, making you feel like you should go and seek warm fellowship with your conspecifics, as long as there is no sex involved? Is it a structure representing all the times you said something stupid at a party and people laughed at you or rejected you, making you socially anxious? Or, do you end up just opening a bag of chips and turning on the television?

This kind of question often seems to come up in the clinical literature, and in some recent research I have been studying social anxiety and social phobia. In this literature it is observed that even if people seem to have, available to them in memory, multiple models of relationships—including some structures representing positive, secure ways of relating to others—still something seems to trigger just the wrong relational schema at just the wrong time, leading them to anticipate rejection or criticism from others. The task for therapy, then, can involve seeking ways to cue positive structures at moments of stress or anxiety. Bringing this challenge into the lab, I have recently been interested in studying triggers for feelings of secure interpersonal acceptance.

When I was in graduate school, my friend Dave Jamieson asked to borrow my vacuum cleaner and tape recorder. He later explained that when he was a child his mother would vacuum the carpet every Saturday morning, and Dave would curl up under the covers and read his comic books, and these were some of his most secure memories. So, in graduate school he made a tape of himself vacuuming his apartment so that whenever he was feeling anxious or stressed he could pop the tape into his stereo and calm his nerves.

Associations such as this, through which relational schemas become activated by specific contexts or otherwise neutral stimuli such as songs on the radio, the smell of a distinctive perfume, or the taste of comfort food, are commonplace. In our recent research, Kelley Main and I have examined the possibility of creating similar associations experimentally (Baldwin & Main, 1998). We have asked whether it might be possible to experimentally create a new association between a relational schema and a neutral cue, such that later presentation of the cue can come to activate the relational schema during an anxiety-provoking social situation.

Participants were 56 undergraduate women. At the beginning of the experimental session, the participant underwent a conditioning procedure. This consisted of completing a bogus computerized questionnaire made up of questions such as, "What is your favorite flavor of ice cream?" They were told that we had already pretested this questionnaire with other university students to find out what kinds of answers they would like someone to give; now we were going to see if the participants' actual opinions matched up with the ones the other students chose as the ideal, or most likeable, answers.

The participants were also told that because people often want to know how well they are doing while answering the questions, they would periodically receive feedback about whether their answers were indeed the socially highly desirable ones. Feedback consisted of a row of approving or disapproving faces (representing matches and mismatches)[3] displayed on the computer screen for 1 s. In fact, the feedback was entirely bogus and was given every few questions in a fixed random order unrelated to the participant's actual answers. The conditioning procedure involved the computer emitting distinctive tone sequences as signals 0.5 s before the faces were displayed. For example, a participant might hear a high tone sequence followed by the approving faces; then a few questions later would hear the other, lower, sequence followed by the disapproving faces. One tone sequence was paired 100% with acceptance feedback; the other sequence was paired 100% with rejection feedback (tones were counterbalanced across participants). By the end of the 60-item, approximately 15-min questionnaire, all participants had been given 10 trials establishing a conditioned stimulus (CS)-acceptance tone sequence and 10 trials establishing a CS-rejection tone sequence.

---

[3] I thank Paula Niedenthal for lending us the stimuli.

Following a 5-min filler task, participants were informed they would be participating in a brief (5-min) conversation with a male experimenter, who in fact was a well-dressed confederate who had been instructed to behave in a reserved but not unfriendly way toward the participants. He was instructed not to initiate the conversation unless there was a pause of longer than 30 s, and was told to allow uncomfortable pauses to occur, based on the procedure used by Stopa and Clark (1993) in their research on social anxiety. Not surprisingly, participants generally found this an anxiety-provoking situation.

During this conversation, the computer on the other side of the room, which an experimenter ostensibly had been working on periodically during the session to develop new programs, repeatedly emitted one of three tone sequences. Depending on experimental condition, the tones were the CS-acceptance tones, the CS-rejection tones, or new control tones unfamiliar to participants. The confederate was unaware of which tones were paired with which faces for each particular participant.

Following the conversation, participants filled out a number of scales assessing their anxiety during the interaction and their metaperceptions of how the confederate probably perceived them. The confederate also filled out measures of how he did in fact perceive the participant.

Our major prediction was that the conditioning procedure would establish associations between the neutral cues and feelings of social acceptance and rejection, so that people who later interacted while the CS-rejection tone played repeatedly in the background would feel more anxious, and people who interacted with the CS-acceptance in the background would feel less anxious, compared with controls.

As we hypothesized, self-reported mood and, specifically, anxiousness were more negative in the CS-rejection, and more positive in the CS-acceptance, conditions. Participants' metaperceptions, or ratings of how the confederate saw them on dimensions of interestingness, confidence, outgoingness, and so on, were more positive in the CS-acceptance than in the other two conditions. These findings supported the general effectiveness of the cued-activation procedure. There were more complex findings, however, once individual differences in social-evaluative anxiety were factored in.

In their influential model of social anxiety, Schlenker and Leary (1982) held that anxiety arises from a combination of two factors: having negative expectations about how one is going to be evaluated and being highly concerned about that evaluation. Participants were designated as dispositionally high or low on the premeasured Public Self-Consciousness (PSC) Scale (Fenigstein, Scheier, & Buss, 1975) following a median split procedure. On self-reported anxiousness during the interaction, low-PSC participants reported little anxiousness across the board, presumably because of their generally low concern with creating a good impression. High-PSC participants reported more anxiety, particularly in the CS-rejection condition. In the CS-acceptance condition, on the other hand, high-PSC participants reported anxiousness levels virtually identical to those of the low-PSC participants. Thus, the CS-acceptance condition, which was designed to cue feelings of secure social acceptance, seemed to override any dispositional feelings of social anxiety (see Figure 5.3).

Similar interaction effects between the cue condition and level of PSC showed up on a number of other measures as well. Importantly, there was evidence that the cued feelings had an impact on participants' social behavior. Similar to participants' self-reports, the confederate's ratings of the participants' interaction anxiousness were lowest for high-PSC participants in the CS-acceptance condition. Thus, the activation manipulation not only affected participants' feelings and cognitions about others' views but actually influenced their behavior as perceived by an interaction partner.

FIGURE 5.3

Interaction anxiousness as a function of experimental condition and public self-consciousness (Baldwin & Main, 1998). CS = conditioned stimulus.

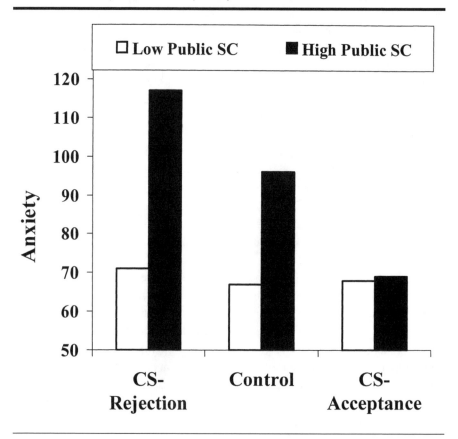

So it seems that not only is it possible to activate relational schemas fairly directly in the lab by using guided visualizations and primes of names or pictures, but it is also possible to create associations to otherwise neutral cues that can then act as indirect triggers. As Zajonc has shown in so much of his work, very subtle, simple factors can have a surprising influence on one's social and emotional lives.

My hope for this type of research is that it may evolve into an experimental analogue for some key elements of intervention. I would not envision a direct application—I'm not sure I would want to go to parties, for example, where people were walking around with computerized beepers going off at regular intervals while they conversed with others. The general question, however, of how positive (i.e., therapeutic, secure, or otherwise functional) structures, rather than dysfunctional structures, get activated during a social interaction could be studied in this type of research.

Who is in the Back of *Your* Mind?

Now let me return to my question from the title of this chapter. Do you—especially if you were a student at Michigan—ever experience Bob Zajonc watching you from the back of your mind, perhaps like some Orwellian Big Brother? When you think about a research idea, do your thoughts take the form of an internal dialogue in which you imagine what Bob would say? Does this make you work harder and think smarter? If you were not a Michigan student, who do you find in your private audience?

FIGURE 5.4

Warm, vodka-sharing Bob.

Of course, the internal presence of authority figures, mentors, and others need not be a bad thing. I think of my own big brother. I, as a later-born, grew up under and still feel the influence of my big brother, who, yes, sometimes used to criticize and tease me. He also used to give me advice, though, pointing me in the right direction. He used to inspire me to do better and provoke me if I became complacent. He used to give me support if things went wrong or I did not understand something. As the social anxiety study showed, activation of this kind of relational schema can definitely have a positive impact.

All of which makes me wish there had been a large enough sample size in the earlier study I did at Michigan so that I could have used a picture of Bob smiling as one of my experimental stimuli. Then I might have tapped into the positive associative links his students had in their self-with-Bob relational schemas which led them—and, one might surmise, still lead them—to feel inspired, encouraged, motivated, and enlightened as they felt his internal presence in the back of their mind (see Figure 5.4).

References

Andersen, S. M., & Cole, S. W. (1990). "Do I know you?": The role of significant others in general social perception. *Journal of Personality and Social Psychology, 59*, 384–399.

Baldwin, M. W. (1992). Relational schemas and the processing of social information. *Psychological Bulletin, 112*, 461–484.

Baldwin, M. W. (1994). Primed relational schemas as a source of self-evaluative reactions. *Journal of Social and Clinical Psychology, 13*, 380–403.

Baldwin, M. W. (1997). Relational schemas as a source of if-then self-inference procedures. *Review of General Psychology, 1*, 326–335.

Baldwin, M. W., Carrell, S. E., & Lopez, D. F. (1990). Priming relationship schemas: My advisor and the Pope are watching me from the back of my mind. *Journal of Experimental Social Psychology, 26*, 435–454.

Baldwin, M. W., & Holmes, J. G. (1987). Salient private audiences and awareness of the self. *Journal of Personality and Social Psychology, 53*, 1087–1098.

Baldwin, M. W., & Main, K. (1998). Cued activation of relational schemas in social anxiety, Unpublished research data, University of Winnipeg, Manitoba, Canada.

Bargh, J. A., & Pietromonaco, P. (1982). Automatic information processing and social perception: The influence of trait information presented outside of conscious awareness on impression formation. *Journal of Personality and Social Psychology, 43*, 437–449.

Fenigstein, A., Scheier, M. F., & Buss, A. H. (1975). Public and private self-consciousness: Assessment and theory. *Journal of Consulting and Clinical Psychology, 43*, 522–527.

Fiske, A. P. (1992). The four elementary forms of sociality: Framework for a unified theory of social relations. *Psychological Review, 99*, 689–723.

Higgins, E. T., & Rholes, W. S. (1978). "Saying is believing": Effects of message modification on memory and liking for the person described. *Journal of Experimental Social Psychology, 14*, 363–378.

Horowitz, M. J. (1988). *Introduction to psychodynamics.* New York: Basic Books.

Levine, L. M., Bogart, L. M., & Zdaniuk, B. (1996). Impact of anticipated group membership on cognition. In R. M. Sorrentino & E. T. Higgins (Eds.), *Handbook of motivation and cognition* (Vol. 3, pp. 531–569). New York: Guilford Press.

Mitchell, S. A. (1988). *Relational concepts in psychoanalysis.* Cambridge, MA: Harvard University Press.

Murphy, S. T., & Zajonc, R. B. (1993). Affect, cognition, and awareness: Affective priming with optimal and suboptimal stimulus exposures. *Journal of Personality and Social Psychology, 64*, 723–739.

Ogilvie, D. M., & Ashmore, R. D. (1991). Self-with-other representation as a unit of analysis in self-concept research. In R. C. Curtis (Ed.), *The relational self* (pp. 282–314). New York: Guilford Press.

Planalp, S. (1985). Relational schemata: A test of alternative forms of relational knowledge as guides to communication. *Human Communication Research, 12*, 3–29.

Polanyi, M. (1966). The logic of tacit inference. *Philosophy, 41*, 1–18.

Safran, J. D. (1990). Towards a refinement of cognitive therapy in light of interpersonal theory: I. Theory. *Clinical Psychology Review, 10*, 87–103.

Schlenker, B. R., & Leary, M. R. (1982). Social anxiety and self-presentation: A conceptualization and model. *Psychological Bulletin, 92*, 641–669.

Stern, D. N. (1985). *The interpersonal world of the infant.* New York: Basic Books.

Stopa, L., & Clark, D. M. (1993). Cognitive processes in social phobia. *Behaviour Research and Therapy, 31*, 255–267.

Wegner, D. M., & Giuliano, T. (1982). The forms of social awareness. In W. J. Ickes & E. S. Knowles (Eds.), *Personality, roles, and social behavior* (pp. 165–198). New York: Springer-Verlag.

Zajonc, R. B. (1960). The process of cognitive tuning in communication. *Journal of Abnormal and Social Psychology, 61*, 159–167.

Zajonc, R. B. (1980). Feeling and thinking: Preferences need no inferences. *American Psychologist, 35*, 151–175.

Zajonc, R. B., & Adelmann, P. K. (1987). Cognition and communication: A story of missed opportunities. *Social Science Information, 26*, 3–30.

PART 2

Affect and Cognition

CHAPTER 6

The Nature of Pleasure

Nico H. Frijda

The nature of pleasure is a central issue for the psychology of emotion, or at least it should be. Pleasure is one of the most elementary of emotional processes, but its nature is not really transparent. What is pleasure? What does the response consist of, and what does the process consist of that gives rise to it?

Pleasure is one of the faces of affect, and affect is central in Zajonc's research. Pleasure is most readily defined as a feeling, but some of Zajonc's research has shown that positive affect can exist without conscious awareness. It can influence the pleasantness of stimuli that as such do not arouse it. What, therefore, is "it"? What can it be when it can be unconscious?

The notion of pleasure has a multitude of aspects and meanings. Not all of these are caught in the English word *pleasure*. Some are present in words in other languages with a roughly similar meaning. The French concept *plaisir*, for instance, implies a richness and fullness that are not present in the English word which has more the overtone of a dry, positive, hedonic quality. The French word suggests that one devotes oneself to it and hints at a communion between the subject and whatever or whoever spends the *plaisir*—whether something you can eat or drink or a person with whom you are together, one feels enveloped by it. It may well be that *plaisir* provides better cues to the nature of pleasure than does the word *pleasure*, as do the Polish words *przyjemnosc* and *rózkosz*, which more or less cover the same domain (A. Wierzbicka, personal communication, March 25, 1998). In this chapter, I do not examine all that richness. I concentrate on the basic psychological process that is involved in pleasant tastes, in elementary likings, and in positive emotions.

I argue that pleasure is most fruitfully defined, not as a feeling but as a process of stimulus or state acceptance that may result in feelings as well as in other effects. I seek to explain the process by examining the different kinds and sources of pleasure. I propose that most or all of them result from well-functioning of the organism's actions or action potentialities.

The Experience of Pleasure

What is pleasure? The first answer may be that it is a feeling, just as pain (in the extended sense) is. But what is a feeling? According to introspective psychology, feelings are forms of awareness different from sensations, including those of warmth, touch, and body sensations, and different from memory images (Titchener, 1908; Wundt, 1902) and thoughts (K. Bühler, 1907). Feelings of pleasure and pain were supposedly *qualia*, irreducible mental qualities, the only *qualia* not reducible into sensations, images, or thoughts.

Feelings were esteemed to have specific characteristics that make them distinct from the other forms of awareness or "elements of consciousness." They cannot be localized in space or in some sense organ; they are subjective and evaluative "comments" to sensations, memory images, or thoughts; and they are "evanescent," that is, they evaporate or disappear whenever attention is focused on them (Titchener, 1908).

These characteristics of affective feeling would seem to be valid. Yet, there are all sorts of things wrong or problematic with designating "pleasure" and "pain" as feelings in this way.

Take their evanescence. Indeed, pleasure is evanescent when attention is directed on it. The same would seem to hold for pain, as is suggested by Buddhist meditation exercises of "mindfulness." However, there is little evanescence when attention is not directed on it. Pleasure may make people act in a particular direction, with "control precedence"; pleasurable events and foresights may fill the mind and usurp attention, and such activities may continue indefinitely as long as pleasure is there, in interpersonal contact, in sex, in gluttony, in listening to music, in play. One of the major characteristics of pleasure of some intensity is its motivating power. It pushes and clamors for continuation, it instigates desire, it is at the root of human passion. But indeed pleasure evaporates when attention is directed, not toward the event, but toward the feeling. When you focus attention on the pleasure produced by a sweet substance, all that remains is the experience of a sweet substance. When you focus on what is so nice about a familiar stimulus, it just becomes a stimulus; it may not even appear familiar any longer. But who would focus on the feeling, under normal circumstances? Directing attention toward one's feelings of pleasure interrupts the interaction. It takes attention away from the pleasure. It may thereby drastically alter the very experience.

There are other problems surrounding the nature of the experiences of pleasure as irreducible experiential *qualia*. They may be irreducible, but much can be said about them.

Feelings Are Not Sensations

It is true that the experiences of pleasure and of pain cannot be reduced to other kinds of awareness, such as body sensations or thoughts (Arnold, 1960). Yet, they are structured experiences. They certainly are not themselves sensations of some sort, as Hume (1739/1740) considered them to be. They are not closed in themselves, as sensations of red or of light pressure are (Nafe, 1924). They have some sort of meaning. They point beyond themselves. As Wilhelm Wundt initially preferred to say, experiences of pleasure or pain are "carried" by sensations, they are a "comment" on those sensations. That is, they are felt by the experiencer as signifying something in his or her relationship to an object or one's state.

Intentionality

More precisely, experiences of pleasure are intentional. They usually are about something. Something is liked or disliked, attractive or repulsive. Feelings are evanescent precisely because directing attention on them cuts the tie with the intentional object; the relevant aspect of feeling is precisely that it is about something other than itself. "Feeling" that is focused on is like the sound of one hand clapping.

The intentionality of feelings of pleasure or pain—their having some sort of meaning—applies even to objectless moods. Moods may have no object (Frijda, 1993), but they still are experiences of *my* state, of my momentary relationship with the world as a whole or with myself. Feeling light in the morning is not like feeling weight loss in a zero-gravity machine. Being in a good mood is okay; being in a bad mood is something *I* want to get rid of.

Are Pleasure and Pain ''Feelings''?

The intentionality of feeling highlights a major question about pleasure and pain: *Are* they feelings? In other words, are pleasure and pain experienced as subject-connected inner experiences that float around in the mind or are they necessarily so experienced? It may just be a myth to talk about feelings in this way. Is there an experience of pleasure, or of pleasantness? Does one exist? Does one find such an experience when looking inward? When hearing music, or seeing a beautiful person, is there pleasure or pleasantness in the air? Is there a little experiential gem that one cherishes in one's experience purse?

No, usually there is not, if only because "an experience of pleasure" is not a natural given. It is a mental construction. All states of consciousness are constructions, as has been forcefully argued by Marcel (1983) and others. Conscious experiences do not just reflect underlying information states and need not be isomorphic to those states. An "experience of pleasure," in fact, is a product of a particular mental attitude, a reflective attitude. One looks inward, inspecting how one feels. The more natural attitude during affective experience is a quite different one. One's attention is toward the object with its demand character[1]: what it wants from you, what it

---

[1]Demand character, or *Aufforderungs-charakter*, was originally introduced by Lewin (1926) to denote what events appear to invite a person to do, notably in emotional contexts. It was not restricted to confounding test contexts.

may do to you, or what it seems to offer you. And affective experience first of all consists of experiencing a liked or a disliked object.

In other words, affective experience in its most elementary form consists of experiencing objects with meanings. Sartre (1948) labeled it *irreflexive experience*; certain current philosophers call it *immersed experience*. Irreflexive or immersed emotional experience is experience of an object charged with affective meaning. It is not an affective experience disjointed from an object and a momentary state of *me*. The experience of pleasure, most of the time, is the experience of something pleasant: of a wonderful person, a delightful experience, a liked Chinese ideograph, one's charming, beautiful, and endearing baby—of a *plaisir*, and not of a feeling of pleasure.

Subjectivity

In one sense, therefore, pleasure is not "subjective." Usually, the subject plays no part in his or her experience, nor does he or she need to be aware of the fact that the experience depends on himself or herself. The newborn baby *is* indubitably charming. Its beauty and endearingness appear as intrinsic qualities. But in another sense, reference to oneself is a component of experience. Affect is felt as affecting oneself; that is indeed where the word *affect* came from. One does not choose to like or dislike. Affect imposes itself, and beyond a certain intensity it takes over: That is to say that affect restricts the felt spontaneity of "the self as actor," in William James's sense. It intrudes on initiatives. That reference to oneself comes to the fore in a different way when it is lost, as happens in dissociation experiences. Sometimes, in fever or during traumatic events, events and objects suddenly turn "strange," which reveals that they were sensed as familiar before. Even emotions may become strange in that fashion. Franz Kafka described a man who "opened his mouth so that his excitement might leave him by his mouth"; and pain is often suffered during torture with a similar strangeness. Perhaps pleasure too can become strange, or perhaps it disappears in dissociation.

Evaluative Nature

The core of affective experience, whatever its guise, is its evaluative nature. Affect introduces value in a world of factual perceptions and sensations. It creates preferences, manifest or experienced palatability and aversiveness of stimuli, and behavioral priorities other than as are based on habit strength. Pleasure is good, and pain is bad, and so are their objects. But what does that mean? Good and bad do not involve cognitive anticipation of what may happen next. Apart from its psychological implausibility, this would lead to infinite regress. What the good and bad of affect mean can best be inferred from how they function in a person's life from what they tell the person to want to do and what he or she then usually indeed does: And what the person wants to do and does is: accept or not accept the experience, or the object that it comes from, or a particular activity.

This is the demand character of the objects experienced as pleasant or unpleasant, and it is what forms the core of the experiences of pleasure and pain. Objects appear as to-be-dwelt-with or to-discontinue-interaction-with, as acceptable or not acceptable. Activities are experienced as to-be-continued or to-be-terminated. In pleasure, the object or activity is experienced as consonant, as one that one could stay with. Aristotle defined pleasure as the sense of unimpeded functioning. Pleasure is felt as giving access or approval to any event or activity that enhances interaction with the intentional object or one's momentary state, just as pain is felt as giving access or approval to any event or activity that decreases interaction with the intentional object or one's state.

Pleasure Without Pleasant Feeling

In immersed or irreflexive experience, pleasure thus is not, properly speaking, a conscious experience. It dissolves into the apparent valued nature of object, activity, or state. But even that valued nature does not need to be conscious in the sense of being an object of awareness. When interacting with pleasure, one may have other things to do than to notice one's like or dislike. One interacts. One willingly enters the interaction, and one willingly continues to interact. For instance, is sexual interaction pleasurable? Well, it most certainly is when engaged in freely, but it is only *felt* as pleasurable after having withdrawn from full engagement, and having taken some distance, which one often would not do until orgasm is over. Hence the old paradox of true happiness: One can never be truly happy and know it until afterward because one was immersed in it. And yet one would have prolonged it if one could, and one would do it again.

The example suggests that pleasure without a distinct experience of pleasure is not a rare occurrence, due only to subliminal stimulation or backward masking (making a brief stimulus invisible by showing something else a millisecond after). That this indeed is so shows most clearly in the occurrences of compelling eagerness to engage in certain interactions and of eagerness to prolong them, and which often are not accompanied by pleasant feelings. I am referring to what Csikszentmihalyi called instances of *optimal experience* or *experiences of flow* (e.g., Csikszentmihalyi & Csikszentmihalyi, 1988).

For example, scientists who tirelessly work through the night trying to solve a problem, and mountain climbers who work themselves into a sweat and run grave risks, do so until the work is finished or a goal is accomplished. Whether they do it for the sake of pleasure, or in view of the experience or anticipation of pleasure, is uncertain. People may seek an experience even when they suffer from it. The experience of pleasure felt at certain moments is a confirmation that what they did was worth doing.

Still, such work represents optimal experience. Behaviorally, it answers the criteria for pleasure: One is at it and remains at it. But the experience is not one of pleasure. The only major aspect of the experience is, I think, that the task is felt by the person to entice him or her to hang on, to stay with it. The task manifests that demand character, and the people do conform. And only under particular circumstances do the experiences of pleasure arise—for instance, when one steps back and takes stock of one's progress, or when the work is over and one looks back on it and sees that it is good.

Why then did the scientist work in a chilly laboratory, or why did the mountain climber climb that slippery mountain in icy rain? There is only one answer: Because they liked it. That answer is to be taken seriously. The activities may ultimately give rise to pleasurable emotions, to joy and celebration and drinking champagne, but those are mere confirmations of the immersion that went before, implicit in the sense of flow, the full sense of unimpeded functioning.

Similar constellations are present elsewhere. Take the joy of friendship under harsh circumstances, such as the friendships and the joys of intense interaction under conditions of war or political resistance. These friendships may give pleasure in a strict sense, but only retrospectively. Before that, they had filled life. The fullness became evident *post hoc* in that sense of emptiness that befell so many resistance fighters after the fighting was won, in the same way as the common sense of familiarity with one's surroundings becomes evident only in an experience of derealization.

Some events are pleasurable while conscious feeling is that of pain. One may cry for a piece of music or a painting because it is almost unbearably beautiful. The constellation is not dissimilar to that of certain states of being in love that are painful and agitated, and that one yet would not want to miss for anything. Of course, all this is not really surprising, considering that emotions are "multicomponential processes" in which the various response components are only weakly correlated (e.g., Scherer, 1984). Emotional experience is just one component among others.

The Pleasure Process

The conclusion is that there can be pleasure, whether one is aware of it or not. An inner process may be going on, whether one is aware of it or not, that leads to certain motivational and behavioral propensities and, in the event, to certain feelings. *Pleasure, positive affect,* or *pleasure state* all can be used as names for this process. The propensities are those for continuation of interaction with the stimulus, engagement in the activity, or continuation of the state, and for expending efforts toward such continuation: for be-with and stay-with behaviors, and for attention toward the stimulus as may be helpful for such efforts. Likewise, *pain* may refer to the process for termination of the interaction or a decrease in its intensity.

There are, of course, many behavioral phenomena that call for such a process as their explanation, and where the assumption of conscious feeling is hazardous. A rat may show activities that are geared to get more of the stimulus involved, such as sniffing, attentional focusing, and behavioral activation; the activities tend to parallel neuronal processes and in normal circumstances precede actual efforts to obtain more of the stimuli (Berridge, 1999). Other phenomena concern behaviors of animals exposed to prolonged stress that humans would find highly aversive and that are best explained as endeavors to block internal, subjective consequences of that stress. Battery animals engage in behaviors such as fighting, inflicting self-injury, and biting inedible objects until the mouth is bleeding. Such behaviors have been found to increase endorphin release, which decreases experience of pain in humans and the consequences of harmful stimulation in animals.

What the pleasure process does corresponds to the functional nature of pleasure. Not only does it command stimulus acceptance and continuation of activity, but it also involves a global attunement of the organism, at least when it has a certain strength. It induces the stimulus or activity with attractiveness, that is, with incentive power to continue interaction. It sets preferences: If it comes to action, that action is more likely to deal with the accepted than the nonaccepted stimuli, and it tends to produce changes in control precedence of the corresponding interactional behaviors or goals. It tends to facilitate certain classes of actions. The behavioral or motivational implications of pleasure as such are not easily distinguished from those of pleasure embedded in a certain context, and where the responses are to be distinguished as particular emotions such as joy, positive desire, enjoyment, fascination, pride, bliss, happiness in its deeper sense, "being moved," or as mere states of liking. What would seem to be common to all is a threshold decrease for all sensory and bodily actions geared to maintaining or enhancing interactions, and an increased sensitivity for relevant stimuli and thoughts. The latter is suggested by the greater accessibility of pleasant memories during pleasant moods (see Frijda, 1993, for a review). It may modify the mode of cognitive interaction, as suggested by the findings on less-focused cognitive strategies during positive mood (Frijda, 1993). It may decrease general muscular control, which is suggested by the often decreased rate of respiration and the probably less angular form of the respiration curves (Boiten, Frijda, & Wientjes, 1994).

When exceeding a certain intensity, affect is a process that influences widely divergent responses, such as attention, resource distribution over various functions, behavior threshold changes, and certain sensory thresholds, as when negative affect modifies those for pain.

Pleasure thus can be conceptualized in several correlated but distinct fashions. It can be conceived as a conscious state with a number of properties. It can also be conceived as a mental process, itself as unconscious as any other mental process, that changes the tuning for inputs and behavioral inclinations. The process of a whole is a stimulus-acceptance or activity-acceptance process, parallel to pain as a stimulus-rejection process.

The characterization of pleasure as a stimulus-acceptance process and of pain as a nonacceptance process differs from the more traditional one that links pleasure and pain to approach and avoidance. It is more precise in several regards. Approach and avoidance may exist without pleasure or pain. They may reflect desire, not pleasure. Pleasure and desire can be uncoupled (Berridge, 1999). Also, there are other behaviors that enhance or weaken interaction than approach and avoidance. What is essential for affect is the relational function, not the spatial movement.

Awareness of pleasure would seem to depend on various conditions. One is event magnitude, or response intensity. Another is focus of attention, on the object, on one's reaction, or on one's feeling. The nature of attention determines the nature of the experience, as a perceptual, an immersed, or a reflexive one—a "feeling." Awareness of pleasure, in any form, I think, is the condition that enables preferences and motivational persistence over time.

What Elicits Pleasure?

Why are certain events or activities acceptable and others not? What is it that arouses pleasure, and why does it?

Discussions of what elicits pleasure are often uniquely about relatively elementary sensory stimuli such as pleasant smells and tastes, or pleasing things such as the appearance of potential sexual partners, just as discussions of unpleasantness tend to be concerned only with unpleasant smells and physical pain. Or the discussions tend to focus on the still rather simple fact that familiar stimuli tend to be pleasant and novel ones unpleasant. Evolutionary explanations come easily, too easily perhaps. It may indeed well have been advantageous, in the evolutionary past, that certain stimuli were sought or preferred. Sugar is good for energy, and so evolution made humans like sweet things; familiar stimuli tend to be safe ones, and thus liking them makes a person stay close to home. From the perspective of understanding the processes of liking or disliking, this means that certain stimuli are pleasant or unpleasant just because they happen to be. Other stimuli may then become pleasant or unpleasant through association to the unconditioned ones.

But sensory stimuli and relatively simple stimulus constellations such as familiarity constitute only a fraction of what is actually felt as pleasant. Equally important are activities. People take pleasure in things they do as much as in things they see, hear, or eat. In addition, many or most pleasures do not derive from an affective sensitivity to particular stimuli involved, neither directly nor indirectly by conditioning, as I will try to show. Sensory stimuli may not be typical or paradigmatic for what gives rise to pleasure.

Indeed, one can distinguish several kinds of pleasure. Rozin (1999), for instance, distinguished between pleasures of sense, aesthetic pleasures, and pleasures of mastery. I distinguish the following:

- sensory pleasures
- relief and increase pleasures

- achievement and mastery pleasures
- activity pleasures
- social pleasures
- aesthetic pleasures

Sensory Pleasures

Certain stimuli are pleasant by themselves, regardless of association to other stimuli. Moderately sweet substances appear to be universally liked (Young, 1959). Drops of sucrose solution tend to quieten a crying newborn baby (Blass & Shah, 1995), so do caresses. Sexual smells and sights arouse pleasure in humans, as well as presumably animals, under appropriate conditions of receptivity. The examples suffice to make the point: There do exist inherently pleasurable stimuli. Their range needs to be scrutinized, however, because many stimuli that appear as inherently pleasant may not be. Most taste aversions, and perhaps also taste likings, are learned and thus depend on example, although some of them may rest on preparedness (Rozin, Haidt, & McCauley, 1993). Familiar stimuli of course tend to be liked more than unfamiliar ones (Zajonc, 1968), but familiarity is not a stimulus variable, as it depends on some input-memory comparison, and its liking is often replaced by liking for the novel.

Many pleasures of the senses, in fact, are not fully accounted for by their sensory nature. They are pleasures that depend on overall states of the organism or on being immersed in emotions of different sorts. One example is orgasm, perhaps the most sensory of pleasures, which nevertheless does not involve a particular sense, and in which, moreover, the pleasure is maximal when the whole body is given over to it, and still more when intimacy has been achieved. Another is provided by some "pleasures of the mind" as described and named by Kubovy (1999). They are pleasures that come from the confluence of impacts, such as dining and drinking with good friends in a good restaurant. These pleasures, too, present problems to understanding. How can one conceive the way that these pleasures emerge?

Relief and Increase Pleasures

A large class of pleasurable events is formed by "relief pleasures" (Kubovy, 1999): the pleasures evoked by the termination of aversive stimulation. It was one of the major classes of emotional conditions in behaviorist analyses of the conditions for reinforcement. It is a true source for pleasure, not just a decrease in pain. Schopenhauer (1994) argued that pleasure consists only of temporary diminishment of unhappiness, but I do not think that is correct. There exists good argument: Relief may lead to the manifestations of positive emotion. The joys of relief are often manifest in deep sighs, smiling, exuberance, laughter, and celebration, as Gregory (1924) showed by a wealth of anecdotes.

Termination of pain is not a stimulus in any real sense. Its affective impact cannot be understood as a stimulus effect or by conditioning. Relief pleasure results from a constellation involving an unpleasant stimulus and an event in which it is expected but does not occur. Understanding its affective value calls for a somewhat involved explanation, such as that of drive reduction theory. The pleasurable nature of diminishment of pain has a deep and general significance. It was the basic mechanism for aesthetic pleasure in Berlyne's (1960) theory of the arousal jag (an increase of arousal followed by a steep drop), and it fits (perhaps not in the temporal sequence mode) the pleasures derived from aversive experiences, as in roller coasters and parachute jumping, or perhaps even those gained from eating hot Mexican peppers (Rozin, 1999). Relief pleasures are a subclass of a much larger class of affect antecedents—that of discrepancies with regard to standards of comparison, including expectancies (see Frijda, 1988, where this constellation is discussed as "The Law of Comparative Feeling"), or from norms (Kahneman & Miller, 1986). In the negative affective domain, this includes the pains of loss, in particular those of sadness and grief, as well as regret (Kahneman & Tversky, 1982). For positive affect, it includes the pleasures of being more than someone else or having more than someone else. Degrees of pleasure do not as a rule correspond to the magnitude of actual satisfactions involved, but also, or more so, on surpassing standards of comparison. Why? I return to it later.

Achievement and Mastery Pleasures

The pleasures from having achieved a major goal, or from making clear progress, form another major class of nonstimulus pleasures. In fact, several emotion theorists (e.g., Oatley, 1992) regard all positive emotions to result from this contingency.

The notion of *goal* may not be the most appropriate to explain positive emotions and their pleasantness. It would be better to expand the condition to include motives, interests, and values, for which I use the word *concerns*. A very large number of pleasures result from events satisfying concerns, or from promises of gratification. These include the pleasures of reuniting with one's beloved, hearing that one's child passed an exam, being praised in public, being comfortably warm, and being together with friendly people. The events satisfy the concerns of attachments, self-esteem or social esteem, and bodily comfort. Anything that one values can become the basis of pleasure, when something happens that brings it nearer, improves it, or restores it.

The important point is that most of these valued conditions cannot be traced back to pleasurable sensory stimulations, and thus the pleasures cannot be. There is nothing sensorily pleasant in self-esteem, in the approval of others, in having gained knowledge and insight, in sense of mastery, or in the satisfaction of "effectance motivation" (White, 1959) that underlies such a large share of anticipatory as well as of achievement pleasures. Sports, of course, yield achievement pleasures, even when the goals set for achievement are private and trivial by external standards.

More telling still is the pleasure of rough-and-tumble play, which is perhaps the truly paradigmatic situation of positive affect. What is so nice about it? Rough-and-tumble play is almost universal among young mammals, at least among the young males of the species (Panksepp, 1998). It may be evolutionarily useful, but that is not what drives the children; it is not what makes them happy. Rather, it is the doing of playing; it is the game of challenges and meeting challenges, and if one does not meet them, then of being able to fail gracefully and believing that your turn will come. Much of its pleasure comes from a continuous game with small achievements: kicking well, tricking someone else, getting the better of someone else, and all this supported by the achievement when you win.

Pleasure in successful goal achievement extends to any goal-directed action that is successfully performed when such performance is not taken for granted and perceived as a challenge. This is the domain of mastery pleasures, to which most or all activities lead to flow and optimal experience belong. But *mastery* can be taken to include modest masteries. A boring job such as constructing a fence can be turned into fun when the goal is set to have all nails straight and neat.

Mastery is often subtle and intangible, if indeed it is the source of cognitive satisfactions. What is the fun of obtaining and enlarging knowledge? Whence the fascination exerted by almost any story, as told or as watched on television? What is the source of the potent curiosity of the young of most species and of some of the older ones, or of the attractions yielded by novel stimulation? Certainly all these may ultimately help adaptation, but that is not what one cares about when reading or watching with abandonment. What, exactly, causes these satisfactions?

And there are many other concerns that yield pleasure when satisfied, and where the nature of the satisfaction and the mechanisms involved are rather obscure. What is the source of the pleasures of self-loss or loss of identity, as obtained in mystic experiences and mystic forms of religion, in the seductions of hashish, and in participating in collective enthusiasm and admiration (Baumeister, 1991)? In effect, what does it mean in this context when we say that a concern is satisfied?

Activity Pleasures

The pleasure produced by progress toward a goal or by achievement depends on the value of the goal. However, there seems to be pleasure in goal achievement per se. Any goal that one has set produces some satisfaction on its being reached; any progress that is made with some degree of effort provides some degree of pleasure. One is reminded of Aristotle's definition of pleasure, as the sense of unimpeded functioning. This sense may indeed come just from such unimpeded functioning.

Having set a goal with some involvement would seem to suffice, to judge from negative affect. Any interruption of progress toward a goal tends to produce irritation and the need to resume (Zeigarnik, 1927). It seems to apply to even the lowest levels of goal-setting. Almost invariably, negative feelings are aroused by obstruction of planned movement. You try to grasp your coffee cup, and someone holds your hand in midway. You write a sentence and the point of the pencil snaps off. The most elementary anger is perhaps that evoked by movement restraint. It was the prototypical anger stimulus for Watson, the behaviorist, and the elementary stressor used by Selye in his early stress research. So its inverse, unencumbered goal achievement, may very well be a sufficient condition for pleasure.

But it is obvious that this is not always the case. Unencumbered goal achievement does not invariably produce pleasure. One walks, eats, and breathes with no affect. However, unencumbered activity does give one pleasure when reaching the goal or completing one's actions is not entirely self-evident—when it represents a challenge, proceeds not entirely smoothly, or was not to be taken for granted. Unhampered respiration yields positive pleasure after one has had a cold or has been in a badly ventilated space. Arguably, it is not only the relief but the mere exercise and successful completion of the simple actions. Walking becomes a pleasure when illness had prevented one from doing it for some time. It also can be a pleasure when one has set one's mind to it, just as watching and seeing novel things can be pleasant when one has the mind for it. One has the mind for it I think when one is free from other engagements and preoccupations, as well as free to attend to exercising those activities. The pleasure of exercise may extend to sensory sensations. Not only is the grass greener at the other side of the fence: I, one day had never seen grass as green, truly and sensory green, as that of a little park that one crossed right after release from a week of unsolicited confinement.

All this goes beyond effectance pleasures, or comes before it. It is part of the larger domain of what Charlotte Bühler (1931) labeled as "function pleasure," or *Funktionslust*, pleasure in just doing. Presumably, it comes from doing the things that you can do while there still is some challenge involved, a little uncertainty about whether you can indeed do it, or do it as well as you can envisage.

Much action appears to be a source of pleasure, for its own sake, irrespective of further concerns such as increase in self-esteem or sense of competence that goes beyond the actual moment. I think the clearest instance is dancing. You dance, you danced well, you had a wonderful evening. Dancing well means performing well and with precision the movements that you wanted to perform which requires constant control, and at their best, constant control that manages itself and that represents "flow." The same goes for singing, when it succeeds, if only a little. You come home happy from your choir's exercise. The pleasures, no doubt, also feed on the erotic and social aspects of the dancing and the singing, but they do not live by it. In fact, both are behaviors from the play repertoire. Doing them with reasonable success represents *funktionslust*.

Social Pleasures

Quite diverse forms of social interaction, too, produce pleasure by themselves, and also not so much for the secondary profits they may yield. The pleasures may well be as basic and elementary as those of the senses. Among them are those of being together with people one loves or is familiar with and from whom one receives affection; they are the pleasures of satisfaction of desires for social bonding (Baumeister & Leary, 1995). They include the pleasures of emotional exchange and emotional proximity, mentally or physically huddling together as sparrows on a telephone line. They also include the pleasures of intimacy with a particular individual—the pleasures deriving from attachments. One variant consists of the pleasure of being dependent on that individual, being the target of nurturance, and being able to abandon to it as well as returning it, as expressed in the Japanese notion of *amae* (Markus & Kitayama, 1991). Social pleasures also include those at the other extreme of relationships: exerting power over others and seeing them at one's feet. It is perhaps as elementary a pleasure as that of *amae*. Finally, there is the pervasive pleasure of just watching others, knowing about them regardless of the relationship, regardless of what advantages of knowing about them may produce. They are the satisfactions that must reside in the willingness to view for hours the fates and adventures of indifferent people in television serials, the eagerness with which one listens to the social sharing of emotions by others and with which one shares those shared emotions with third parties (Rimé, 1995).

As before, these activities and the pleasures rest on concerns that may derive from their survival value during evolution. However, evolution only explains the origin of the concerns, and not how and why, by what process and in what functional role, pleasures are evoked by the occurrence of particular activities and stimulus events.

Aesthetic Pleasures

Aesthetic pleasures are distinguished from other pleasures by Kubovy (1999) and Rozin (1999), among others. By aesthetic pleasures I mean "disinterested pleasures" (the designation comes from Kant), that is, pleasures resulting from perceiving objects or events without a direct gain or interest being at stake. The designation is not unproblematic, because aesthetic pleasures blend over into the pleasures elicited by recognizing fit objects for concerns, such as erotic beauty, and certain sensory pleasures, such as smelling a delicate perfume (Plato gave the example of smelling the roses in his garden in the early morning).

Are they on a par with sensory pleasures, and due to innate preferences? For some, this may be true, or some aesthetic objects may be derivatives of stimuli for which innate likings exist. The point has been argued for female beauty and the pleasingness of curves in other contexts, such as those of an iMac computer. But it is unlikely that this one principle covers a large part of the sources of aesthetic pleasure in particular because deviation from accepted patterns plays such an important role in them (Gaver & Mandler, 1987), and because of the very large variety of aesthetic objects and of properties making them pleasurable.

A stimulus-based explanation of all aesthetic pleasures in unlikely also because a person's attitude toward the objects may be more decisive for the emergence of pleasure than the nature of the objects. All aesthetic objects may fail to evoke pleasure; and there are indications that every object may become an object of aesthetic emotion under certain conditions. The role of attitude is implicit in the conception of disinterested pleasure. It suggests that the moment interest enters, this pleasure may disappear. Generally, conditions under which aesthetic pleasure is expected to arise are designed to bock interested interaction with the objects. Footlights are interposed between spectators and spectacles, paintings are put in frames. "Aesthetic distance" is a major concept from aesthetic theory. One can argue that aesthetic emotions are witness–emotions, not participant emotions (Tan, 2000). Conversely, there are indications that a certain distance, a certain contemplative attitude, may make any object one of beauty and thus a spender of pleasure. Such an attitude is facilitated by the footlights and the frames. Put a frame around any ordinary object and it becomes a candidate for representing a more general meaning and to being pleasurable. This hypothesis comes from the aesthetic value of ordinary objects as in still life paintings, in photography, in pop arts, and in artistic displays of "found objects" (*objets trouvées*), as well as from studying the antecedents of emotions of being moved. The importance of the perceptual attitude for the emergence of aesthetic pleasure underscores the problem of explaining that emergence. How does it come about and why?

Explaining Pleasures

The pleasures of achievement and mastery arise because a goal has been reached, a situation is mastered, or an action is performed when it was not performed in routine fshion, by habit, or sheer training. One may say that the pleasures result from the well-functioning of a behavior system for which there is a criterion of well-functioning: the goal, the mastery, the proper or perfect execution and completion of the action. In all the examples given, pleasure results from well-functioning when this is not self-evident and involved some uncertainty that has been overcome or some challenge met. These qualifications hold for the action pleasures. Singing and dancing, however badly done, may be done, and may be done at the fringe of one's capability. To remain pleasurable, the activities must remain at that fringe. One arranges little contests with oneself, one seeks for a difficult note to be sung purely, or one seeks for a novel mountain to climb. Some activities by their very nature require constant ad hoc adaptations, as in dancing. In short, pleasure comes from doing things that one is just able to do. It comes from monitoring the achievement of the criterion of well-functioning of a capability or of a closed action sequence.

This analysis also applies to the social pleasures. People may like to talk together, be together, and seek one another because they are able to do so. They have it in them to be able to do so. They live together because they are able to do so, at least to some degree and for some period of time. They are provided with entire repertoires of social abilities, as are many animals. One can argue that that is the source of the pleasures: exercising a whole repertoire of things one is capable of doing and that lead to further conditions that one can handle well, where being together or interacting is the criterion of having completed the social actions.

Together, this leads to the idea that all sources of pleasure other than sensory pleasures can perhaps be subsumed under one common conception. They all involve the well-functioning of an individual's major action or processing systems. Pleasure means to the person that things are functioning well: The event encountered is good because it enables some action system, or the action it suggests and enables is good because it represents a challenge that appears manageable, or the ongoing or planned action, while taxing the system, is running reasonably smoothly.

In other words, pleasure signals the well-functioning of action or processing systems of the individual, when such well-functioning has not been routine. It is the positive outcome of constant monitoring of one's well-functioning or of one's subsystems. This conception can cover all affect. Affect signals changes in the well-functioning of the individual's action and processing systems. Positive affect signals return to, promises of, or increase in well-functioning, and negative affect signals its obstruction.

The conception is not novel. Pribram (1970) once proposed that feelings are monitors—monitors of adequate functioning. Aristotle, as indicated earlier, defined pleasure as the sense of unimpeded functioning, and Spinoza defined it as increase in the power of acting. Pain was defined in corresponding but opposite fashion: as sense of impeded functioning or loss in the power of acting.

Monitoring of well-functioning can be assumed to go beyond monitoring progress and achievement. One may reasonably suppose that it extends to detecting occasions for using the system's provisions, for their coming alive. This would be meaningful for autonomous provisions, such as those for processing unfamiliar information or the sexual system. These systems start operating upon recognition of fit objects: novel information and attractive people. Both give pleasure. Pleasure occurs at the front end of action systems as well as at the rear end. Pleasure arises when things go well and when they do not.

The clearest examples come from the domain of sex. Men take pleasure in watching women, particularly those experienced as pretty women. Why would that be? One might suppose that the pleasure results from anticipating sexual satisfaction, but I doubt that that is the proper explanation. Considering the realities of life, anticipations would rather confer a frustration character on them, since most of such anticipations would be met with disappointment. Instead, one might argue that certain appearances appear as pretty, and thus pleasant, as a consequence of evolutionary processes: Female beauty might correlate with reproductive fitness. This indeed is one of the theories. But why and how would that make beauty be pleasant to watch? One may venture this hypothesis: Because or when beauty is attractive. That people are experienced as attractive means that they activate the sexual behavioral system, with its various components such as drawing attention, pursuit, flirting, and beyond. The question appears legitimate: Do people feel attracted because they like the appearance, or do they like the appearance because they are attracted? Which comes first? I would think attractiveness. Remember that most if not all beauties are felt as affordances: as skin to be stroked, as lips to be kissed, as bodies to embrace, as persons to interact closely with, physically or otherwise.

Interestingly, not only starting conditions and terminal conditions (those that end the system's activation) are liked, but also all intervening stimuli or activities that open up successive steps in the path from start to finish. Flirting is pleasant. Necking is pleasant. Caresses are pleasant. Eyeplay is fun, and foreplay is fun. All this implies that what enables a function to operate generates pleasure, its smooth functioning itself generates pleasure, and reaching its terminal state generates pleasure. Well-functioning monitoring, one might say, functions as if foresight was involved. One likes pretty people and all the intervening steps because of what they seem to promise in the end. Such foresight, of course, is not always absent; relevant thoughts and images cross people's minds. But all these likings and enjoyments are present even in relatively naive humans and animals. And the pleasures are positive; they reside in the appearances and intermediate activities. Pretty is pretty, regardless of anticipations, or else it is the prettiness that evokes the anticipations. The anatomy of the action systems seems to take care of what foresights may not always be capable of ensuring.

The monitoring interpretation fits the various other categories of pleasure. It provides a satisfactory framework for understanding the relief pleasures. Relief pleasure comes from restoration of smooth functioning after actual or expected malfunctioning. Progress toward a goal or achieving it by definition involves functioning according to what one had set out to do. In fact, monitoring goal progress and completion may be the most general and most elementary instance of well-functioning monitoring. Completion of intentional action is obviously monitored, because action terminates when the goal is reached. It occurs at the most elementary levels. In voluntary movement, for instance, movement stops when muscle tension sensors matches the setting made by the anticipation of the movement to be made in certain nerve cells called gamma fibers. I already mentioned the frustration felt when voluntary movement is interrupted midway; it is an obvious instance of malfunctioning with respect to a well-functioning criterion. "Satisfaction" when the criterion is actually reached, or when progress is smooth, does not usually enter awareness. However, it does when, during execution, problems or uncertainty about completion has occurred. It is often also felt when progress is faster than expected; Carver and Scheier (1990) identified it as the cause for positive affect.

It is interesting to ponder the intensification of emotion by comparisons with standards or normality in this connection. The comparison introduces concerns in addition to those that make the event pleasant or unpleasant in the first place; it favors or harms comparative social standing. Even without that, however, it makes failure or success in reaching a goal more salient; experimental research indeed shows salience to be the major factor (Kahneman & Tversky, 1982; Landman, 1993).

The social pleasures also fit the scheme. The underlying concerns for social contact, proximity, intimacy, and the like are best viewed as representations of the desired situations, and these, in turn, are best viewed as representations of the termination points of action repertoires for achieving proximity, intimacy, and so on, much as the set-point for body temperature represents the termination point of the body temperature regulation mechanisms (Frijda, 1998a). Humans seek the social things they seek because they have the capacity to do so, as well as the sensitivity to make them do so. People have the repertoires to reach proximity and intimacy, and the sensitivity to recognize the objects that might offer that: other people in general, attachment figures in particular, and certain individuals most particularly—those they then fall in love with. The repertoires include sensitivities for recognizing specific signs relevant to successful deployment of the action system. A smiling face is rated positively, just as an angry face is usually rated negatively, probably because a smiling face is an affordance for contact-establishing approach actions.

Even narcissistic pleasures may be regarded as resulting from the well-functioning of action systems. What are narcissistic strivings for? Why does one cherish self-esteem? Probably for having a general background of confidence in the success of one's actions, primarily of one's social actions or interactions (and such confidence estimations belong to the elementary ingredients of action planning, in animals as well as in humans). Enhancing self-esteem thus means enhancing the efficiency of all the action systems involved in social interaction.

The affective value of both familiarity and novelty can be derived from the same perspective. Why are familiar stimuli liked more than novel ones, at least at certain ages and under certain conditions (Bornstein, 1989; Zajonc, 1968)? Is there a "sensitivity to familiarity," a sensitivity inherent in the organism? Is the organism biased to react with pleasure to zero input, as Cacioppo, Gardner, and Berntson (1997) suggested, because of the usefulness of such bias: It evokes confrontations with what is novel but harmless? Perhaps. But one thing seems certain. Humans (and animals) have a capacity for cognitive integration. They use that capacity automatically; one cannot help but recognize a familiar object and perform what old-time psychology called the *Höffding-step*, matching the input to some memory trace. When the object is familiar, the process succeeds, which in the event may be signaled by the liking. And it fails when the object is unfamiliar, leading to some failure signal, neophobia. When failure leads to the engagement of available correction capacities, however, it again leads to positive affect: to curiosity. The operation of cognitive integration processes thus may lead to the pleasure in, rather than the dislike of, novelty—when the stimuli represent a challenge for cognitive capacities, for exercising them with a fair chance of success after an acceptable amount of effort.

The proposed conception also fits the pleasures of the mind that Kubovy (1999) discussed. Pleasures of the mind, in Kubovy's sense, are the epitome of well-functioning. They are pleasures that come from the confluence of impacts that themselves can be pleasurable as well as painful. Earlier, the example was given of dining and drinking with good friends in a good restaurant. Other examples that Kubovy gave include recalling the friendships and interactions from the battlefield or secret freedom fighting, and the prevailing willingness for sacrifice; remembering the difficulties, solutions, and mixed results of having raised one's children that over a period gave sense and direction to life; and working to achieve optimal experience. They all constitute pleasures of great magnitude because one functioned on many channels simultaneously with full engagement of one's resources and without reticence.

Perhaps the present conception of pleasure also offers a way to understand the intense and powerful emotions in epileptic auras. MacLean (1990) reviewed reports on such emotions. They include experiences of extreme bliss and cosmic satisfaction, as well as experiences of panic and anguish, again often with existential overtones, such as the experience of doom or catastrophe. Perhaps the limbic stimulations imply a sense of effortless access to coping procedures, or, by contrast, a complete absence of such access. Sense of power and competence are elementary gratifications that may also occur during drug and alcohol intoxication. Sense of access to coping procedures is an elementary kind of information processing, a "knowledge by acquaintance" that is needed in any behavior programming at whatever level; it represents finding access to the action programs. The scope of the anguish and bliss match the extremity of the well-functioning monitoring outcomes.

The Problem of Aesthetic Pleasures

Aesthetic pleasure forms a problem and a challenge for any theory of pleasure or emotion. Why and how do objects that are useless for the practical conduct of life generate pleasure? But perhaps even aesthetic pleasures, or some of them, may fit into the present explanatory schema. Indeed, some of the extant theories come close to the perspective that is being developed here. Meyer (1956) and Mandler (Gaver & Mandler, 1987) related the pleasure taken in music in challenging and then satisfying expectations or the deviation from schemas: the expectancy-confirmation or discrepancy-arousal-and-solution approach. Even if such a mechanism is involved, it cannot be the entire explanation, because it predicts boredom when the music becomes familiar. Narmour (1990) then modified the theory. He argued that arousal and tension spring from difficulties in integrating deviations from innate schemas into the expectations that those schemas evoke. Deviations from schemas invite their integration, and when that succeeds, it evokes pleasure, as is generally a result from unity-in-complexity relationships. It thus again appears that the pleasure does not so much come from the stimuli themselves, but from succeeding in work and goal achievement, and thus from succeeding in what one can do, but not without effort. Even familiar music may require integrative effort; namely when attention must remain focused on a number of features simultaneously.

This brings aesthetic pleasures, or at least some of them, close to the pleasures of familiarity and curiosity: cognitive operations that succeed. But the success is not only that of cognitive operations. The integrations are more "relational" than merely cognitive, more akin to assimilation and making the stimulus a part of oneself. Cognitive integration readily means having relevant motor responses available (if only in imagination) and knowing what to do with the stimulus event, how to handle it, and how to stand toward it.

The Problem of Sensory Pleasures

Sensory pleasures do not fit this explanation. They cannot in any obvious way be seen as indicating well-functioning, except by circular reasoning. There is, of course, no reason why there should not be more than one pleasure mechanism. But a single principle would satisfy a theorist, and maybe a single principle indeed applies. With regard to sensory pleasures, as I did with regard to erotic attraction: Do we consider certain foods palatable because we like them, or do we like them because they are palatable, that is, because in some way they fit the food-ingestion system?

Simple sensory pleasures are not always as simple as they might seem. They are not entirely pre-prepared hedonic responses to given types of stimuli. Their pleasantness depends on stimulus intensity, resulting in the well-known Wundt curve: Stimuli of moderate intensity tend to be liked, and both those that are weaker and that are more intense less so or not at all (Beebe-Center, 1932/1966; Wundt, 1902). It sometimes also depends on the state of deprivation or satiation of the organism, with respect to the substance concerned, or with respect to its adaptation level for the stimulus class (Pfaffman, 1960; Young, 1959).

But one may go further. I am not aware of any theory of the mechanism of sensory liking. In any case, one has to postulate a mechanism that "recognizes" the stimulus as pleasant or unpleasant. Perhaps such a mechanism can indeed be viewed as recognizing the stimulus as a fit or unfit object for the system concerned—the ingestion system, the body-integrity-sensing system (Archer, 1976), the maintaining optimal body temperature system, or whichever. A fit is communicated to the subsystem-progress monitor as pleasure. A misfit results in displeasure. No fit, no misfit, or just not engaging the system results in neutrality. Remember that when unipolar scales are used, the combined positive–negative Wundt curves do not show some point of neutrality, but a region of ambivalence or suggestions of a sudden flip-over (Lehmann, 1914).

Conclusion

Pleasure, according to the view put forward in this chapter, is the process signaling stimulus acceptance or continuation of current activity, as well as preparing for such acceptance or continuation. It does so because it mirrors the well-functioning of the person's actions, action potentialities, and processing provisions. Well-functioning is represented by stimulus events that enable particular processes or by processes proceeding smoothly, previous or current uncertainty notwithstanding.

In this chapter, I explored the scope and limits of this conception of pleasure. As it stands, it certainly is incomplete. There are many things that people can do, that they can do with some degree of uncertainty, and that give little or no intrinsic pleasure in doing them. Some actions are taken for granted at some moments and not at other moments. Walking is a case in point. Some further specifications are needed. As I suggested, pleasure depends on the actions, processes, or action systems being in some way "closed," carrying a criterion for well-functioning or accomplishment. For the proposed concept, criteria for well-functioning and closedness are needed that allow one to predict what does and does not generate pleasure; only then can one determine whether all pleasures (or all pleasures other than elementary sensory ones) fit into it.

It has probably become clear from the preceding considerations what motivated this theoretical exploration. It was to understand the nature and functional roles as well as the occurrences of pleasure, without circularity. In other words, I tried to avoid as much as possible the "explanation" that certain things are pleasant because they are—because evolution made them pleasant. For most occurrences of pleasure, that explanation is implausible. Avoiding circularity also motivated the desire to analyze concerns or goals: Pleasure comes from satisfying a concern or goal, but is not achieving a goal desired because it yields pleasure? This issue is touched in the present analysis only tangentially; it is more focally discussed elsewhere (Frijda, 1998a). But it underlies the attempt in this chapter to explain certain pleasures by the proper functioning of an action system, like that of sex or of assimilating incoming stimuli. An additional aim was to restore action to the forefront, in explaining affective phenomena. Emotions as well as affects, I am convinced, come from actions that are possible or impossible, as much or more than from stimulus events encountered or obtained.

One of the difficulties one encounters in analyzing pleasure is to get a clear view of the relations between pleasure and action that results from it. On the one hand, pleasure is closely linked to approach. On the other hand, pleasure and action are not too intimately connected. Pleasure can be calm and serene, as well as take exuberant forms in the gaiety of play and the buoyancy of relief or lead to powerful passions of desire. One has to separate the process of positive affect from that which generates action or the impulse to act. It is the latter in particular that is connoted by the word "emotion" (Frijda, 1986). Different action dispositions constitute different emotions, such as joy, pride, enjoyment, happiness, greed, sexual excitement, humble *amae*, or the glow of friendship, and each is due, apart from positive affect, to different antecedent conditions. Pleasure as such does not imply approach. As Berridge (1999) made clear, liking and wanting are separable, both conceptually and empirically. Liking involves the enhanced salience of stimuli experienced as acceptable, but the waiting or the desire that may follow is a different process.

The pleasure process is just that: a process to activate stimulus salience and acceptance behavior or readiness for continuation of ongoing interaction. As such, it does not necessarily extend into behavioral activation. Nor does it include representation of what object or action instigated it, or even what the object for acceptance tuning is to be. That is, the pleasure process and its outputs in feeling and behavior may involve no trace of the cognitive processes that led to it, nor those that identify what it is about. In other words, different processes are involved in linking awareness of pleasure to awareness of their object. Russell (in preparation) had been suggesting this for some time: Affect response is separate from attributing it to some object. Shizgal (1999) made the same suggestion, based on the study of rewarding brain stimulation, and so did Reisenzein (1998), on theoretical grounds. "Pleasure" may remain without an object, or its object may be other than the object that actually aroused it, as demonstrated in Murphy and Zajonc's (1993) studies. I do not think that attribution is the best word for designating the processes that link pleasure to an object. More automatic processes, more akin to those involved in perceptual causality and less to propositional knowledge, will usually be involved.

All this can yield different conscious experiences. Conscious experience always is the product of some constructive process; it is not a direct reflection of the underlying process, and it is likely that it changes something in that underlying process. As Zajonc (Murphy & Zajonc, 1993) made plausible, it limits the diffuseness of the underlying process; the same happens with semantic processes, as Marcel (1983) has shown. One would have to believe, I think, that it is so by necessity. Constructing consciousness is a process that may well preempt some of the resources that otherwise the nonconscious process would have available, and that now are put at the disposition of whatever consciousness is for and enables the person to do.

Does all this account for *le plaisir*? Well, indirectly. Pleasure becomes *plaisir* when several behavior systems come together and all run off impeccably: those for receiving sensory sensation, those for relishing sensory sensation, those involved in producing interpersonal intimacy, and those that account for integrating those pleasures into a momentary evaluation of a piece of existence as a whole—that is, when they blend into a pleasure of the mind.

References

Archer, J. (1976). The organisation of aggression and fear in vertebrates. In P. P. G. Bateson & P. Klopfer (Eds.), *Perspectives in ethology* (Vol. 2, pp. 231–298). New York: Plenum.

Arnold, M. B. (1960). *Emotion and personality* (Vol. 1). New York: Columbia University Press.

Baumeister, R. F. (1991). *Escaping the self: Alcoholism, spirituality, masochism, and other flights from the burden of selfhood.* New York: Basic Books.

Baumeister, R. F., & Leary, R. M. (1995). The need to belong: Desire for interpersonal attachment as a fundamental human motivation. *Psychological Bulletin, 117,* 497–529.

Beebe-Center, J. G. (1966). *The psychology of pleasantness and unpleasantness.* New York: Russell & Russell. (Original work published 1932)

Berlyne, D. E. (1960). *Conflict, arousal and curiosity.* New York: McGraw-Hill.

Berridge, K. C. (1999). Pleasure, pain, desire, and dread: Hidden core processes of emotion. In D. Kahneman, E. Diener, & N. Schwarz (Eds.), *Foundations of hedonic psychology: Scientific perspectives on enjoyment and suffering* (pp. 525–557). New York: Russell Sage.

Blass, E. M., & Shah, A. (1995). Pain reducing properties of sucrose in newborns. *Chemical Senses, 20,* 29–35.

Boiten, F. A., Frijda, N. H., & Wientjes, C. J. E. (1994). Emotions and respiratory patterns: Review and critical analysis. *International Journal of Psychophysiology, 17,* 103–128.

Bornstein, R. F. (1989). Exposure and affect. Overview and meta-analysis of research, 1968–1987. *Psychological Bulletin, 106,* 265–289.

Bühler, C. (1931). *Kindheit und Jugend* [Childhood and youth]. Leipzig, Germany: Hirzel.

Bühler, K. (1907). Tatsachen und Problemen zu einer Psychologie der Denkvorgänge: I. Über Gedanken [On thoughts]. *Archive für die gesamte Psychologie, 9,* 297–365.

Cacioppo, J. T., Gardner, W. L., & Berntson, G. G. (1997). Beyond bipolar conceptualizations and measures: The case of attitudes and evaluative space. *Personality and Social Psychology Review, 1,* 1–18.

Carver, C. S., & Scheier, Z.M.F. (1990). Origins and functions of positive and negative affect: A control-process view. *Psychological Bulletin, 97,* 19–35.

Csikszentmihalyi, M., & Csikszentmihalyi, I. S. (1988) (Eds). *Optimal experience: Psychological studies of flow in consciousness.* Cambridge, England: Cambridge University Press.

Frijda, N. H. (1986). *The emotions.* Cambridge, England: Cambridge University Press.

Frijda, N. H. (1988). The laws of emotion. *American Psychologist, 43,* 349–358.

Frijda, N. H. (1993). Moods, emotion episodes, and emotions. In J. Haviland & M.Lewis (Eds.), *Handbook of emotions* (pp. 381–403). New York: Guilford Press.

Frijda, N. H. (1998a, September). *What comes first: Emotion or striving?* Paper presented at the Sixth Annual Meeting of the European Society for Philosophy and Psychology, Lisbon, Spain.

Frijda, N. H. (1998b). What comes first: emotion or striving? In A. Fischer (Ed.), *ISRE '98: Proceedings of the 10th conference of the International Society for Research on Emotions* (pp. 34–36).

Gaver, W. W., & Mandler, G. (1987). Play it again, Sam: On liking music. *Cognition and Emotion, 1,* 259–282.

Gregory, J. C. (1924). *The nature of laughter.* London: Kegan Paul.

Hume, D. (1739–1740/1969). *A treatise of human nature.* Harmondsworth, England: Penguin Books.

Kahneman, D., & Miller, D. T. (1986). Norm theory: Comparing reality to its alternatives. *Psychological Review, 93,* 136–153.

Kahneman, D., & Tversky, A. (1982). The simulation heuristic. In D. Kahneman, P. Slovic, & A. Tversky (Eds.), *Judgment under uncertainty: Heuristics and biases* (pp. 201–208). New York: Cambridge University Press.

Kubovy, M. (1999). On the pleasures of the mind. In D. Kahneman, E. Diener, & N. Schwarz (Eds.), *Foundations of hedonic psychology: Scientific perspectives on enjoyment and suffering* (pp. 139–154). New York: Russell Sage.

Landman, J. (1993). *Regret: The persistence of the possible.* New York: Oxford University Press.

Lehmann, A. (1914). *Die Hauptgesetze des menschlichen Gefühlslebens* [The principal laws of human feeling]. Leipzig, Germany: Reisland.

Lewin, K. (1926). Wille, Vorsatz und Bedürfnis [Will, intention, and needs]. *Psychologische Forschung, 7,* 294–385.

MacLean, P. (1990). *The triune brain in evolution: Role in paleaocerebral functions.* New York: Plenum Press.

Marcel, A. (1983). Conscious and unconscious perception: An approach to the relations between phenomenal experience and perceptual processes. *Cognitive Psychology, 15,* 238–300.

Markus, H. R., & Kitayama, S. (1991). Culture and the self: Implications for cognition, emotion, and motivation. *Psychological Review, 98,* 224–253.

Meyer, L. B. (1956). *Emotion and meaning in music.* Chicago: University of Chicago Press.

Murphy, S. T., & Zajonc, R. B. (1993). Affect, cognition, and awareness: Affective priming with optimal and suboptimal stimulus exposures. *Journal of Personality and Social Psychology, 64,* 723–739.

Nafe, J. P. (1924). An experimental study of the affective qualities. *American Journal of Psychology, 35,* 507–544.

Narmour, E. (1990). *The analysis and cognition of basic melodic structures: The implication-realization model.* Chicago: University of Chicago Press.

Oatley, K. (1992). *Best laid schemes: The psychology of emotions.* Cambridge, England: Cambridge University Press.

Panksepp, J. (1998). *Affective neuroscience. The foundations of human and animal emotions.* Oxford, England: Oxford University Press.

Pfaffman, C. (1960). The pleasures of sensation. *Psychological Review, 67,* 253–268.

Pribram, K. H. (1970). Feelings as monitors. In M. B. Arnold (Ed.), *Feelings and emotions: The Loyola symposium* (pp. 39–54). New York: Academic Press.

Reisenzein, R. (1998). A theory of emotional feelings as metarepresentational states of mind. In A. Fischer (Ed.), *ISRE '98: Proceedings of the 10th conference of the International Society for Research on Emotions* (pp. 186–190).

Rimé, B. (1995). Mental rumination, social sharing, and the recovery from emotional exposure. In J. Pennebaker (Ed.), *Emotion, disclosure, and health* (pp. 271–291). Washington, DC: American Psychological Association.

Rozin, P. (1999). Pleasure. In D. Kahneman, E. Diener, & N. Schwarz (Eds.), *Foundations of hedonic psychology: Scientific perspectives on enjoyment and suffering* (pp. 100–133). New York: Russell Sage.

Rozin, P., Haidt, J., & McCauley, C. R. (1993). Disgust. In M. Lewis & J. M. Haviland (Eds.), *Handbook of emotions* (pp. 575–594). New York: Guilford.

Russell, J. A. (in preparation). *Affect and the psychological construction of mood and emotion.* Manuscript.

Sartre, J. P. (1948). *The emotions.* New York: Philosophical Library.

Scherer, K. R. (1984). Emotion as a multicomponent process: A model and some cross-cultural data. In P. Shaver (Ed.), *Review of personality and social psychology* (Vol. 5, pp. 37–63). Beverly Hills, CA: Sage.

Schopenhauer, W. (1859/1994). *Die Welt als Wille und Vorstellung* [The world as will and mental image]. Zurich: Hoffmann.

Shizgal, P. (1999). On the neural computation of utility: Implications from studies of brain stimulus reward. In D. Kahneman, E. Diener, & N. Schwarz (Eds.), *Foundations of hedonic psychology: Scientific perspectives on enjoyment and suffering* (pp. 500–524). New York: Russell Sage.

Tan, E. S. H. (2000). Emotion, art, and the humanities. In M. Lewis & J. M. Haviland, (Eds.), *Handbook of emotions* (2nd ed., pp. 116–134). New York: Guilford Press.

Titchener, E. B. (1908). *Lectures on the elementary psychology of feeling and attention.* New York: MacMillan.

White, R. W. (1959). Motivation reconsidered: The concept of competence. *Psychological Review, 66,* 297–333.

Wundt, W. (1902). *Grundzüge der pysiologischen Psychologie* [Foundation of physiological psychology] (Vol. 5). Leipzig, Germany: Engelmann.

Young, P. T. (1959). The role of affective processes in learning and motivation. *Psychological Review, 66,* 104–125.

Zajonc, R. B. (1968). The attitudinal effects of mere exposure. *Journal of Personality and Social Psychology Monograph, 9*(2, Whole No. 2).

Zeigarnik, B. (1927). Das Wiederaufnehmen unterbrochenen Handlungen [The resumption of interrupted actions]. *Psychologische Forschung, 9,* 1–85.

CHAPTER 7

The Affect System and Racial Prejudice

John T. Cacioppo
Gary G. Berntson

In Frank Capra's movie, *It's a Wonderful Life,* George Bailey spends his considerable talent working to make Bedford Falls a better, more progressive place. Bob Zajonc is social psychology's George Bailey. Among his many contributions are fertile research fields on cognitive sets and schema, mere exposure, social facilitation, intellectual development, animal social behavior (including work on cockroaches), emotional expression and experience, collective violence, the interface between cognition and emotion, affect as an identifiable central and coherent system, and affective priming. The landscape of social psychology would be considerably different if not for him.

Zajonc (1980) elevated the affect system to an object of study in his classic article, "Feeling and Thinking: Preferences Need No Inferences." He suggested that the affect system is a primitive, spontaneous, and immediate information-processing system. The affect system, in Zajonc's thinking, is more encompassing than feeling states, just as the cognitive system is more encompassing than thoughts and ideas. Zajonc called on the field to examine the affect system and its operating characteristics with the same care and vigor as has been devoted to the study of the cognitive system, and he reviewed provocative evidence that affect could precede cognition. Studies from behavioral neuroscience (e.g., see LeDoux, 1995) support Zajonc's (1980) suggestion that the structure and function of the affect system is not fully describable in terms of higher level cognitive processes. Our focus in this chapter is on the affect system, some of the features and operating characteristics, and its implications for one's understanding of a continuing problem in society—racial prejudice.

The Affect System

The affect system refers to the components of the nervous system (conceptual and neurophysiological) involved in appetitive and aversive information processing. The affect system has been sculpted by the hammer and chisel of adaptation and natural selection to differentiate hostile from hospitable stimuli and to respond accordingly (Cacioppo & Gardner, 1999; Cacioppo, Gardner, & Berntson, 1999). Although specific behaviors may differ depending on the stimulus and context, there is an underlying commonality to these behaviors. Affective categorizations and responses are so critical that all species have rudimentary reflexes for categorizing certain classes of stimuli and approaching or withdrawing from them, and for providing metabolic support for these actions (e.g., Berntson, Boysen, & Cacioppo, 1993; Davis, 1997; LeDoux, 1995). These rudimentary processes are evident in humans as well, but a remarkable feature of humans is the extent to which the affective categorizations are shaped by learning and cognition (Berntson et al., 1993; Kahneman, Diener, & Schwarz, 1999). An additional adaptive advantage is conferred to species whose individual members have the capacity to learn from the unique environmental contingencies to which they are exposed, to represent and predict events in their environment, to manipulate and plan on the basis of representations, and to exert some control over their attentional and cognitive resources.

To focus on the affect system as an object of study in its own right is not to deny the inextricable links between affect and cognition. Affect directs attention, guides decision making, stimulates learning, and triggers behavior (e.g., Damasio, 1994). Evidence that the neural circuitry involved in computing the affective significance of a stimulus (i.e., evaluative processing) diverges at least in part from the circuitry involved in identification and discrimination was provided by Shizgal (1999) in a series of studies involving brain stimulation in rats as well as in our laboratory in a series of studies of event-related brain potential (ERP) topographies in humans (Cacioppo, Crites, & Gardner, 1996; Crites & Cacioppo, 1996; Cacioppo & Gardner, 1999; Ito & Cacioppo, 1999).

With rapidly developing electrocortical and neuroimaging techniques, views are available of aspects of brain function in conscious individuals during a variety of cognitive and affective activities. These techniques, together with more basic studies of cellular processes and behavioral analyses of evaluative processes and predispositions, should provide the tools for a truly interdisciplinary study of the affect system. For instance, evaluative categorizations have been found to be measurable using ERPs, and these measures have been found to be relatively insensitive to response (e.g., selection/execution) processes (Cacioppo, Crites, Berntson, & Coles, 1993; Crites, Cacioppo, Gardner, & Berntson, 1995). In a typical study, participants are exposed to sequences of six traits and perform a dichotomous evaluative categorization task. Evaluative inconsistency may be varied by embedding, for instance, very positive, moderately positive, moderately negative, and very negative traits in sequences containing predominantly very positive traits. Results have shown that highly and moderately (evaluatively) inconsistent traits, compared with mildly inconsistent or consistent traits, evoke a larger amplitude late positive potential (LPP) that is maximal over centroparietal scalp regions. Furthermore, extremely inconsistent traits evoke a larger amplitude LPP than moderately inconsistent traits even though both sets of traits are judged to be negative (Cacioppo, Crites, Gardner, & Berntson, 1994). Research has also shown that the amplitude of the LPP is larger when participants evaluatively categorize inconsistent rather than consistent affective stimuli even when they intentionally misreport their feelings about the stimulus (Crites et al., 1995).

Furthermore, investigations of the spatial distribution of LPPs across the scalp have revealed a right lateralization of affective categorizations, whereas the spatial distribution of the LPP associated with nonaffective categorizations is more symmetrical (Cacioppo et al., 1996). Whether participants performed affective or nonaffective categorizations of stimuli was manipulated by Crites and Cacioppo (1996), who similarly obtained a symmetrical topography of LPPs when a nonaffective categorization is performed (e.g., Is the food item a vegetable?) but a right lateralized topography of LPPs with an affective categorization (e.g., Is the food item positive?). This asymmetrical activation is consistent with the importance of the right hemisphere in emotion (see Tucker, 1981; Tucker & Frederick, 1989). When highly emotional stimuli served as experimental stimuli, the ERP topographies were right lateralized whether the participants' task was to perform evaluative or nonevaluative categorizations, suggesting that emotionally charged stimuli are categorized evaluatively, immediately, and automatically (Ito & Cacioppo, 1999). Considerable similarities in the ERPs were observed as well, consistent with the notion that affective and nonaffective appraisals rely on a number of common information-processing operations.

The affect system evolved to foster adaptive action in varying contexts. The form of the information processing that fosters this adaptive action differs across levels of the neuraxis. Although behavioral expression—the outcome of a series of information-processing operations on which evolution operates—may be limited by physical constraints to a bipolar (approach–withdraw) organization, the operations of the underlying mechanisms are not. When the appetitive and aversive features of stimuli are first being determined, for instance, these rapid, critical evaluations can occur in parallel, at least in part. Consequently, the potential affective space can be depicted as being bivariate, with appetitive and aversive information processed somewhat differently (Cacioppo & Berntson, 1994; Cacioppo, Gardner, & Berntson, 1997). As behavioral responses to the stimuli are formulated, the antagonistic effects of the activation of appetitive and aversive motivational forces are integrated to form a net action. Figure 7.1 depicts the potential combinations of appetitive (positivity) and aversive (negativity) activation as a bivariate plane, and the subsequent net predisposition to respond as the overarching surface.

The z-axis is depicted in this fashion because behavior in many cases is inherently bipolar: one can approach, one can withdraw, or one can stand in the middle in indifference or in indecision. In each case, the behavioral response can be depicted along a bipolar dimension. An organism that has no evaluation of environmental stimuli, and that neither approaches nor withdraws, is not likely to respond adap-

FIGURE 7.1

Illustrative bivariate evaluative space and its associated affective response surface. This surface represents the net predisposition of an individual toward (+) or away from (−) the target stimulus. This net predisposition is expressed in relative units, and the axis dimensions are in relative units of activation. The point on the surface overlying the left-axis intersection represents a maximally positive predisposition, and the point on the surface overlying the right-axis intersection represents a maximally negative predisposition. Each of the points overlying the dashed diagonal extending from the back to the front-axis intersections represent the same middling predisposition. Thus, the nonreciprocal diagonal on the evaluative plane, which represents different evaluative processes (e.g., neutral to ambivalence), yields the same middling expression on the affective response surface. Dashed lines (including the coactivity diagonal) represent isocontours on the evaluative plane, which depict many-to-one mappings between the affective response surface and the underlying evaluative space. These isocontours are illustrative rather than exhaustive. From "Relationship between attitudes and evaluative space: A critical review, with emphasis on the separability of positive and negative substrates," by J. T. Cacioppo & G. G. Berntson, 1994, Psychological Bulletin, 115, 401–423, figure appears on p. 412. Copyright 1994 by the American Psychological Association. Reprinted with permission.

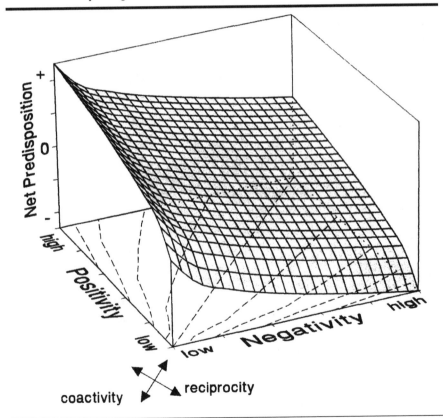

tively, at least in the long run. Thus, species have evolved mechanisms for differentiating appetitive from aversive events, for approaching the former and avoiding the latter, and, at least in the case of humans, for doing so deliberately as well as automatically. LeDoux (1995), for instance, reviewed evidence showing that sensory information going through the thalamus is routed to the amygdala and to the cortex. At the amygdala, a quick, inexact assessment of potential danger is performed and a series of reactions commensurate with this assessment is initiated. Cortical brain areas send a slower, more detailed account of the pending threat to the amygdala. If the information confirms that the stimulus is a threat, additional signals of action are triggered; if not, the threat response is terminated.

The Multiplicity of Evaluative Processes

We have discussed elsewhere the separability of positive and negative affective processing, the differential activation functions for positivity and negativity, and the various modes of evaluative activation (Cacioppo & Berntson, 1994; Cacioppo et al., 1997, 1999). Our emphasis here is on another feature of the affect system—the multiplicity of and interactions among evaluative mechanisms. As illustrated by LeDoux (1995), assessments of the potential hostility (or hospitality) of a stimulus can unfold at different levels of the neuraxis.

The highest levels of the central nervous system (CNS) show the greatest expansion and elaboration through both the development of the individual (ontogeny) and that of the species (phylogeny) and serve to differentiate the adult human from the infant, and from other animals. In contrast, lower levels of the CNS (e.g., the spinal cord) evidence a more common, primordial organization throughout ontogeny and across phylogeny. Basic approach–withdrawal dispositions, however, are intrinsic to all levels of CNS organization, as documented by both experimental studies in animals and clinical findings in humans with spinal cord injuries. Cord transections isolate spinal networks from higher neural influences, leaving the lower regions of the body (e.g., the legs and trunk) under the exclusive control of spinal mechanisms. Despite this loss of higher neural controls, the spinal cord is intrinsically capable of supporting reflexive limb withdrawal from a noxious stimulus. This response is mediated, in part, by a relatively simple three-neuron circuit. The simplicity of this basic reflex circuit, however, does not imply an immutability of spinal networks. Just as evaluative dispositions are subject to change, so are spinal dispositions. For instance, spinal networks can learn to withdraw from innocuous stimuli which, although not painful themselves, come to predict the occurrence of pain stimuli through Pavlovian conditioning (for review, see Berntson et al., 1993).

Animal studies provide support for Zajonc's (1980) suggestion that the structure and function of the affect system is not fully describable in terms of higher level cognitive processes (Berntson et al., 1993). The isolated spinal cord, for instance, can evidence primitive approach responses, as indicated by basic genital reflexes to tactile stimulation (erection, pelvic thrusting, and ejaculation). Basic approach—withdrawal behaviors can be seen not only in the simplest of organisms but also at the lowest level of organization in the mammalian CNS. These basic approach—withdrawal dispositions such as spinal reflexes are clearly subject to learned modification with experience. At the same time, no one would mistake the primitive responses of the isolated spinal cord for the richness of the reactions of an intact organism to aversive or sexual contexts. There are two fundamental distinctions between these classes of reaction: (a) stimulus dependence and response variability and (b) the level of contextual control.

The first striking difference between an organism with a lesion separating the spinal cord from the brain and an organism with an intact connection between the brain and spinal cord is the repertoire of responses to, for example, an aversive stimulus. Although a spinal organism may show limb withdrawal, the intact organism also exhibits more global escape and avoidance responses, aggression, vocalization, or instrumental responses that serve to eliminate or diminish the aversive stimulus. A related difference is apparent in the persistence of behavioral responses. Although the spinal withdrawal is highly stimulus-bound, the intact organism may evidence behavioral activation, agitation, and escape attempts that persist well after the pain stimulus is withdrawn. Thus, the aversive reaction of the intact organism is less dependent on the immediate sensory environment.

This latter feature anticipates the second major distinction in the approach—withdrawal responses of spinal and intact organisms. That difference is in the complexity of contextual controls over behavior. The approach—withdrawal responses of the spinal organism appear to be sensitive only to relatively simple dimensions of a stimulus, such as its modality, intensity, or body location. In contrast, the aversive or sexual reactions of an intact organism frequently depend on highly complex relational features of the social context. In the intact organism, sexual arousal may not require direct tactile stimulation but may be manifest in the presence of a specific individual, or by the thought of a specific individual, in an appropriate social context.

Studies of decerebrate organisms further illustrate the increased behavioral flexibility and the expansion of relational contextual controls over behavior that result from higher order neural organizations. The decerebrate organism, deprived of the cerebral hemispheres, can display orofacial consummatory responses such as chewing and swallowing when palatable items are placed within the mouth, and vigorous rejection responses to nonpalatable items placed in the mouth. These approach—withdrawal behaviors parallel the basic capacities of the spinal preparation but evidence a degree of complexity and integration beyond that characteristic of spinal systems. Moreover, these complex reflexive responses are influenced not only by immediate sensory features of the stimulus such as palatability but are also sensitive to internal motivational conditions such as food deprivation. Thus, although mechanisms for reflex ingestive responses to palatable foods may be relatively hardwired, their ultimate expression is further controlled by an additional class of internal stimuli.

Although decerebrates are sensitive to metabolic needs and are capable of competent ingestive (i.e., approach–withdrawal) responses in the presence of a suitable goal object, they still fail to adequately regulate food intake or maintain body weight in typical environments. What appears to be lacking in these organisms is the ability to anticipate metabolic need, to evidence goal-searching behavior in the absence of an immediate stimulus for ingestion, or to respond to the normal contextual controls over food intake (e.g., social convention, passage of day, and consideration of caloric need). These controls require a contextual representation that transcends simple dimensions of environmental stimuli such as the presence of food and entails relational aspects among stimuli (e.g., hunger together with the memory of the location of food). It is this latter class of contextual controls, entailing relational features among stimuli or transcendent representations of the environment, that liberates an organism from the immediate dictates of the sensory environment and confers what has been interpreted as deliberative or goal-directed action.

The progression of increased behavioral flexibility and the expansion of relational contextual controls over behavior constitute hallmarks of higher level neural organizations. It is here that one sees the affect system working hand in glove with the cognitive system to appraise the significance of stimuli and to execute appropriate actions. It directs attention, guides decision making, stimulates learning, and triggers behavior. The neurological case of Elliot, reported by Damasio (1994), is illustrative. Elliot was a businessman who developed a brain tumor that damaged his prefrontal cortex. Following the damage to the prefrontal cortex by the brain tumor and the subsequent surgery, Elliot began behaving irrationally. The testing of Elliot revealed that his intelligence, attention, and memory were unaffected. Elliot, however, had lost the ability to experience emotion; and without emotion there were no affective responses to foster learning or decision making. As Damasio (1994) noted, decision making for Elliot became a dangerous game of roulette.

The higher level systems in the brain appear to be organized partly in a heterarchical fashion, and both extend the sensory processing of lower systems and expand on the motor repertoire and flexibility of lower mechanisms. Importantly, this heterarchical organization permits multiple levels of analysis and control over behavioral processes. In response to a pain stimulus, for example, lower level processing may predominate initially, resulting in a rather stereotyped but highly adaptive, short-latency limb withdrawal. The significant advantage of lower level processing is that, although somewhat inflexible, it is highly efficient and places minimal burdens on higher level processing substrates. Indeed, for the initial protective response, elaborate processing of the stimulus is not necessary, and in fact may be maladaptive. Lower level processing, however, does not preclude further analysis at higher perceptual levels. In the case of a pain stimulus, this further analysis may be manifest in subsequent emotional reactions (e.g., fear and anxiety), which may motivate subsequent behavior (e.g., avoidance and aggression).

This pattern of multiple-level analysis and control confers significant advantages. By their nature, higher level organizations must integrate information from varied modalities and sources and exert control over diverse aspects of behavior. This convergence of sensory information, the need for integration with prior memories, and the divergence of output control can create a processing bottleneck that taxes the information-processing capacity of neural networks. Consequently, these higher level systems may be more likely to require active attentional focus and may have limited capacity for multiple concurrent activities than lower level systems. Those stimuli or conditions that do not effectively compete for attentional resources may be subject to only lower level processing or to fairly elementary processing by higher level neural networks. An important question, and an actively researched area, relates to the determinants of which stimuli are selected for further processing.

Being of Two Minds at Once

The multiplicity of evaluative representations does not reflect a simple redundancy. Because the capacity for stimulus processing differs across neuraxial levels, these evaluative mechanisms may be sensitive to distinct or only partially overlapping features of the social context. Moreover, because evaluative mechanisms may have differential access to levels of organization within response systems, their behavioral manifestations may be rather disparate. As we discuss in the next section, the coexistence of multiple evaluative (e.g., attitudinal) representations toward the same classes of stimuli has implications for one's understanding of stereotypes and prejudice. We first, however, review experimental evidence that primates can indeed be of two minds at once and, more specifically, that the relatively emotional and the relatively thoughtful representations can be elicited under specifiable conditions that engage primarily lower level versus higher level brain systems, respectively.

Specifically, the multiple levels of evaluative processes, their differential sensitivities to features of the environmental context, and their divergent behavioral manifestations raise the possibility of interactions among evaluative dispositions. The heterarchical features of neural organization are consistent with the descending biases exerted by higher systems on lower evaluative mechanisms (Berntson et al., 1993). An example of the biasing operations of higher evaluative mechanisms on lower reflex mechanisms is provided by Lang and colleagues' work on startle modulation (Lang, 1995; Lang, Bradley, & Cuthbert, 1990, 1992). In an illustrative study, Vrana, Spence, and Lang (1988) had participants view a series of positive, negative, and neutral slides for 6,000-ms each. The slides were selected from the International Affective Picture System (IAPS; Lang, Bradley, & Cuthbert, 1995), a set of nearly 550 color images used widely in emotion research in general, and in startle reflex research in particular. Normative ratings from college-age samples for self-reported bipolar valence and arousal are available for the IAPS images and were used to select slides in Vrana et al.'s study. The positive and negative slides were equated for mean arousal, and both valent categories were more arousing than the neutral slides. An unsignaled 50-ms noise burst was presented during presentation of a subset of slides. Participants were instructed to attend to the slides and ignore noises in their headphones. The magnitude of the blink response, measured by miniature electrodes placed over the muscle under one of the eyes, was inversely related to the valence of the affective foreground. Specifically, blinks elicited during the presentation of negative slides were augmented relative to those elicited during neutral slides. Blinks elicited during positive slides, in contrast, were inhibited relative to the neutral slides. Lang and his colleagues (Lang, 1995; Lang et al., 1990, 1992) have explained startle blink modulation as a function of affective foreground in terms of motivational priming.

Lang's explanation presumes two motivational systems, one appetitive and concerned with rewarding stimuli that results in a currency function we have termed *positivity*, and the other aversive and concerned with defensive responses that results in a currency function we have termed *negativity* (Cacioppo et al., 1997; Lang et al., 1990). Affective stimuli are thought to prime associations, representations, and actions programs that are associated with one or the other system. Such priming is thought to increase the likelihood and potential strength of responding for the activated system while simultaneously decreasing the likelihood and potential strength of responding for the nonengaged system (i.e., reciprocal activation). A negative stimulus that precedes a startle probe is therefore thought to activate the aversive system. The subsequent match between the already primed aversive system and the defensive startle reflex results in potentiation of startle eyeblinks (reflex–affect match). By contrast, a positive affective foreground results in a mismatch between the valence of the affective foreground and the reflexive response, resulting in inhibition of startle eyeblinks (a reflex–affect mismatch).

Relatively primitive evaluative dispositions can also have an impact on complex, acquired behaviors. Ohman, Hamm, and Hugdahl (2000), for instance, review evidence demonstrating that humans show enhanced electrodermal conditioned responses to a conditioned stimulus having inherent "fear relevance" (e.g., spiders, snakes), compared with neutral or "fear-irrelevant" stimuli (e.g., flowers, mushrooms). In studies of monkeys, Cook and Mineka (1989, 1990) reported enhanced observational learning of fear responses to a toy snake or crocodile than to flowers or a toy rabbit. Importantly, the monkeys in Cook and Mineka's studies had no experience with the experimental stimuli prior to testing, and all of the experimental stimuli were shown to support comparable appetitive conditioning, ruling out explanations based on general salience or conditionability of the stimuli.

Primitive evaluative dispositions can also exert powerful influences on behavior. Boysen, Berntson, Hannan, and Cacioppo (1996) provided a powerful demonstration of this principle in a study of chimpanzees who had been trained extensively in simple arithmetic operations (counting, addition, and subtraction) using Arabic numerals. The participant could see two reinforcement pans, each of which was baited with different quantities of candies on each trial. A reversed reinforcement contingency was implemented such that the participant received the candies from the pan to which they did not point. Thus, it was in the participant's best interest to select the smaller of the two candy arrays to obtain the remaining, larger quantity. Even after hundreds of training trials across dozens of sessions, the chimpanzees' performances were significantly below chance. Moreover, their performance worsened at higher reward ratios—where they stood to benefit the most. This was true for all chimps in the study. As was noted concerning 2 of the participants, Sarah is perhaps the most celebrated chimpanzee in the animal cognition literature, with demonstrated competence in ratio judgments and analogical reasoning. Sheba has the documented ability to count from 1 to 9, use transitive inference, accurately derive the sum of two quantities, and flexibly use number symbols. Yet neither of these animals could consistently select the smaller of two candy arrays, even after hundreds of training trials (Berntson et al., 1993, p. 91).

We posited that the inherent evaluative disposition based on the perceptual features of the candy arrays interfered with optimal performance based on the underlying rule structure of the task (Boysen et al., 1996). To test this hypothesis, we conducted an experiment in which the chimps performed the same task, but rather than using candy arrays as stimuli, placards with corresponding Arabic numerals were substituted. Thus, the participant received the number of candies that corresponded to the nonselected numeral. This change led to an immediate above-chance performance. When the candies were again used as experimental stimuli, performance fell immediately to below chance levels; when the Arabic numerals were used, performance rose immediately to above chance. These results suggested that the chimps had acquired the rules of the task but this knowledge, or at least its effect on behavior, was obscured by a potent competing disposition arising from the intrinsic incentive properties of the candy arrays. Lower level evaluative processing is generally adaptive, but there are situations in which it is not. It is thus interesting to note that these data further suggest that humans evolved the capacity to work with symbolic representations of the world because symbols helped minimize the powerful and sometimes maladaptive dictates of lower evaluative dispositions.

Although the evaluative disposition studied by Boysen et al. (1996) may have been inherent to chimps, acquired evaluative dispositions in humans can operate similarly. We have shown that evaluative predispositions (attitudes) can be formed in humans through a form of classical conditioning termed *latent inhibition* (Cacioppo, Marshall-Goodell, Tassinary, & Petty, 1992). The experimental stimuli were neutral words and pronounceable nonwords, which were matched in terms of structural features and participants' prior attitudes and affect. A differential conditioning procedure was used such that the word was paired with electric shock, the nonword was paired with electric shock, or the word and nonword were paired randomly with electric shock. A simulation experiment in which participants read descriptions of the conditioning procedures revealed that they expected (and believed the experimenter anticipated) simply that whatever stimulus was paired with electric shock would become disliked. In accord with latent inhibition, however, we posited that conditioning would be more apparent for nonwords than for words because of the preexposures to the latter class of stimuli. Results confirmed that more negative attitudes were formed when the nonwords were paired with electric shock than when the words were paired with the electric shock.

Animal research by LeDoux and colleagues on conditioned fear reactions to acoustic stimuli indicates that projections from the auditory processing areas of the thalamus to the amygdala bypass the cortex and constitute a subcortical mechanism for affective learning (e.g., LeDoux, Iwata, Cicchetti, & Reis, 1988; see LeDoux, 1995). LeDoux, Romanski, and Xagorasis (1989) used visual rather than auditory stimuli to determine whether affective memory was limited to the auditory modality. Furthermore, the visual cortex was ablated in half of the rats to determine whether classically conditioned affective responses to visual stimuli were dependent on the visual cortex. Animals were given either paired or random presentations of a flashing light and a footshock. Classically conditioned responses were found following the pairing of the light and footshock whether or not the visual cortex had been destroyed, although the presence of the visual cortex greatly slowed extinction to the conditioned response. These data are consistent with the thesis that the acquisition and representation of affective (evaluative) dispositions can operate at multiple, interrelated levels of the neuraxis.

These data are reminiscent of Nisbett and Wilson's (1977) and Gazzaniga and LeDoux's (1978) proposition that individuals can come to feel certain ways about stimuli and can even construct rationalizations for their feelings, while not really knowing why they came to feel as they do about people, objects, or events around them. The results of our simulation study indicated that people's declarative knowledge about classical conditioning led them to believe that whatever stimulus was associated with electric shock would also become disliked. Our results, however, conformed to animal studies showing that individuals felt more negatively about a novel than familiar stimulus that was paired with electric shock. These data suggest a process by which individuals can come to feel differently toward stimuli in their world even though they do not comprehend the true basis for these differential feelings. Work on split-brain patients further suggests that people spontaneously confabulate to explain their feelings. To the patient who is trying to construct a meaningful world from disparate parts, the confabulations are sensible and sober (Gazzaniga, 1985).

Implications for Explaining and Minimizing Racial Prejudice

Open racial prejudice has declined over the past half century, but prejudice and discrimination still emerges when, for instance, people are emotionally engaged (e.g., Rogers & Prentice-Dunn, 1981; Stroessner & Mackie, 1993) or pressed for time (Kaplan, Wanshhula, & Zanna, 1993) or when discriminatory behavior can be masked by some other motive (Gaertner & Dovidio, 1986; Meertens & Pettigrew, 1997). Social psychologists have focused in recent years on explaining prejudice in terms of a natural side effect of cognitive processing. The present analysis of the multifarious structure and operation of the affect system suggests another explanation, one with implications for the understanding and treatment of racial prejudice.

To illustrate, consider children living in an egalitarian society who are exposed to relatively familiar and unfamiliar races in film, television, and the news media. These children are exposed in daily life to many more majority than minority members, but members of each race periodically are associated with negative events (e.g., assault, homicide, and victimization) in the media. Thus, different exemplars of racial categories (conditioned stimulus) are paired periodically with inherently frightening or aversive events (unconditioned stimulus). Our classical conditioning studies suggest that greater prejudice should develop toward the race about which the children have little knowledge or contact (i.e., racial minorities) and that these children will not appreciate the subtle manner in which their social environment has produced these prejudices. Consider, further, that as these children go through socialization, they may initially articulate prejudicial beliefs to justify the differential feelings they hold toward majority and minority groups. In an egalitarian society, these prejudicial beliefs are challenged and undergo correction during socialization. One possible outcome is that these children become socialized to inhibit *expressions* of their true beliefs and prejudices. A second possible outcome, however, is that the egalitarian beliefs they are taught also produce corresponding changes in verbal beliefs, attitudes, and prejudices, but that the classically conditioned evaluative predisposition remains in place at a lower level of the neuraxis.

The evidence reviewed above suggests racial prejudice rests in part on the conditioned evaluative predispositions that coexist with egalitarian beliefs, leaving people unwittingly of two minds about members of racial minorities. Accordingly, the verbal beliefs and evaluative attitude representations are more likely to influence and predict behavioral intentions, whereas the lower level (e.g., conditioned) evaluative predisposition is more likely to influence a variety of affective and "unintentional" behaviors—the kinds of behaviors that have been shown to be most likely to reveal prejudice in contemporary research on stereotypy (see Clark & Squire, 1998). Contrary to the notion in modern racism that people are of one mind but two faces, the current analysis raises the possibility that individuals who report being egalitarian but find themselves acting in a discriminatory fashion are speaking truthfully, in a sense, when they say that their actions were not really "them." Their actions may not reflect what they see to be the behavioral implications of their beliefs. In a sense, a lower evaluative predisposition had usurped volitional control of their behavior, just as had candies over the chimps' selections. Symbolic representations provided a different glimpse into the minds of the chimps; similarly, words and rating scales may provide an accurate yet incomplete glimpse into human prejudices.

An obvious difference among these explanations of racial prejudice comes from the expected effectiveness of various interventions. If racial prejudice at higher levels of evaluative processing has declined over the past 50 years while conditioned racial prejudice remains problematic, extensive neutral (i.e., nonpunished) exposures of young children to numerous exemplars of minority races should help diminish the strength of the conditioned prejudicial responses. If, in contrast, stereotyping and racial prejudice are natural side effects of the cognitive system, or reflect people's true feelings but these are hidden to avoid social sanctions, then such an intervention would be ineffective. The key may be to start young, before latent inhibition operates to foster the development of racial prejudices.

Conclusion

Among Zajonc's many contributions were his generative hypotheses about the affect system. He suggested, for instance, that the operation of the affect system is separable from traditional mindful cognitive operations and that the latter are the consequences as (or more) often as the antecedents of affective operations. We reviewed evidence here that there is "localization" of functions and that these functions are distributed broadly and are re-represented across levels of the neuraxis. Among the re-representation of functions are core components for the maintenance of life (brain stem), species adaptive behaviors (limbic region), and creative adaptations based on individual and cultural influences (neocortex). Similarly, cognitive and affective mechanisms are not localized at a specific neuraxial level but are represented throughout the CNS. At progressively higher organizational levels, there is a general expansion in the range and relational complexity of contextual controls and in the breadth and flexibility of discriminative and adaptive responses. Although these levels of representation often act in concert, this need not be the case. Illusory correlations and latent inhibition, for instance, both may contribute to implicit prejudice even in individuals who by explicit measures appear to be egalitarian. Such complexities owe much to Zajonc, whose example of looking beyond the singular, linear, and self-evident solution laid the groundwork for contemporary studies of the social mind.

References

Berntson, G. G., Boysen, S. T., & Cacioppo, J. T. (1993). Neurobehavioral organization and the cardinal principle of evaluative bivalence. *Annals of the New York Academy of Sciences, 702,* 75–102.

Boysen, S. T., Berntson, G. G., Hannan, M. B., & Cacioppo, J. T. (1996). Quantity-based choices: Interference and symbolic representations in chimpanzees (*Pan troglodytes*). *Journal of Experimental Psychology: Animal Behavior Processes, 22,* 76–86.

Cacioppo, J. T., & Berntson, G. G. (1994). Relationship between attitudes and evaluative space: A critical review, with emphasis on the separability of positive and negative substrates. *Psychological Bulletin, 115,* 401–423.

Cacioppo, J. T., Crites, S. L. Jr., Berntson, G. G., & Coles, M. G. H. (1993). If attitudes affect how stimuli are processed, should not they affect the event-related brain potential? *Psychological Science, 4,* 108–112.

Cacioppo, J. T., Crites, S. L., Jr., & Gardner, W. L. (1996). Attitudes to the right: Evaluative processing is associated with lateralized late positive event-related brain potentials. *Personality and Social Psychology Bulletin, 22,* 1205–1219.

Cacioppo, J. T., Crites, S. L. Jr., Gardner, W. L., & Berntson, G. G. (1994). Bioelectrical echoes from evaluative categorizations: I. A late positive brain potential that varies as a function of trait negativity and extremity. *Journal of Personality and Social Psychology, 67,* 115–125.

Cacioppo, J. T., & Gardner, W. L. (1999). Emotion. *Annual Review of Psychology, 50,* 191–214.

Cacioppo, J. T., Gardner, W. L., & Berntson, G. G. (1997). Beyond bipolar conceptualizations and measures: The case of attitudes and evaluative space. *Personality and Social Psychology Review, 1,* 3–25.

Cacioppo, J. T., Gardner, W. L., & Berntson, G. G. (1999). The affect system: Form follows function. *Journal of Personality and Social Psychology, 76,* 839–855.

Cacioppo, J. T., Marshall-Goodell, B. S., Tassinary, L. G., & Petty, R. E. (1992). Rudimentary determinants of attitudes: Classical conditioning is more effective when prior knowledge about the attitude stimulus is low than high. *Journal of Experimental Social Psychology, 28,* 207–233.

Clark, R. E., & Squire, L. R. (1998). Classical conditioning and brain systems: The role of awareness. *Science, 280,* 77–81.

Cook, M., & Mineka, S. (1989). Observational conditioning of fear to fear-relevant versus fear-irrelevant stimuli in rhesus monkeys. *Journal of Abnormal Behavior, 98,* 448–459.

Cook, M., & Mineka, S. (1990). Selective associations in the observational conditioning of fear in rhesus monkeys. *Journal of Experimental Psychology: Animal Behavior and Processes, 16,* 372–389.

Crites, S. L., Jr., & Cacioppo, J. T. (1996). Electrocortical differentiation of evaluative and nonevaluative categorizations. *Psychological Science, 7,* 318–321.

Crites, S. L., Jr., Cacioppo, J. T., Gardner, W. L., & Berntson, G. G. (1995). Bioelectrical echoes from evaluative categorization: II. A late positive brain potential that varies as a function of attitude registration rather than attitude report. *Journal of Personality and Social Psychology, 68,* 997–1013.

Damasio, A. R. (1994). *Descartes' error: Emotion, reason, and the human brain.* New York: Grossett/Putnam.

Davis, M. (1997). The neurophysiological basis of acoustic startle modulation: Research on fear motivation and sensory gating. In P. J. Lang, R. F. Simons, & M. Balaban (Eds.), *Attention and orienting* (pp. 69–96). Mahwah, NJ: Erlbaum.

Gaertner, S. L., & Dovidio, J. F. (1986). The aversive form of racism. In J. F. Dovidio & S. L. Gaertner (Eds.), *Prejudice, discrimination, and racism* (pp. 61–89). Orlando, FL: Academic Press.

Gardner, W. L., & Cacioppo, J. T. (in press). A brain based index of evaluative processing: A late positive brain potential reflects individual differences in the extremity of a negative evaluation. *Social Cognition.*

Gazzaniga, M. S. (1985). *The social brain: Discovering the networks of the mind.* New York: Basic Books.

Gazzaniga, M. S., & LeDoux, J. E. (1978). *The integrated mind.* New York: Plenum Press.

Ito, T. A., & Cacioppo, J. T. (1999). The psychophysiology of utility appraisals. In D. Kahneman, E. Diener, & N. Schwarz (Eds.), *Well being: The foundations of hedonic psychology* (pp. 470–488). New York: Russell Sage Foundation.

Kahneman, D., Diener, E., & Schwarz, N. (1999). *Understanding quality of life: Scientific perspectives on enjoyment and suffering.* New York: Cambridge University Press.

Kaplan, M. F., Wanshula, L. T., & Zanna, M. P. (1993). Time pressure and information integration in social judgment: The effect of need for structure. In O. Svenson & J. Maule (Eds.), *Time pressure and stress in human judgment and decision making* (pp. 255–267). Cambridge, England: Cambridge University Press.

Lang, P. J. (1995). The emotion probe: Studies of motivation and attention. *American Psychologist, 50,* 372–385.

Lang, P. J., Bradley, M. M., & Cuthbert, B. N. (1990). Emotion, attention, and the startle reflex. *Psychological Review, 97,* 377–395.

Lang, P. J., Bradley, M. M., & Cuthbert, B. N. (1992). A motivational analysis of emotion: Reflex–cortex connections. *Psychological Science, 3,* 44–49.

Lang, P. J., Bradley, M. M., & Cuthbert, B. N. (1995). *International affective picture systems (IAPS): Technical manual and affective ratings.* Gainesville, FL: The Center for Research in Psychophysiology, University of Florida.

LeDoux, J. E. (1995). Emotion: Clues from the brain. *Annual Review of Psychology, 46,* 209–235.

LeDoux, J. E., Iwata, J., Cicchetti, P., & Reis, D. J. (1988). Different projections of the central amygdaloid nucleus mediate autonomic and behavioral correlates of conditioned fear. *Journal of Neuroscience, 8,* 2517–2529.

LeDoux, J. E., Romanski, L., & Xagorasis, A. (1989). Indelibility of subcortical emotional memories. *Journal of Cognitive Neuroscience, 1,* 238–243.

Meertens, R. W., & Pettigrew, T. F. (1997). Is subtle prejudice really prejudice? *Public Opinion Quarterly, 61*, 54–71.

Nisbett, R. E., & Wilson, T. D. (1977). Telling more than we can know: Verbal reports on mental processes. *Psychological Review, 84*, 231–259.

Ohman, A., Hamm, A., & Hugdahl, K. (2000). Cognition and the autonomic nervous system: Orienting, anticipation, and conditioning. In J. T. Cacioppo, L. G. Tassinary, & G. G. Berntson (Eds.), *Handbook of psychophysiology* (pp. 533–575). New York: Cambridge University Press.

Rogers, R. W., & Prentice-Dunn, S. (1981). Deindividuation and anger-mediated interracial aggression: Unmasking regressive racism. *Journal of Personality and Social Psychology, 41*, 63–73.

Shizgal, P. (1999). On the neural computation of utility: Implications from studies of brain stimulation reward. In D. Kahneman, E. Diener, & N. Schwarz (Eds.), *Hedonic psychology: Scientific perspectives on enjoyment, suffering, and well-being* (pp. 500–524). New York: Cambridge University Press.

Stroessner, S. J., & Mackie, D. M. (1993). Affect and perceived group variability: Implications for stereotyping and prejudice. In D. M. Mackie & D. L. Hamilton (Eds.), *Affect, cognition, and stereotyping: Interactive processes in group perception* (pp. 63–86). San Diego, CA: Academic Press.

Tucker, D. M. (1981). Lateral brain function, emotion, and conceptualization. *Psychological Bulletin, 89*, 19–46.

Tucker, D. M., & Frederick, S. L. (1989). Emotion and brain lateralization. In H. Wagner & A. Manstead (Eds.), *Handbook of social psychophysiology* (pp. 27–70). Chichester, England: Wiley.

Vrana, S. R., Spence, E. L., & Lang, P. J. (1988). The startle probe response: A new measure of emotion? *Journal of Abnormal Psychology, 97*, 487–491.

Zajonc, R. B. (1980). Feeling and thinking: Preferences need no inferences. *American Psychologist, 35*, 157–193.

CHAPTER 8

How and When Preferences Influence Inferences: A Motivated Hypothesis-Testing Framework

Yaacov Trope
Melissa J. Ferguson

Bob Zajonc (1980) convincingly demonstrated that people's wants are not always based on what they believe. Instead, people's preferences concerning a stimulus can sometimes apparently preempt any conscious cognitive appraisal of that stimulus and persist even in the absence of any explicit recognition. Although it thus seems quite plausible that people's preferences about a stimulus can develop and endure independently of their inferences about that stimulus, Zajonc and colleagues (Winkielman, Zajonc, & Schwarz, 1997) conducted further work suggesting that some inferences themselves seem to depend on one's preferences. Evidently, not only can preferences about a stimulus sometimes be orthogonal to explicit beliefs about the stimulus, but beliefs about a stimulus might to some extent depend on the corresponding preferences.

We would like to extend and argue for the possibility that what people believe often seems to depend on what they want. There is much research in social psychology showing that people believe what they want to believe. The tendency for preferential believing is manifested in judgmental biases involving both the self and others as well as predictions concerning the future.

Still, despite the evidence for such wishful thinking, people regularly come to believe things that they surely do not prefer. That is, other than perhaps those who are afflicted with delusional belief systems, people seem ultimately unable to construct their world solely on the basis of their preferences. Though it might be nice to live in a world in which everything that is preferred is also evident, people's conceptions of their surroundings are informed and curtailed by reality.

Indeed, the New Look perspective in perception in the 1940s and 1950s (e.g., Bruner, 1957; Bruner & Postman, 1947) and the reemergence of the movement in the 1970s (Erdelyi, 1974) burst the bubble of naïve realism by demonstrating the influence of needs and wants (i.e., preferences) on perception. And yet, the constructivist elements in this work were always constrained by parameters of objective reality. Just as one cannot transform a quarter into a dollar bill by sheer will, social judgments correspond to at least ambiguously related data in the real world (see Higgins, 1996).

With these limitations of preferential believing in mind, a consequent question therefore concerns precisely how and when people's inferences are guided by their preferences. In this chapter, we explore this by first considering the evidence for preferential believing and then by describing and applying a framework of how people identify and test their inferences. This framework incorporates both motivational and cognitive aspects of such a testing procedure and explains why people may tend to confirm the hypotheses that they test. Given the supposition that people tend to test preferred rather than nonpreferred hypotheses, which is discussed, this framework provides one explication for the phenomenon of preferential believing.

Evidence for Preferential Believing

I'm Okay, You're Not Okay!

Although traditional views of people's belief systems largely downplayed the degree to which people interpret themselves and their worlds through rose-tinted glasses (e.g., Fiske & Taylor, 1991; Nisbett & Ross, 1980; see Taylor & Brown, 1988, for a review), more recent conceptualizations reflect the vast amount of evidence that people believe good things, particularly about their own traits and behaviors as well as the groups to which they belong (e.g., Greenwald, 1980; Kruglanski, 1989; Kunda, 1987; Pyszczynski & Greenberg, 1987; M. Ross & Sicoly, 1979; Taylor & Brown, 1988). Most people tend to rate themselves as being above average on a variety of desirable skills and traits compared with others. For example, people often report that they are above average with regard to driving ability, intelligence, and humor (Brown 1986; Campbell, 1986; Weinstein, 1982).

People also tend to attribute their successes more to their stable personality traits and abilities and their failures to situational glitches compared with how they explain another's successes and failures (Miller & Ross, 1975; L. Ross, 1977; Zuckerman, 1979). For example, whereas one's stellar performance on a test must be due to one's vast wisdom, a poor performance is undoubtedly the result of an unfairly difficult test, coupled with the cold and rainy weather on the day of the test and the alignment of the stars. Another person's failure on the test, however, might be more readily explained by his or her inadequate knowledge base.

People also predict that they will enjoy a more optimistic future compared with the present (Markus & Nurius, 1986). For instance, when asked to predict the probability of possessing both positive and negative traits sometime in the future, participants both thought about acquiring positive traits more so than negative traits and reported that the attainment of positive traits was more probable compared with the attainment of negative traits.

Us Versus Them

People's glowing appraisals of themselves and their futures are also graciously extended to the members of the groups to which they belong. The propensity for people to favor those in their in-group compared with those in their out-group has been documented in a number of ways over the last several decades by researchers in social psychology. For example, people often explain the successes and failures of those with whom they associate in a similar fashion to how they causally attribute their own successes and failures (Taylor & Kouvumaki, 1976). As long as a close other does not succeed in a personally important realm (e.g., Cialdini et al., 1976; Tesser, 1986; Tesser, Millar, & Moore, 1988), people seem to give those in their group the benefit of the doubt when they fail and the benefit of faith when they succeed. Moreover, people frequently view others in their own group as displaying more desirable traits and abilities (Brown, 1986) than those in the out-group.

The basis of group membership need not be enduring or meaningful for members to view each other in a more positive light than how they perceive those outside of the group. Research from the minimal group paradigm, for instance, has demonstrated that in-group favoritism can emerge on the basis of random assignment to arbitrary groups (Tajfel & Turner, 1986). It seems then that simply designating someone as a group member is enough to provoke a positivity bias similar to that which people use when evaluating themselves.

Illusion of Control: ''I Can Do It!''

People also apparently overestimate the degree to which they are able to exert control over phenomena in their lives. When asked to decide between a randomly chosen lottery ticket and one they themselves had chosen, participants overwhelmingly wanted to keep the one they had chosen, irrespective of the superstition underlying such a preference (Langer, 1975). This and related findings have been interpreted as indicating people's unwarranted beliefs that they can control actually uncontrollable outcomes (see also Miller & Ross, 1975; Taylor & Brown, 1988).

Beyond exerting control over events in the world, people also seem to believe that they can control their ability to make rational (i.e., unbiased) decisions, even when exposed to evidence that they previously recognized as biased toward one choice option of a decision. In one study, Wilson and Brekke (1994) presented participants with evidence both in favor of and against a product. Even when participants identified some of the evidence as sensationalistic, misleading, and ultimately uninformative, they still chose to evaluate the evidence in more detail before making a decision about the product, believing that they would be able to resist the influence. Their decisions in fact indicated that they were swayed by the misleading information, suggesting that their confidence in their ability to make rational decisions was unwarranted. Presumably, people would prefer to believe that they are able to arrive at unbiased judgments.

Research also suggests that although people may believe that they know the reasons for their decisions, they may in fact be unaware of them (e.g., Nisbett & Wilson, 1977; Wilson & Schooler, 1991). Nisbett and Wilson (1977) reported research showing how people promptly offered explanations and predictions of their choices and behavior and that those explanations were typically inaccurate and misguided. The reference to this research in the context of preferential believing is based on the conjecture that people would prefer to think that they know the reasons for their decisions and behavior.

Relatedly, Wegner and his colleagues have developed a research program dedicated to examining the extent to which people think they have more control over their mental processes than they apparently do (Wegner, 1994; Wegner & Bargh, 1997). People seem frequently ill-equipped to suppress unwanted thoughts when under attentional duress (see also Macrae, Bodenhausen, Milne, & Jetten, 1994). For instance, participants attempted to suppress thoughts about sexist behaviors, and those who were instructed to immediately complete sentence stems emitted more sexist responses compared with participants who were allowed to complete the sentence stems within ten seconds (see Wegner, 1994). Wegner and his colleagues, among others, have extended this line of work by proposing that people falsely believe that they are capable of willful behavior (Ansfield & Wegner, 1996; Christensen & Turner, 1993; Prinz, 1997; Wegner & Wheatley, 1999). Both of these lines of research about how people believe that they can control their mental lives and exert their will strongly suggest that many of people's inferences are based on what they would prefer to be true.

In a similar vein, participants often report being nonprejudiced and strongly committed to egalitarianism and nondiscriminatory behaviors (e.g., Bodenhausen & Macrae, 1998; Devine, 1989). Yet, some research has shown that people's beliefs in their own inclination toward nonprejudiced behavior may be overly optimistic. People sometimes display prejudiced behavior even after explicitly endorsing nonprejudiced ideals (e.g., Banaji, Hardin, & Rothman, 1993; Bargh, 1999; Fazio, Jackson, Dunton, & Williams, 1995). For example, White participants who identified themselves as nonracist subsequently behaved in a prejudiced manner toward an African American experimenter and displayed implicit attitudes consistent with a negative affective orientation toward images of African Americans (Fazio et al., 1995).

This set of findings across such a broad spectrum of domains suggests that people believe that they have control over their reasoning, introspective ability, willful intent, and behavior when in fact they may not. Therefore, people may be unduly confident in their abilities to predict, interpret, and control their own behavior (e.g., Vallone, Griffin, Lin, & Ross, 1990). Irrespective of the veridicality of their beliefs, then, many people's inferences seem intertwined with their preferences. This concomitance of preferences and inferences, in the face of possible overconfidence and inaccuracy, highlights the need to explore how inferences might emerge, albeit sometimes inappropriately, from preferences.

''But I'm Not Always Okay''

Although there is clearly ample evidence for wishful thinking in many areas of research in social psychology, there are also limitations to believing what one wants to believe. Although some people may inhabit worlds colored almost exclusively by what they want, most people endorse many beliefs that they do not prefer. People are bombarded daily with evidence that confirms facts and phenomena that are undeniably undesirable, such as the suffering that results from natural disasters, personal tragedies, and societal ills, for example. When faced with evidence concerning such undesirable occurrences, people frequently incorporate the corresponding evidence into their belief systems. This seems self-evident.

Researchers in social psychology regularly rely on this capacity to accept nonpreferred propositions when trying to examine various effects of negative feedback on behavior. For instance, although people typically exhibit a self-serving bias by explaining away their failures and taking credit for their success, this is not always the case. People are vulnerable to negative feedback about themselves and their abilities, and researchers regularly make use of this vulnerability when trying to study the implications of depressed self-esteem or induced negative moods. In short, people are limited in their ability to engage in exclusively preferential believing, as implied by both anecdotal evidence to the contrary and empirical work in social psychology.

A Hypothesis-Testing Framework

Although the preceding review is far from exhaustive, it should be clear from the review that there is a large amount of research showing that people often, but not always, infer what they prefer. One question remains open, however: What are the mechanisms that underlie these phenomena? In this chapter, we attempt to address this question by using a motivated hypothesis-testing framework (Trope & Liberman, 1996). This framework rests on the assumption that people are motivated to test the validity of hypotheses to avoid the consequences of holding false beliefs. When these corollaries of being inaccurate are sufficiently aversive, people will actively test the validity of their hypotheses. Conversely, when the consequences of making erroneous judgments are minimally aversive or not aversive at all (from the perspective of the person), one will be less motivated to be accurate and may not even bother to test the validity of the respective hypotheses.

Central to the present idea that people may believe what they want to believe is the possibility that people tend to accept the hypotheses that they test. There are both cognitive and motivational mechanisms that can guide the process of testing a hypothesis and thus contribute to this tendency. People may be likely to accept the hypotheses that they test because they fall prey to evidential biases that arise owing to the accessibility of information related to the hypothesis. This can occur regardless of how much effort a person invests in hypothesis testing.

In addition, the costs of arriving at an inaccurate decision about a hypothesis, namely, the costs of a false acceptance and false rejection of the hypothesis, can sometimes induce a biased search and evaluation of evidence concerning the hypothesis. This can occur because of the differential costliness of the two errors. When the consequences of a false rejection (error of omission) are graver than those of a false acceptance (error of commission), the two costs will be asymmetric. This results in the person adopting a lenient criterion for supportive evidence and a strict criterion for unsupportive evidence concerning the hypothesis. This differential scrutiny of evidence means that the person will more easily accept than reject the possibility being tested. The nature of such a biased process can sometimes lead to a proclivity to confirm one's hypothesis.

This propensity to accept whatever hypothesis one is testing renders preferential believing likely to the extent that people are more likely to test preferred rather than nonpreferred hypotheses. People may indeed tend to test preferred hypotheses for at least two reasons (see Kruglanski, 1989; Kunda, 1990; Trope & Liberman, 1996). One such reason is that it seems more enjoyable to entertain preferred versus nonpreferred hypotheses (Kunda, 1990; Pyszczynski & Greenberg, 1987). Because people seem motivated to either maintain a positive affective state or achieve one (Wegener & Petty, 1996; Wegener, Petty, & Smith, 1995), and because what people think about ostensibly influences their mood, it seems reasonable to assume that people tend to think about preferred outcomes and possibilities rather than nonpreferred ones. This proposed proclivity to ruminate about preferred possibilities may lead one to test preferred hypotheses more frequently than nonpreferred ones.

Another reason for testing preferred versus nonpreferred possibilities concerns the conjecture that people maintain and aspire to desirable versus undesirable goals; because they tend to behave in ways that allow them to achieve such goals, and hence may be preoccupied with their goals, preferred hypotheses may be more accessible than nonpreferred ones (Trope & Liberman, 1996). Goals ostensibly guide and determine people's behavior, and it would seem productive to focus on preferred states rather than nonpreferred ones (see also Carver & Scheier, 1981). If one's goal is to learn how to play bass guitar, one may be more likely to concentrate on preferred states such as being able to buy a guitar and securing a suitable and reliable teacher. These possibilities may be more accessible, therefore, then a nonpreferred possibility such as never learning how to use a pick or not being able to read notation (these may be considered, albeit perhaps to a lesser extent than preferred possibilities).

Mechanisms Producing Confirmation of Preferred Hypotheses

Let us turn now to the mechanisms that lead people to accept preferred hypotheses. One mechanism, evidential biases, concerns the tendency to perceive evidence as consistent rather than inconsistent with one's hypothesis. The other mechanism, asymmetric error costs, concerns the tendency to perceive errors of omission as costlier than errors of commission.

Evidential Biases

When people have ample time and cognitive resources, they may engage in diagnostic testing by taking into account both the hypothesis and its alternatives in seeking information to test their hypothesis (Trope & Bassok, 1982). However, under less optimal conditions, people may resort to a simpler, more heuristic search, called *pseudodiagnostic testing* or *positive testing* (see Klayman & Ha, 1987; Trope & Liberman, 1996). Here, people focus on their hypothesis, ignore alternatives, and seek evidence that is consistent with the focal hypothesis. In itself, pseudodiagnostic testing does not guarantee hypothesis confirmation because the evidence may turn out to be inconsistent with the hypothesis. However, biases in the interpretation of incoming evidence make it likely that a pseudodiagnostic search will actually result in hypothesis confirmation.

One factor that may bias the evidence people obtain from others is acquiescence bias, or the tendency to answer questions with "yes" rather than with "no" (see Zuckerman, Knee, Hodgins, & Miyake, 1995). This bias results from people's assumption that another person's questions represent that person's underlying expectations. Because people often try to confirm another's expectations, they may respond to queries with "yes" for the sake of pleasing the questioner, irrespective of the truth of the answer. If a person asks a question that is consistent with her or his focal hypothesis, the respondent's tendency to acquiesce to the question will result in evidence that suggests the truth of the hypothesis. Therefore, affirmative answers to questions may be construed as supportive evidence when in fact they reflect interpersonal dynamics between the person asking the question and the respondent.

Evidence may also be interpreted as consistent with one's hypothesis because of assimilative encoding and retrieval biases. When information is ambiguous, it will often be encoded in terms of whatever representations in memory are most highly activated, which are due to prior recent or chronic use (Higgins, King, & Mavin, 1982; Higgins, Rholes, & Jones, 1977; Srull & Wyer, 1989). Because of this, if one is testing a hypothesis concerning friendliness, ambiguous behavior may be identified as friendly because the representations concerning friendly are accessible and active in memory. This means that evidence can be interpreted as consistent with the hypothesis even when it might otherwise be interpreted as ambiguous or inconclusive with respect to the hypothesis (i.e., if the hypothesis was not being tested). Furthermore, retrieval biases can also make confirmation of a hypothesis more likely because evidence that is consistent with the hypothesis may be retrieved from memory more easily than evidence that is inconsistent with the hypothesis (see Koehler, 1991; Snyder & Uranowitz, 1978).

Another evidential bias that can lead to the misidentification of evidence as supportive rather than unsupportive is affirmation bias, or the tendency to attribute more importance to affirmations rather than negations (Newman, Wolff, & Hearst, 1980; Zuckerman et al., 1995). Given that people tend to make queries about information that is consistent with their hypotheses, the tendency to assign greater weight to affirmative than negative answers favors hypothesis confirmation more so than disconfirmation. For example, if one is testing the hypothesis that a coworker is hardworking, one may attend to instances during which the coworker expended a lot of effort but ignore or dismiss many instances when the person did not expend a lot of effort. Thus, an affirmative bias, when coupled with searching for evidence consistent with the hypothesis, may result in confirmation of a hypothesis whenever there exists some evidence in support of the hypothesis.

Importantly, these evidential biases can occur outside of people's awareness and thus influence hypothesis testing even when a person is testing a hypothesis in an effortful manner. Attentional and motivational resources may enable people to test their hypotheses diagnostically, namely, to take into account alternatives to their focal hypothesis. But even in diagnostic testing, the focal hypothesis is likely to be considered first and to receive more attention than alternative hypotheses. As a result, the focal hypothesis is likely to retain an advantage in search and processing of information. Thus, diagnostic testing may attenuate, but not entirely eliminate, evidential biases in favor of hypothesis confirmation.

Although our present discussion suggests that evidential biases are likely to favor preferred conclusions, sometimes confirmation biases will actually work against positivity biases. Some individuals may start hypothesis testing with negative possibilities seeming more probable and accessible than positive possibilities. This may result from chronic orientation toward avoiding negative outcomes rather than approaching positive outcomes, a history of negative outcomes, or a contextually induced framing of decisions in terms of negative outcomes (see Higgins, 1987; Tversky & Kahneman, 1981). For example, individuals who are chronically depressed may habitually expect and frame events in terms of negative possibilities (see Andersen, Spielman, & Bargh, 1992). For these individuals, evidential biases will favor confirmation of undesired conclusions. That is, they are likely to seek evidence that is consistent with their negative hypothesis and interpret the actually obtained evidence as confirming this hypothesis.

For example, a person who is more chronically predisposed toward maximizing security than aspiring to self-growth and achievement (see Higgins, 1987) may test the hypothesis that he made a fool of himself at the office dance-a-thon rather than the hypothesis that he impressed other people. The testing process of the focal hypothesis, that he acted foolishly, will fall prey to the same evidential biases that have been described, including acquiescence, assimilation and retrieval biases, and affirmation bias. These biases make it likely that he will interpret relevant evidence as being consistent with the undesirable hypothesis, just as evidential biases can lead one to interpret evidence as consistent with a desirable hypothesis.

In sum, evidential biases, such as acquiescence, assimilative encoding, and affirmation bias, favor confirmation of one's hypotheses. Assuming that people frequently, though not always, test preferred versus nonpreferred hypotheses, as previously discussed, evidential biases may often enable preferences to influence inferences.

Asymmetric Error Costs

The aforementioned evidential biases are not the only factors that can lead to the confirmation of a preferred hypothesis. This framework also postulates that people may conduct a biased search for and evaluation of evidence germane to the hypothesis because of different anticipated costs of making an error (i.e., error of commission or omission). Such biased hypothesis testing may result in the confirmation of the hypothesis when a person is testing a preferred hypothesis. We first describe the role of error costs in hypothesis testing in more detail, and then we describe the implications of testing a preferred possibility for hypothesis confirmation.

Error Costs and Confidence Thresholds

There are four possible outcomes of testing any proposition, two of which are accurate (see Table 8.1). People make accurate judgments when they accept a true hypothesis and reject a false hypothesis. The two other possible outcomes constitute errors in judgment and occur when people believe a false proposition (i.e., the error of commission, or false acceptance; Type II error in statistical testing) and disbelieve a true proposition (i.e., the error of omission, or false rejection; Type I error in statistical testing).

The two possible errors each has associated costs for the person in terms of potential harm or loss caused by being inaccurate rather than accurate. For instance, the implications of rejecting the possibility that an acquaintance is friendly when in fact she is friendly (false rejection) may result in a missed opportunity for friendship and camaraderie. Conversely, accepting the possibility that the acquaintance is friendly when she really is unfriendly (false acceptance) may lead to making unsuc-

TABLE 8.1

Decision Matrix in Hypothesis Testing

		ACTUAL STATE OF AFFAIRS	
		Hypothesis True	**Hypothesis False**
DECISION	**Accept Hypothesis**	Correct acceptance	False acceptance (Error of commission)
	Reject Hypothesis	False rejection (Error of omission)	Correct rejection

cessful overtures of friendship, for instance. The costs related to each of the possible errors are independent and comprise the main motivation for beginning to test a hypothesis.

But once one begins to test a hypothesis, what is the criterion by which one decides that she or he can stop searching and evaluating evidence and make a decision? This framework asserts that people adopt two thresholds of confidence that correspond to the costs of the two possible errors. The more costly the error associated with one decision, the higher the confidence needed to make a decision (i.e., either reject or accept). These confidence thresholds are crucial because they determine when a person will stop the hypothesis-testing process. People will stop when one of their confidence thresholds has been reached with regard to one of the two possible decisions.

Because the two error costs are independent, the two corresponding confidence thresholds can be characterized by their extremity and the degree to which they are symmetric. The extremity of each confidence threshold will be directly proportional to the cost associated with the error. If the cost of a false rejection is particularly troublesome, the confidence threshold for rejection will be especially stringent (compared with a situation in which the cost is trivial), resulting in a critical and effortful evaluation of relevant, unsupportive evidence. In contrast, when the cost of a false rejection is rather low, the associated confidence threshold for rejection will be low, and thus one will tend to reject the hypothesis on the basis of less diagnostic, unsupportive evidence. These implications of a high versus low confidence threshold similarly apply to the decision to accept the hypothesis.

An overall indication of how much effort a person will invest in hypothesis testing can be appreciated by combining the two confidence thresholds. If the two thresholds are extreme, the person will need to see a lot of evidence before making either a reject or accept decision. If the two costs are insignificant, the person will not expend much time and energy in assessing the validity of the proposition, and in fact may not test the hypothesis in the first place. Even if one decided to test a hypothesis in such a case, she or he might not invest that much effort and thus might tend to make a decision on the basis of very little either confirming or disconfirming evidence.

Asymmetry of Error Costs

The overall extremity of the two confidence thresholds will determine the extent to which the person is motivated to be accurate (i.e., by not making errors in judgment). However, in addition, the separability of the two confidence thresholds means that the two thresholds can sometimes be asymmetric rather than symmetric. The two thresholds will differ in extremity when the costs implied by one error loom larger than the costs implied by the other. Such asymmetry in costs may be quite common. A discrepancy in the costs of the two errors should lead to different ways of testing a hypothesis, depending on the direction of the asymmetry between the confidence thresholds. If the cost of false rejection is greater compared with the cost of a false acceptance, one would be more concerned with making sure that the hypothesis is false before rejecting it. Comparatively, the same person would not be as concerned with making sure that the hypothesis is true before accepting it. In short, when there is an asymmetry between the costs (and thus between the confidence thresholds), the amount and strength of evidence needed to accept the hypothesis will differ compared with that which is needed to reject the same hypothesis.

For instance, if someone is testing the hypothesis that an acquaintance is friendly, the cost of a false rejection may be greater than the cost of a false acceptance (i.e., one could lose the opportunity to establish a friendship if one falsely rejects the hypothesis but simply make unsuccessful attempts at friendship if one falsely accepts the hypothesis). Consequently, one might adopt a higher confidence threshold for rejection compared with acceptance and thus demand more diagnostic and plentiful unsupportive evidence before rejecting. Thus, one might accept the validity of the hypothesis on the basis of evidence (e.g., Jeffrey offered his chair at the lecture) that is nondiagnostic, or one might be unable to distinguish between the focal hypothesis (i.e., Jeffrey is friendly) and alternative hypotheses (e.g., Jeffrey did not want to sit on the broken chair). The same person might choose to reject the hypothesis only after considering numerous pieces of diagnostic evidence (e.g., Jeffrey is cold, insensitive, and uncaring to nearly everyone).

The presence of an asymmetry between the two thresholds therefore results in a biased testing process. The testing process can be qualified as biased when a person has differential criteria for searching for and assessing supportive versus unsupportive evidence. An unbiased process would presumably involve the same criteria for extensiveness of the search, regardless of the nature of the evidence and its implications for the person.

It should be noted that biased hypothesis testing does not imply inaccuracy. According to this framework, accuracy and bias are independent. For example, if the two costs of the two possible errors are equivalent, the testing process could be considered unbiased because presumably the person would evaluate both unsupportive and supportive evidence with a similar degree of scrutiny. However, because accuracy is determined by the combined extremity of the two thresholds, one may conduct an unbiased and accurate search (i.e., the two thresholds are equal and extreme) or an unbiased and inaccurate search (i.e., the two thresholds are equal and inextreme). It is also possible to conduct a biased and accurate search (i.e., unequal and extreme thresholds) and a biased and inaccurate search (i.e., unequal and inextreme thresholds).

Asymmetric Error Costs and Preferred Hypotheses

In our model, the desirability of a hypothesis (i.e., the extent to which one wants it to be true) can influence confidence thresholds for accepting and rejecting a hypothesis, based on the costs of errors of omission and commission, respectively. The two thresholds may either be symmetric (equally stringent) or asymmetric. Because the costs of the two possible errors may differ, one's acceptance threshold may differ from one's rejection threshold. For a variety of reasons, people may set their rejection thresholds more stringently than their acceptance thresholds. The desirability of the hypothesis is one of the factors that may lead to asymmetric confidence thresholds.

Why should desired hypotheses tend to have more lenient acceptance than rejection criteria (and the opposite for undesired hypotheses)? First and foremost, as discussed earlier, individuals are likely to think more about the state of affairs in which their hypothesis is true rather than false. This means that failing to recognize a true desired hypothesis (error of omission) will be more salient than failing to reject a false hypothesis (error of commission). For example, when testing the hypothesis that an acquaintance is friendly, one is likely to focus on the hypothetical situation that she is indeed friendly. Given this focus, one would be primarily concerned with the potential future relationship one may miss by failing to recognize this possibility. Thus, with a desired hypothesis, the costs of erroneously rejecting the hypothesis (errors of omission) are likely to loom larger in one's mind than the costs of erroneously accepting the hypothesis (errors of commission). In testing a desirable hypothesis, one would be primarily motivated to minimize errors of omission and would, therefore, set more stringent confidence thresholds for rejecting the hypothesis than for accepting it.

Second, the positive affect associated with accepting a desired hypothesis may attenuate the cost of a false acceptance, whereas the negative affect associated with rejecting a desired hypothesis may augment its costs. Thus, when someone aspires to achieve some goal, believing that the goal is achievable is more pleasing, at least in the short term, than believing that it is not (see Friedrich, 1993).

Third, falsely rejecting a desired hypothesis often means missing an opportunity to reach a desired goal and thus may be more costly to a person compared with falsely accepting the hypothesis. I may miss the opportunity to learn how to play the piano if I erroneously decide that I lack musical talent; I may miss the opportunity to get well if I erroneously decide that treatment is ineffective; and I may miss the opportunity to solve a problem if I wrongly decide that it is unsolvable. When such goals are personally significant, missing the opportunity to reach them (the cost of an error of omission) may seem worse than a futile attempt to reach them (the cost of an error of commission).

In short, when a conclusion is desired, the cost of false acceptance may seem lower than the cost of false rejection, leading to asymmetric confidence thresholds. One's overall motivation for accuracy may be quite high, but it may primarily stem from one's wish to avoid false rejection of the desired hypothesis. Consequently, desired conclusions may be accepted more quickly and on the basis of less information and hypothesis testing than would be necessary to reject them. Moreover, perceivers may selectively seek information that minimizes false rejections rather than false acceptances. Several lines of research bear on this analysis.

Earlier Termination Following Evidence Supporting Desired Hypotheses

The assumption that desired hypotheses have costlier false rejection errors than false acceptance errors implies that people should engage in more extensive and analytic processing before rejecting a desired hypothesis than before accepting it. Thus, evidence will often be evaluated more critically when it is inconsistent rather than consistent with a desired hypothesis. Evidence supporting the desired hypothesis is likely to bolster one's confidence and lead to earlier termination of the hypothesis-testing sequence than evidence refuting it.

A number of studies on evaluation of self-relevant tests support this prediction. For example, Wyer and Frey (1983) and Pyszczynski, Greenberg, and Holt (1985) tested participants and gave them either positive or negative feedback. Participants then read reports concerning the tests' reliability. Those who had received positive test results judged reports supporting the tests as stronger, whereas those who had received negative test results judged reports refuting the tests as stronger. In these studies, then, participants seemed more sensitive to unreliability when the test results were inconsistent rather than consistent with positive self-beliefs.

Comparable results have been found with evaluations of evidence concerning health issues. Kunda (1987) and Liberman and Chaiken (1992) had coffee drinkers and nondrinkers read research reports concerning risks of drinking coffee. Coffee drinkers judged results indicating that coffee was dangerous as weaker than did noncoffee drinkers, despite being matched on prior beliefs concerning coffee's health risks (Liberman & Chaiken, 1992). When exploring the mediating processes underlying these self-serving conclusions of coffee drinkers, Liberman and Chaiken found evidence that coffee-drinking participants scrutinized the data more carefully and detected more flaws in the evidence.

Similarly, Ditto and Lopez (1992) told participants about a purportedly danger-ous medical condition that increases one's chances of pancreatic disease, "TAA deficiency." They then gave participants yellow test papers to test their own saliva for TAA. Some participants were told that the paper would turn green if they had the condition, whereas others were told that it would turn green only if they did not have the condition. Participants were also told that the test's accuracy might be affected by irregularities in lifestyle, such as in their diets or sleep. When participants tested their own saliva, none of the test papers changed color because they were actually just slips of yellow construction paper. When then asked whether they had any life irregularities that might render the test inaccurate, participants whose tests implied that they had (vs. did not have) TAA deficiency generated more life irregulari-ties and rated the test as less accurate. Again, participants seemed more sensitive to alternative interpretations when evaluating evidence that favored rejection of desired self-relevant hypotheses.

These findings are consistent with the idea that in testing desired hypotheses people are primarily concerned with minimizing false rejections. As a result, they require a smaller amount of information and less critical hypothesis-testing proce-dures to accept a desired hypothesis than to reject it.

Biased Information Search

Asymmetric confidence thresholds for desired hypotheses may produce asymmetric information search. Specifically, the stringent threshold for rejecting a desired hypothesis favors a search that is unlikely to leave the hypothesis undetected (i.e., unlikely to falsely reject the hypothesis). Consider, for example, the desired hypothe-sis that one's child is athletic. The primary concern here is to minimize the likelihood of undetected athletic ability. Given this goal, the hypothesis tester will observe the child performing tasks in which it is relatively easy to succeed. In such tasks, failure is unlikely to occur unless the child is really incompetent. The likelihood of false rejection of the hypothesis that the child is talented is thus minimized. Stated otherwise, success, the likely outcome, is not very diagnostic, but it may be sufficient to exceed the lenient threshold for attributing athletic ability to one's child. Failure is less likely and can occur only if the child is athletically incompetent. This makes failure sufficiently diagnostic to exceed the stringent threshold for rejecting the competence hypothesis.

Similarly, the hypothesis tester may search his or her memory by first looking for instances of successful athletic performances because retrieving few successes may be sufficient to accept the competence hypothesis, whereas many more failures would have to be retrieved to reject this hypothesis. Such testing is unlikely to miss the possibility that a desired hypothesis is true, but it may miss the possibility that a desired hypothesis is false (see Sanitoso, Kunda, & Fong, 1990).

A study by Quattrone and Tversky (1984) illustrated these biased information search strategies in self-testing behavior. Participants in this study immersed their hands in cold water longer when they were told that high cold tolerance (vs. low cold tolerance) was indicative of longevity. In our terms, Quattrone and Tversky's participants were testing the desired hypothesis that their true cold tolerance is high. By making an effort to tolerate the cold water, participants in effect minimized the likelihood of false rejection of this hypothesis. If the participant's true cold tolerance was high, her or his efforts ensured that it will be expressed in the test results. This, however, could come at the expense of detection of low cold tolerance; that is, with sufficient effort, even a participant with low cold tolerance could still obtain favorable test results. Thus, participants' self-testing behavior was biased against detection of the undesired possibility. In our framework, this is due to the fact that they were more concerned with missing the possibility that they have a desired physical attribute (high cold tolerance) than with missing the possibility that they have an undesired physical attribute (low cold tolerance).

In sum, research on motivationally biased information search and processing is consistent with the present error cost analysis. For a variety of reasons, failing to detect that a desired possibility is true is subjectively costlier than failing to detect that it is false. These asymmetric error costs lead to setting asymmetric confidence thresholds for accepting and rejecting a desired possibility, with acceptance thresholds becoming increasingly more lenient relative to rejection thresholds as the hypothesis becomes more desired. In the present hypothesis-testing framework, biased search and processing of information are direct consequences of this asymmetry.

Asymmetry of Error Costs and Nonpreferred Hypotheses

We have argued that people will most often, but not necessarily always, test preferred hypotheses. Therefore, surely people sometimes test nonpreferred possibilities. When this occurs, there may be implications for the error costs. The cost associated with failing to detect a true hypothesis is greater for those who focus on negative hypotheses compared with those who focus on positive hypotheses. Although hypothesis testing by those with a positive outcome focus may be primarily designed to detect desired possibilities, hypothesis testing by those with a negative outcome focus may be primarily designed to detect undesired possibilities. Negatively focused individuals will thus put a premium on minimizing omission errors rather than commission errors in making a decision regarding negative possibilities. As a result, these individuals will seek more information and subject the information to more critical scrutiny before rejecting a negative conclusion than before accepting such a conclusion. For example, the person who is figuring out whether he acted foolishly at the dance-a-thon might dismiss a lot of unsupportive evidence (e.g., everyone complemented him on his dancing prowess) as insufficient to reject the hypothesis and accept supportive evidence, even if weak (e.g., one person started laughing while he was dancing), as validating the hypothesis.

Conclusion

In this chapter, we proposed a hypothesis-testing framework in an attempt to explain when and why people tend to infer what they prefer. This framework described both cognitive and motivational mechanisms that can produce hypothesis confirmation. First, a host of evidential biases, including the tendency to acquiesce to questions, assimilation and retrieval biases, and affirmation bias, can cause one to misinterpret evidence as supportive and thus lead to the confirmation of the hypothesis. Importantly, these often automatic processes can render hypothesis confirmation likely regardless of the degree to which the person invests time and effort in the process of testing the hypothesis.

Second, confirmation of a hypothesis is also likely, according to the present framework, when one differentially scrutinizes supportive versus unsupportive evidence concerning the hypothesis. This bias emerges when there is an asymmetry in the error costs such that the cost of a false rejection looms larger than the cost of a false acceptance. Such a direction of asymmetry means that people will search and process information less critically and extensively before accepting their hypothesis than before rejecting their hypothesis. People will, thus, accept their preferred hypotheses more easily compared with rejecting them because of a lenient criterion for supportive evidence and a strict criterion for unsupportive evidence.

These arguments for the likelihood of confirmation bias alone have no immediate bearing for preferential believing. However, given the conjecture that people may test preferred hypotheses more frequently than nonpreferred hypotheses, as previously discussed, the pattern of findings concerning preferential believing can now be conceptually integrated and explained, at least tentatively. Given that people seem to test what they prefer, and given that people tend to infer what they test, it seems likely that people will infer what they prefer.

Prompted by previous research (Winkielman et al., 1997; Zajonc, 1980), this chapter outlined an argument suggesting that people's inferences might sometimes be derivatives of their preferences. Not only might people's simple beliefs about a stimulus rely to some extent on their preference for the stimulus, but the ways in which they test even a complex hypothesis might be influenced and curtailed by their wish that the hypothesis is true. On the basis of this analysis of the cognitive and motivational mechanisms of preferential thinking, it seems that although people's preferences need no inferences (Zajonc, 1980), their inferences do seem to depend on their preferences.

References

Andersen, S. M., Spielman, L. A., & Bargh, J. A. (1992). Future-event schemas and certainty about the future: Automaticity in depressives' future-event predictions. *Journal of Personality and Social Psychology, 63,* 711–723.

Ansfield, M. E., & Wegner, D. M. (1996). The feeling of doing. In P. M. Gollwitzer & J. A. Bargh (Eds.), *The psychology of action* (pp. 482–506). New York: Guilford Press.

Banaji, M. R., Hardin, C., & Rothman, A. J. (1993). Implicit stereotyping in person judgment. *Journal of Personality and Social Psychology, 65,* 272–281.

Bargh, J. A. (1999). The cognitive monster. In S. Chaiken & Y. Trope (Eds.), *Dual process theories in social psychology* (pp. 361–382). New York: Guilford Press.

Bodenhausen, G. V., & Macrae, C. N. (1998). Stereotype activation and inhibition. In R. S. Wyer (Ed.), *Advances in social cognition* (Vol. 11, pp. 1–52). Mahwah, NJ: Erlbaum.

Brown, J. D. (1986). Evaluations of self and others: Self-enhancement biases in social judgments. *Social Cognition, 4,* 353–376.

Bruner, J. S. (1957). On perceptual readiness. *Psychological Review, 64,* 123–152.

Bruner, J. S., & Postman, L. (1947). Emotional selectivity in perception and reaction. *Journal of Personality, 16,* 69–77.

Campbell, J. D. (1986). Similarity and uniqueness: The effects of attribution type, relevance, and individual differences in self-esteem and depression. *Journal of Personality and Social Psychology, 50,* 281–294.

Carver, C. S., & Scheier, M. F. (1981). *Attention and self-regulation: A control-theory approach to human behavior.* New York: Springer-Verlag.

Christensen, S. M., & Turner, D. R. (1993). *Folk psychology and the philosophy of the mind.* Hillsdale, NJ: Erlbaum.

Cialdini, R. B., Bordern, R. J., Thorne, A., Walker, M. R., Freeman, S., & Slone, L. R. (1976). Basking in reflected glory: Three (football) field studies. *Journal of Personality and Social Psychology, 34,* 366–375.

Devine, P. G. (1989). Stereotypes and prejudice: Their automatic and controlled components. *Journal of Personality and Social Psychology, 56,* 5–18.

Ditto, P. H., & Lopez, D. F. (1992). Motivated skepticism: Use of differential decision criteria for preferred and nonpreferred conclusions. *Journal of Personality and Social Psychology, 63,* 568–584.

Erdelyi, H. M. (1974). A new look at the New Look: Perceptual defense and vigilance. *Psychological Review, 81,* 1–25.

Fazio, R. H., Jackson, J. R., Dunton, B. C., & Williams, C. J. (1995). Variability in automatic activation as an unobtrusive measure of racial attitudes: A bona fide pipeline? *Journal of Personality and Social Psychology, 69,* 1013–1027.

Fiske, S. T., & Taylor, S. E. (1991). *Social cognition* (2nd ed.). New York: McGraw-Hill.

Friedrich, J. (1993). Primary error detection and minimization (PEDMIN) strategies in social cognition: A reinterpretation of confirmation bias phenomena. *Psychological Review, 100,* 298–319.

Greenwald, A. G. (1980). The totalitarian ego: Fabrication and revision of personal history. *American Psychologist, 35,* 603–618.

Higgins, E. T. (1987). Self discrepancy: A theory relating self and affect. *Psychological Review, 94,* 319–340.

Higgins, E. T. (1996). Knowledge activation: Accessibility, applicability and salience. In E. T. Higgins & A. W. Kruglanski (Eds.), *Social psychology: Handbook of basic principles* (pp. 133–168). New York: Guilford Press.

Higgins, E. T., King, G. A., & Mavin, G. H. (1982). Individual construct accessibility and subjective impressions and recall. *Journal of Personality and Social Psychology, 43,* 35–47.

Higgins, E. T., Rholes, W. S., & Jones, C. R. (1977). Category accessibility and impression formation. *Journal of Personality and Social Psychology, 13,* 141–154.

Klayman, J., & Ha, Y. (1987). Confirmation, disconfirmation, and information in hypothesis-testing. *Psychological Review, 94,* 211–228.

Koehler, D. J. (1991). Explanation, imagination, and confidence in judgment. *Psychological Bulletin, 110,* 499–519.

Kruglanski, A. W. (1989). *Lay epistemics and human knowledge.* New York: Plenum.

Kunda, Z. (1987). Motivated inference: Self-serving generation and evaluation of causal theories. *Journal of Personality and Social Psychology, 53,* 636–647.

Kunda, Z. (1990). The case for motivated reasoning. *Psychological Bulletin, 108,* 480–498.

Langer, E. J. (1975). The illusion of control. *Journal of Personality and Social Psychology, 32,* 311–328.

Liberman, A., & Chaiken, S. (1992). Defensive processing of personally relevant health messages. *Personality and Social Psychology Bulletin, 18,* 669–679.

Macrae, C. N., Bodenhausen, G. V., Milne, A. B., & Jetten, J. (1994). Out of mind but back in sight: Stereotypes on the rebound. *Journal of Personality and Social Psychology, 67,* 808–817.

Markus, H. R., & Nurius, P. (1986). Possible selves. *American Psychologist, 41,* 954–969.

Miller, D. T., & Ross, M. (1975). Self-serving biases in the attribution of causality: Fact or fiction? *Psychological Bulletin, 82,* 213–225.

Newman, J. P., Wolff, W. T., & Hearst, E. (1980). The feature-positive effect in adult human subjects. *Journal of Experimental Psychology: Human Learning and Memory, 6,* 630–650.

Nisbett, R. E., & Ross, L. (1980). *Human inference: Strategies and shortcomings of social judgment.* Engelwood Cliffs, NJ: Prentice Hall.

Nisbett, R. E., & Wilson, T. D. (1977). Telling more than we can know: Verbal reports on mental processes. *Psychological Review, 84,* 231–259.

Prinz, W. (1997). Explaining voluntary action: The role of mental content. In M. Carrier & P. Machamer (Eds.), *Mindscapes: Philosophy, science, and the mind* (pp. 153–175). Konstanz, Germany: Universitaetsverlag.

Pyszczynski, T. A., & Greenberg, J. (1987). Toward an integration of cognitive and motivational perspectives in social inference: A biased hypothesis-testing model. In L. Berkowitz (Ed.), *Advances in experimental social psychology* (Vol. 20, pp. 297–334). New York: Academic Press.

Pyszczynski, T. A., Greenberg, J., & Holt, K. (1985). Maintaining consistency between self-serving beliefs and available data: A bias in information evaluation. *Personality and Social Psychology Bulletin, 11*, 179–190.

Quattrone, G. A., & Tversky, A. (1984). Causal versus diagnostic contingencies: On self-deception and on the voter's illusion. *Journal of Personality and Social Psychology, 46*, 237–248.

Ross, L. (1977). The intuitive psychologist and his shortcomings: Distortions in the attributional process. In L. Berkowitz (Ed.), *Advances in experimental social psychology* (Vol. 10, pp. 174–221). New York: Academic Press.

Ross, M., & Sicoly, F. (1979). Egocentric biases in availability and attribution. *Journal of Personality and Social Psychology, 37*, 322–337.

Sanitoso, R., Kunda, Z., & Fong, G. (1990). Motivated recruitment of autobiographical memories. *Journal of Personality and Social Psychology, 59*, 229–241.

Snyder, M., & Uranowitz, S. W. (1978). Reconstructing the past: Some cognitive consequences of person perception. *Journal of Personality and Social Psychology, 36*, 941–950.

Srull, T. K., & Wyer, R. S. (1989). Person memory and judgment. *Psychological Review, 96*, 58–83.

Tajfel, H., & Turner, J. C. (1986). The social identity of intergroup behavior. In S. Worchel & W. Austin (Eds.), *Psychology of inter-group relations* (pp. 7–24). Chicago: Nelson-Hall.

Taylor, S. E., & Brown, J. D. (1988). Illusion and well being: A social psychological perspective on mental health. *Psychological Bulletin, 110*, 67–83.

Taylor, S. E., & Kouvumaki, J. H. (1976). The perception of self and others: Acquaintanceship, affect and actor–observer differences. *Journal of Personality and Social Psychology, 33*, 403–408.

Tesser, A. (1986). Some effects of self-evaluation maintenance on cognition and action. In R. M. Sorrentino & E. T. Higgins (Eds.), *Handbook of motivation and cognition: Foundations of social behavior* (pp. 435–464). New York: Guilford Press.

Tesser, A., Millar, M., & Moore, J. (1988). Some affective consequences of social comparison and reflection processes: The pain and pleasure of being close. *Journal of Personality and Social Psychology, 54*, 49–61.

Trope, Y., & Bassok, M. (1982). Confirming and diagnosing strategies in social information gathering. *Journal of Personality and Social Psychology, 43*, 22–34.

Trope, Y., & Liberman, A. (1996). Social hypothesis-testing: Cognitive and motivational mechanisms. In E. T. Higgins & A. W. Kruglanski (Eds.), *Social psychology: Handbook of basic principles* (pp. 239–270). New York: Guilford Press.

Tversky, A., & Kahneman, D. (1981). The framing of decisions and the psychology of choice. *Science, 211*, 453–458.

Vallone, R. P., Griffin, D. W., Lin, S., & Ross, L. (1990). Overconfident prediction of future actions and outcomes by self and others. *Journal of Personality and Social Psychology, 58*, 582–592.

Wegener, D. T., & Petty, R. E. (1996). Effects of mood on persuasion processes: Enhancing, reducing, and biasing scrutiny of attitude-relevant information. In L. L. Martin & A.

Tesser (Eds.), *Striving and feeling: Interactions among goals, affect, and self-regulation* (pp. 329–362). Mahwah, NJ: Erlbaum.

Wegener, D. T., Petty, R. E., & Smith, S. M. (1995). Positive mood can increase or decrease message scrutiny: The hedonic contingency view of mood and message processing. *Journal of Personality and Social Psychology, 69,* 5–15.

Wegner, D. M. (1994). Ironic processes of mental control. *Psycholgical Review, 101,* 34–52.

Wegner, D. M., & Bargh, J. A. (1997). Control and automaticity in social life. In D. Gilbert, S. Fiske, & G. Lindzey (Eds.), *Handbook of social psychology* (4th ed., pp. 446–496). Boston: McGraw-Hill.

Wegner, D. M., & Wheatley, T. (1999). Why it feels as if we're doing things: Sources of the experience of the will. *American Psychologist, 54,* 480–492.

Weinstein, N. D. (1982). Unrealistic optimism about susceptibility to health problems. *Journal of Behavioral Medicine, 5,* 441–460.

Wilson, T. D., & Brekke, N. (1994). Mental contaminated and mental correction: Unwanted influences on judgment and evaluation. *Psychological Bulletin, 116,* 117–142.

Wilson, T., & Schooler, J. (1991). Thinking too much: Introspection can reduce the quality of preferences and decisions. *Journal of Personality and Social Psychology, 60,* 181–192.

Winkielman, P., Zajonc, R., & Schwarz, N. (1997). Subliminal affective priming resists attributional interventions. *Cognition and Emotion, 11,* 433–465.

Wyer, R. S., & Frey, D. (1983). The effects of feedback about self and others on the recall and judgments of feedback-relevant information. *Journal of Experimental Social Psychology, 19,* 540–559.

Zajonc, R. B. (1980). Thinking and feeling: Preferences need no inferences. *American Psychologist, 35,* 151–175.

Zuckerman, M. (1979). Attribution of success and failure revisited: Or the motivational bias is alive and well in attribution theory. *Journal of Personality, 47,* 245–287.

Zuckerman, M., Knee, C. R., Hodgins, H. S., & Miyake, K. (1995). Hypothesis confirmation: The joint effect of positive test strategy and acquiescence response set. *Journal of Personality and Social Psychology, 68,* 52–60.

PART 3

Personal Agency

CHAPTER 9

Human Infancy and the Beginnings of Human Competence

Jerome Bruner

Robert Zajonc has always stood for the view that it is in the nature of human nature that we have the makings of competent, agentive, proactive creatures. We do not begin unequipped, but are human in our very nature. I admired greatly his respect for the inherently human competence of human beings, and always felt encouraged reading his work. It was always worth discussing ideas with him, and I did so often—though we were rarely working on the same particular matters. And this article is a continuation of our conversations. I want to discuss what might be called "the very beginning," early infancy: what human beings must be like at the very start for them to become the kind of complex, culture-using creatures they end up being. And what might that story lead to? So here goes on the subject of what we have learned about human infancy and what that might tell us about the human condition.

Infancy Research

Never mind the long, long history of ideas about infancy. Philippe Ariès (1962) has told us enough to make us fully aware that any story we tell about human infancy grows as much out of ideological convictions as out of observation—whether it is original sin to be redeemed, innate rationality destined to be smothered by superstition, or primary process to be squelched by the reality principle. What I have to say will, doubtless, also have to be submitted to some close scrutiny, to use the bland phrase from jurisprudence. And that is as it should be, even if I cite buckets of experimental evidence to make my points! So here goes: the story of early infancy that has grown over the last couple of decades, my version of it!

I begin with the research of Bill Kessen (1963) and his group on infant attention: infants deploying their attention *selectively* and under their own control, not just as creatures of the environment. The prototypical experiment is an actual one by Haith and Kessen (Kessen, 1965), showing that the older the infants, the more often and the longer they choose to look at more informationally pregnant, asymmetric or irregular checker-board patterns. What they found was that human information processing capacity not only increases with age, which is old hat, but that infants select pieces of the world to attend to that fit their capacity limits and work within those limits. In a word, human beings dislike confusion right from the start and work to avoid it. Now, in those distant days of the 1960s, this finding was, so to say, so *proactively* agentive, so downright *cognitive* as to upset the apple-cart about infancy as "blooming buzzing confusion" with which we had been saddled by our forebears. I was so bowled over, indeed, that I hopped right on the train to New Haven to have a look! Could it be that young infants were like *other* human beings!

Then came the discovery that infants were capable not only of monitoring their own attention, but quite capable as well of acting instrumentally to *alter* the stimulus world around them to make it fit their attentional requirements. All they needed was the means. Hanus Papousek (1961) duly demonstrated just that. His young infants easily mastered the trick of turning their heads twice in a row to one side in order to cause exciting jazzy lights to flash over their cribs for a few seconds. Only operant conditioning? But what kind of a reinforcer is a jazzy light bank? Infants were turning out to be interested in a little visual excitement, and quickly got skilled in knowing how to get it.

Animal Studies

Aren't Zeitgeists curious! Just about that time, studies by Krech and Rosenzweig (Rosenzweig, 1966) began demonstrating that young rats raised in a Luna Park environment full of engaging sensori-motor razzmatazz grew up much smarter than their litter mates raised in duller settings. And Levine and Alpert (1959), intending to raise animals germ-free and stress-free to see if that affected their later immune reactions, found that animals raised in a state of dull aseptic calm grew up much stupider (and more disease prone at that) than their louche, communally cage dwelling litter-mate controls. Hmmm, again.

Blooming, Buzzing Confusion

How did all this fit into a folk psychology of the infant's world as a "blooming, buzzing confusion?" If young kids started life passively in a featureless *Ganzfeld* of nothingness, how did they ever get out of it? How do you ever get something from nothing? Logic dictates "*nihil ex nihilo.*" A baby has got to have enough structure to provide some working standard of clarity if she is to attend selectively to the world. Without it, she would be lost. Which led my then research assistant, Ilse Kalnins, and I to devise an experiment that, we thought, clinched it (Kalnins & Bruner, 1973). We devised a pacifier nipple, sucking on which would generate a electrical current by compressing a four-legged strain gauge, the more sucking, the more current. God bless piezo-electricity! The current could then be used to control various features of the world—

in this case, to control the focus of a picture of a motherly, smiling woman's face projected on a screen at the infant's eye level. In one condition, sucking on the nipple brought the motherly face from out of focus into focus, the picture drifting out of focus when the baby stopped sucking. In the other condition, an in-focus picture was driven out of focus by sucking, the picture moving automatically back into focus when sucking stopped. The long and short of it was that babies sucked briskly to get a clear picture, but would desist from sucking when it caused the picture to blur (and desisting is not easy when you are a six-month-old performing for a mad psychologist in an unfamiliar room). So much for blooming buzzing confusion! (I recall a visiting New Delhi pediatrician who was observing one of our subjects through a one-way screen. "That's impossible," she said on emerging, "a baby's world is a buzzing blooming confusion.") *Sic transit gloria mundi.*

Infant Competence

By now, of course, we are well into the 1960s, into the New Frontier of President Johnson, into Head Start and into articles in the press about infancy and early childhood, like articles in major papers in American and European cities on the crucial importance of childhood. I mention this here to remind you, Bob, that where the original nature of humankind is concerned, knowledge and ideology quickly begin walking hand in hand.

The next chapter in the story takes a fascinating turn: It is about *"intersubjectivity,"* how we read each others' minds and when we start doing so. It is a topic that began with efforts to understand the blight of childhood autism, but quickly grew to encompass matters as diverse as the evolution of higher primates into hominids and the very nature of human enculturation. I and my gang of irrepressible graduate students and post-docs at Oxford were up to our ears in it—Alison Gopnik, the two Andys, Meltzoff and Whiten, Alan Leslie, Mike Scaife, Paul Harris, George Butterworth, to mention only some of their boisterous number. The experiment that served as the trope was one that Mike Scaife and I (Scaife & Bruner, 1975) did: infants follow an adult's line of regard in search of what the adult is attending to. In the twinkling of an eye, the old philosophical problem of Other Minds got transferred (to be parochial Oxford) from Merton Street to South Parks Road, from the philosopher's study to the psychologist's lab. Within a decade, a thriving cottage industry of baby labs took it over.[1]

---

[1]For a thoughtful overview of this outpouring at mid-voyage, see Feldman (1992). Among the major books on the subject are a half dozen "overview" volumes, ranging from Janet Astington's (1993) first book on the state of the art, through Perner (1991) to Wellman (1990), on to Gopnik and Meltzoff (1997), Moore and Dunham (1995), and Katherine Nelson (1996).

Intersubjectivity

The emphasis had shifted from the competent solo infant mastering the natural world nearly on her own (as a counterpoise to the old "blooming buzzing confusion") to a concern with how we ever come to understand each other's minds well enough to live in a human culture. And it is still shifting. In some ways, this was not altogether a new concern. Remember the old *culture-and-personality* fever?

Research on autism reopened the gate, the wedge study surely being Alan Leslie's (1991) on the absence of pretend play in young autists. His claim was that autism so seriously destroyed an infant's or child's grasp of other minds, that it was impossible for sufferers even to *pretend* to be an Other. It was followed by a flood of research spelling out many of the particulars (see Baron-Cohen, Tager-Flusberg, & Cohen, 1993; Happé, 1994; and Sigman & Capps, 1998, for a sampling of this fascinating literature).

But this work on "theory of mind," as it came to be called, had an impact way beyond the pathogenesis of autism. It renewed speculation in many fields. One of them was primatology where there was already lots of exploratory work on the subject—e.g., Menzel (1974), by Premack and Woodruff (1978). Take as an example Menzel's early work, showing that young primates in a one-acre field anticipated the line of *travel* of one of their number known by them to know where food had been hidden in the field. They did it by monitoring the know-it-all's *gaze* direction and anticipating where he might be going. Or take the work on the use of *deliberate deceit* in primate social interaction (Byrne & Whiten, 1991).

The Evolutionary Dimension

But the real explosion surely began with Sue Savage-Rumbaugh et al.'s study (1993) on the enculturation of the now famous young bonobo, Kanzi. To make a long and incomplete story short and much too conclusive, what has been found is that Kanzi had not only mastered but, equally to the point, he had been brought by his human handlers to a new level of appreciation of their "intentional states": their intentions, desires, expectations, beliefs. Kanzi had, in the *gemutlich* human intersubjectivity of the Georgia State Language Center, taken a giant step toward *enculturation*. To get a creature to that state, in a word, requires "treating somebody like a human in a human setting," which means treating them as if they had mental states and as if they knew that *you* had mental states you expected *them* to understand. It also means appreciating that intentional states mediate what we *do*. To be enculturated, to put it grandly, means to come to share the folk psychology of your culture.

And that places some odd and seemingly incidental observations in a new light, like, for example, Meltzoff and Gopnik's (1993) report that new parents take especial delight in "discovering" that their young babies, in their words, "have minds, just like us." It doesn't really matter whether they do or do not—in either case, parents are doing just the right thing to promote enculturation. And believe me, you'd better act as if your baby has something in mind! If you act otherwise, say by staying "poker faced" in response to your young baby's changing expressions (which itself is difficult to do), you will quickly produce tears and distress, as Stechler and Latz (1966) showed many years ago. And even Kanzi gets frustrated by the lack of enculturated intersubjectivity in his "natural-raised" sister (Savage-Rumbaugh et. al., 1993). For it seems that Kanzi shares enough of the humanoid genome to make him more than a little sensitive to our human way of enculturation. Not all of it, but some.

The Primacy of Intention

Now to the final but incomplete chapter of our story. We humans seem geared from the start to deal with each others' intentions, at least to be enormously sensitive to them in their various guises. Positivist philosophers, like Dan Dennett (1991) may be embarrassed by human intentionality, deep-freezing them as an "intentional stance," but 18-month-olds are not the least so. I refer again to a Meltzoff (1995) finding. Infants imitate the *intended* behavior of an Other and not its surface properties. In brief, if the outcome of an adult's act is thwarted, infants of 18 months will imitate it *as if it had been carried through right to its goal*. Human infants do easily and naturally (and to the delight of their caregivers) what Kanzi does stumblingly, and only if he has the luck of being raised by that gang of very human and dedicated graduate students and post-docs at Georgia State.

Implications of Infancy Research

That is the gist of the story—still very much unfinished, but definitely getting there. Cultural historians find it very much in conformity with their expectations. They see the "discovery" of the informationally active, socially interactive infant mind as reflecting our departure from the Industrial Age with its machine models, and our entry into the new Information Age where cognition, symbol use, and networking are crucial. No doubt they are right and perhaps that is why it is so easy to tell it that way in French!

But I suspect there is another moral to the story too. I suspect that when one enters into a new revolutionary period, as we surely have, a sure sign is that we look afresh at what we mean by the original nature of man and its origins as well. Infancy research has become a new arena for battling out anew *the* classic and enduring issues—human agency, the nature of culture and interdependence, the scope of human meaning making, the interaction of the genetic and the environmental.

No surprise, then, that there is something uniquely consciousness raising and even politically compelling about reflection and research on immaturity and its potentials. It seems able to move mountains, even political ones. I still cannot believe what happened when Urie Bronfenbrenner and I first proposed Head Start to the White House Office of Economic Opportunity. Impossible, had not we ever read the Constitution on who controls schools? Now it is political suicide to suggest cutting it back.

What I would like to think about over the years ahead is how psychology itself enters the ideological equation—not fake or pop or dictator-driven psychology, but honest-to-god, hardworking psychology. I have always held the conviction, as Robert Zajonc has, that at the heart of every coherent system of cultural beliefs, lies a conception of man, his potential and the constraints that limit these. There has never been a political revolution without one such. So given where we have come, given the story I have told, how do we proceed to make it matter in the broader world in which we live? That is a very Zajonc question, and it is altogether fitting that it should be raised in the concluding sentence of a chapter celebrating him!

References

Ariès, P. (1962). *Centuries of childhood: A social history of family life.* New York: Knopf.

Astington, J. W. (1993). *The child's discovery of the mind.* Cambridge, MA: Harvard University Press.

Baron-Cohen, S., Tager-Flusberg, H., & Cohen, D. J. (Eds.). (1993). *Understanding other minds: Perspectives from autism.* Oxford, England: Oxford University Press.

Byrne, R. W., & Whiten, A. (1991). Computation and mind reading in primate tactical deception. In A. Whiten, (Ed.), *Natural theories of mind: Evolution, development and simulation of everyday mind reading* (pp. 127–141. Oxford, England: Basil Blackwell.

Dennett, D. C. (1991). *Consciousness explained.* Boston: Little Brown.

Feldman, C. F. (1992). The new theory of theory of mind. *Human Development, 35,* 107–117.

Gopnik, A., & Meltzoff, A. N. (1997). *Words, thoughts, and theories.* Cambridge, MA: MIT Press.

Happé, F. (1994). *Autism: An introduction to psychological theory.* London: University College Press.

Kalnins, I., & Bruner, J. S. (1973). The coordination of visual observation and instrumental behavior in early infancy. *Perception, 2,* 307–314.

Kessen, W. (1963). Research on the psychological development of infants: An overview. *Merrill-Palmer Quarterly, 9,* 83–94.

Kessen, W. (1965). *The child.* New York: Wiley.

Leslie, A. (1991). The theory of mind impairment in autism: Evidence for a modular mechanism of development. In A. Whiten (Ed.), *Natural theories of mind: Evolution development and simulation of everyday mind reading.* Oxford, England: Basil Blackwell.

Levine, S., & Alpert M., (1959). Differential maturation of the central nervous system. *Archives of General Psychiatry, 1,* 403–405.

Meltzoff, A. N., & Gopnik, A. (1993). The role of imitation in understanding persons and developing a theory of mind. In S. Baron-Cohen, H. Tager-Flusberg, & D. J. Cohen (Eds.), *Understanding other minds: Perspectives from autism* (pp. 335–366). Oxford, England: Oxford University Press.

Meltzoff, A. N. (1995). Understanding the intentions of others: Re-enactment of intended acts by 18-month-old children. *Developmental Psychology, 31,* 938–950.

Menzel, E. (1974). "A group of young chimpanzees in a one-acre field." In M. Schrier & F. Stolnitz (Eds.), *Behavior of non-human primates,* (Vol. 5), New York: Academic Press.

Moore, C., & Dunham P. J., (Eds.). (1995). *Joint attention: Its origins and role in development.* Hillsdale, NJ: Erlbaum.

Nelson, K. (1996). *Language in cognitive development: The emergence of the mediated mind.* New York: Cambridge University Press.

Papousek, H. (1961). Conditioned head rotation reflexes in infants in the first months of life. *Acta Pediat-rica, 50,* 565–576.

Perner, J. (1991). *Understanding the representational mind.* Cambridge, MA: MIT Press.

Premack, D., & Woodruff, G. (1978). Does the chimpanzee have a theory of mind? *Brain and Behavioral Sciences, 1,* 515–526.

Rosenzweig, M. R. (1966). Environmental complexity, cerebral change, and behavior. *American Psychologist, 21,* 321–332.

Savage-Rumbaugh, E. S., Murphy, J., Sevcik, R. A., Brakke, K. E., Williams, S. L., & Rumbaugh, D. L. (1993). Language comprehension in ape and child. *Monographs of the Society for Research on Child Development, 58,* (3–4, Serial No. 233).

Scaife, M., & Bruner, J. S. (1975). The capacity for joint visual attention in the infant. *Nature, 253,* 265–266.

Sigman, M., & Capps, L. (1998). *Understanding autism.* Cambridge, MA: Harvard University Press.

Stechler, G., & Latz, E. (1966). Some observations on attention and arousal in the human infant. *Journal of the American Academy of Child Psychiatry, 5,* 517–525.

Wellman, H. (1990). *The child's theory of mind.* Cambridge, MA: MIT Press.

CHAPTER 10

Control Preferences

Janusz Grzelak

In most interdependence situations, an individual faces a conflict between his or her interest and the interests of others. When, and under what circumstances, does the individual become ready to compromise the two, to care not only for his or her own but also for others' benefits? It seemed simple enough in the beginning. People, as rational and selfish beings, maximize subjective utilities of their own outcomes. It was claimed that they do so by following the rules described by von Neumann and Morgenstern (1944) and Nash (1951).

The first rule, the *maxi-min rule*, is somewhat conservative: Choose an action for which the worst outcome is still better than the worst outcome of any other available action. It is a rule of safety because it secures the best of the worst outcomes one can possibly obtain in a given social interaction. The second rule, most often recommended as a solution, says: Choose an action leading to the outcomes that neither party can improve by switching to the alternative strategy. It is a simplified definition of the equilibrium solution.

The rules appear to be quite intuitive. The problem, however, is that often people do not follow the rules. At least, not when money is at stake. There is a 40%, sometimes more, observed departure from the theoretically rational choice even in a seemingly nonproblematic situation such as the Prisoners Dilemma with dominant strategies. In other words, people often do not choose the strategy that brings about better outcomes regardless of what the partner or partners choose.

How Social is the Self? Social Orientations

Basic Ideas

This leads to a question of whether people are irrational or whether they are rational but different from that assumed in the early studies on conflict of interests. According to Zajonc, it all depends on what people's intentions are while they are interdependent with others. In 1982 he wrote:

Intention is surely a very complex psychological phenomenon, covert and not readily accessible to observation. There is no very satisfactory conceptual language to deal with most of these covert states of the person.

Above all else, "intention" implies that some future states are being anticipated and desired. This feature in itself is fraught with ambiguity. The problem of intention in the case of prosocial behavior is even more complicated because not only one's own future states (that may be brought about by one's own actions) are anticipated and desired, but the states of others as well. (p. 418)

The earliest attempts to answer the question of what people want to maximize in an interaction with others were made more than three decades ago (McClintock, 1972; Messick & McClintock, 1968). In essence, it was found that people satisfy their self-interest, but "self-interest" does not mean the same thing to everyone. How people behave in interdependence situations can be explained only if one assumes that, in an interaction with another person, people tend to achieve goals other than a mere maximization of their own profits.

Although these alternative goals are named differently in various conceptualizations (e.g., social motives, social values, and social orientations), the main idea remains the same: It matters to people not only what they gain (or lose) themselves but also what the others gain (or lose). In other words, the subjective value of outcomes in interdependence situations is a function of both one's own and others' outcomes. Individuals can (a) maximize only their own outcomes (*individualism*), (b) maximize only their partner's outcomes (*altruism*), (c) maximize both outcomes jointly (*cooperative orientation*), (d) create a relative gain, that is, an advantage over their partner (*competitive orientation*), (e) minimize the absolute difference between their own and their partner's outcomes (*equality orientation*), or (f) attempt to achieve still other goals (see, e.g., Wieczorkowska, 1982).

In yet other models of interdependence behavior, the main distinctions are based on a simple but fundamental dichotomy: proself versus prosocial motives (e.g., Caporael, Dawes, Orbell, & van de Kragt, 1989). Individualism and competition fall into the first category, whereas altruism and cooperation fall into the second. Inferences about the type and strength of orientations are most often drawn from the participant's preferences for the suitable differentiated outcome allocations to the self and to another participant (or to the others).

As Kurt Lewin (1947) wrote, people respond to the world as they perceive it, not to the world as it is. In an interdependence situation, people play a matrix subjectively transformed by the interaction actors, not a matrix as is seen by an outside, uninvolved observer. The distinction between the two matrices, the effective matrix and the given one, was made by Kelley and Thibaut (1978) in their theory of social interdependence. One of the main subjective transformations from a given to the effective matrix is that based on both one's own and one's partner's preferences for outcome allocations—that is, on their social orientations. In terms of the theory of interdependence, choosing cooperation in a Prisoners Dilemma-like situation may be a perfectly rational decision given the condition that people involved in the situation care for each other's well-being. Owing to these outcome transformations, the situation is then no longer a dilemma situation. It turns out to be rather a nonconflict situation in which mutual cooperation benefits all those involved. A similar kind of transformation was proposed by Zajonc (1982).

This interpretation of interdependence seems trivial today. However, it was not trivial some years ago, before the concept of matrix transformations and the concept of social orientations had been introduced and developed.

Some Differential Effects of Social Orientations

Social value orientations can be treated as certain temporary psychological states activated by various social cues. They can also be treated in terms of an individual tendency, a generalized inclination to maximize certain allocations rather than others. In other words, an individual enters an interaction, especially an interaction with strangers, with their own personal preferences for the objectives to maximize. These preferences may, of course, change in the course of the interaction as a result of the type of outcomes available, the partner's behavior, and so on.

Studies show that, on the one hand, social orientations are situation dependent (Grzelak, 1991; Grzelak, Poppe, Czwartosz, & Nowak, 1988). They vary depending on the structure of a conflict; number of partners; partners' characteristics such as their intentions, wealth, prestige, and perceived social identity; the type of outcome (e.g., people are more competitive when money is at stake as compared with the amount of work to share); and how the outcomes are represented.

On the other hand, social orientations (either generalized or activated in a given situation) affect people's perception, judgments, and behavior in a social interaction. Poppe, Croon, and Sluytman (1986) found that people have subjective theories of social values—an implicit structure of social motives. An individual's perception of others' social orientations can substantially change (along the cooperative and the competitive dimensions) as the individual moves from one kind of social role or relationship to another.

In one of the earliest studies, Kelley and Stachelski (1970a, 1970b) discovered that competitively oriented people were particularly prone to attribute the same competitive motivation to others, whereas cooperators tended to attribute a competitive as well as a cooperative motivation to others. The cooperators were also more flexible and responsive than the competitors.

These findings have inspired the *triangle hypothesis*, which contradicts the well-known egocentric bias: Competitively oriented people perceive the world as if it were restricted to their own kind, whereas cooperatively oriented people perceive the entire spectrum of the social world and are capable of adapting to different types of partner. The hypothesis has been confirmed in many studies. For instance, Kuhlman and Marshello (1975) showed that cooperators are more flexible than competitors. Maki and McClintock (1983) suggested that both individualists and cooperators are better aware of the heterogeneity of human motivations and can more readily identify such motivations than either altruists or competitors.

However, in the study by Dawes, McTavish, and Shaklee (1977), participants attributed their own motivation to the others four times as often as they attributed a different motivation. Similar results have been obtained in other studies (e.g., Liebrand, 1984). Thus, there seems to be firm evidence in support of the notion of egocentric attribution as well.

Iedema and Poppe (1994) bridged the two seemingly contradictory tendencies. They showed that all people expect others to be individualistic to a high degree. This consensus effect decreases along with the increase of distance between their own orientation and individualism in the authors' proposed geometric space of orientations.

The issue of partners' evaluation is closely related to how partners are perceived, and it has attracted researchers' attention because of, among others, the "might over morality hypothesis." Liebrand, Jansen, Rijken, and Suhre (1986) found that individualists tend to interpret others' cooperative and competitive behavior in terms of power (as "weak" or "strong"), whereas cooperators tend to evaluate others in terms of moral standards (as "bad" or "good"). A series of studies has confirmed the hypothesis. For instance, lists of behaviors generated by cooperators were rated as more differentiated in the moral (good–bad) dimension than those of noncoopera-tors. Another example can be found in Van Lange and Kuhlman's (1994) experiments revealing that cooperators assign higher predictive value to the information about a partner's morality than about their intellectual capacity, whereas competitors and individualists treat the two types of information as equally important.

Finally, a number of experiments show the impact of social orientations on behavior. For instance, in one of the first studies, Kuhlman and Marshello (1975) confronted their participants with a partner playing the Prisoners Dilemma game using one of three strategies: 100% cooperative, 100% competitive, or tit-for-tat choices. In each of the three situations, the highest level of cooperation was displayed by those who had earlier been identified as cooperators, the next lower by individualists, and the lowest by competitive participants; the difference between the two latter groups tended to decrease when the partner behaved in a competitive way. Participants with cooperative orientations were more flexible in their behavior and tended to adjust their behavior to their partners' choices much more than did those with competitive orientations.

Many other studies since then have demonstrated a relationship between social orientations and behavior in a two-person conflict between individual and common interest. Sattler and Kerr (1991) found in some conditions that individualists were more competitive than cooperators in overusing common resources in a "take-some" game (individuals can extract [take] from a common pool). Similar results were found in n-person situations. Liebrand and Van Run (1985) revealed that in *n*-person simulated social dilemmas (limited resource games), the most thrifty (cooperative) were the altruists, followed by the cooperators and the individualists; the competitive participants were the least thrifty. Social orientations appear then to account for a large portion of the variance in social perception and behavior in interdependence situations.

Control Preferences

Basic Ideas

Are there any other motivational factors that may account for diversity of behaviors in interdependence situations? Is there anything else that people seek when they are interdependent with others?

As argued earlier, any interdependence situation is defined not only in terms of outcome allocations but also in terms of who makes decisions about those allocations. Control can be considered as a means, as an ability to change outcomes in a desired direction. It can also be viewed as an end in itself.

The idea of control as a value in itself is deeply rooted in the history of psychology and underlies many psychological theories. One need only mention Adler's (1929) theory of power, White's (1959) theory of effectance motivation, De Charms's (1968) theory of personal causation, Brehm's (1966) theory of reactance, Christie and Geis's (1970) theory of the Machiavellian personality, Burger's (1993) concept of desire for control, or Winter's (1973) theory of the power motive. Although these theories are focused on different types of control motivation, they all share the notion that people value control and that the degree to which control is valued affects people's perception, emotions, and behavior. Differential effects of need for power and fear of power have been shown by Winter and his collaborators in numerous studies (e.g., Winter, 1988), and a generalized desire for control and its consequences were extensively investigated by Burger (1993).

At this point, I present an approach to control that was inspired by Kelley and Thibaut's (1978) theory and that is tailored to the analysis of interdependence. It is claimed, first, that there are six distinct preferences for control corresponding with six types of control defining interdependence structure in Kelley and Thibaut terms.

In an interaction with others, as an interdependence actor, one can try to maximize (a) one's control over one's own outcomes (*self-control preference*), (b) one's control over others' outcomes (*power preference*), (c) others' control over one's own outcomes (*dependence preference*), (d) others' control over others' own outcomes (*respect preference*), (e) joint control over one's own outcomes (*Collaboration Preference A*), and (f) joint control over others' outcomes (*Collaboration Preference B*).

An individual then evaluates any social situation on the basis of the extent that it satisfies his or her preferences. These evaluations may determine the attractiveness of the interaction as much as do evaluations of outcome allocation (i.e., social orientations). In other words, considering control as one of the desired outcomes, preferences for control alter the structure of interdependence.

I suggest that control preferences are one of the crucial determinants of the intersituational mobility of individuals. They also affect the course of any given interaction. For instance, depending on the type of one's preference for control, an individual is either taking their own initiative or giving room for a partner's initiative in decision making. Turn-taking in social interaction may not only be instrumental for the final outcome allocation (Kelley, 1997) but also for control allocation itself.

As in social interactions, control preferences can be considered as (a) a generalized personal inclination to exercise a certain type of control and (b) a psychological state of desire induced in a given situation. The majority of studies performed up to now have been focused on generalized control preferences.

Control Preferences, Social Orientations, and Locus of Control

The hypothesized relation between preferences for outcome allocation and preferences for control distribution was tested in three studies. In the studies by Grzelak (1982) and Grzelak, Kuhlman, Joireman, Shelly, and Doi (1996), the two types of preferences were inferred from participants' evaluations of the attractiveness of two sets of situations varying in both the allocation of outcomes and the allocation of control to the self and to the anonymous other. In Klimpel's (1998) study, social orientation was measured with the same technique used in the previous studies, and a special inventory was designed to measure control preferences. The inventory consists of six scales. Five of them (see Table 10.1) measure preferences for Self-Control, Dependence, Power, Respect, and Collaboration. In the questionnaire study, Collaboration A and Collaboration B were difficult to differentiate and therefore were combined into one scale. Reliability (Cronbach's α) of all scales reached a satisfactory level; in 12 different studies it ranged from .66 to .85.

As shown in Table 10.2, the studies by Klimpel (1998), Slupska (1988), and Ogórek (1998) show that the particular control scales correlate with each other at a relatively low level, below .18 (Pearson's r), except for self-control and respect for others' control ($r = .55$). This last outcome is not surprising. It may be safely assumed that people respecting their own right to control should also respect the right of others.

None of the control scales correlates with social orientation at a level higher than .23. In some more recent studies (Ogórek, 1998; Slupska, 1998) the control scales correlate at a considerably higher level. There is some basis then to treat control preferences as independent from each other; however, the level of that independence varies from one sample to another (and, supposedly, from one population to another).

Finally, the correlation between generalized locus of control and control preferences is nearly null except for self-control. In the latter case it reaches .26 in one

TABLE 10.1

Sample Questions for Five Scales of Control Preferences Inventory

	DESIRE TO MAXIMIZE STATEMENT	SAMPLE STATEMENTS:
Self-control	my control over my outcomes	I like to rely on myself. I enjoy planning what to do in the future.
Power	my control over his/her outcomes	I like to exercise power. I like to decide for others.
Respect	his/her control over own outcomes	I like people who do not ask for advice. I like people who try to do everything themselves.
Dependence	his/her control over my outcomes	I prefer to be guided by other people. It is good when somebody takes care of myself.
Collaboration	joint control over my and his/her outcomes	I like to be in a group in which decisions are made together. I like to work in a team.

TABLE 10.2

Correlation of Control Preferences With Social Orientations and Locus of Control

	SELF-CONTROL	POWER	DEPENDENCE	RESPECT	COLLABORATION
Power	$.21^{(**)}$				
Dependence	$-.38^{(**)}$	$-21^{(**)}$			
Respect	$.54^{(**)}$	$.20^{(**)}$	$-.31^{(**)}$		
Collaboration	$-.06$	$-.12$	$.25^{(**)}$	$.08$	
Individualism	$-.01$	$.22^{(**)}$	$-.03$	$.09$	$-.17^{(*)}$
Equality	$-.06$	$-.12$	$.05$	$-.10$	$.10$
Altruism	$.01$	$-.18^{(**)}$	$.04$	$-.03$	$.12$
Competition	$-.03$	$.23^{(**)}$	$-.07$	$.07$	$-.15^{(*)}$
Cooperation	$.07$	$.02$	$.03$	$.06$	$.03$
Locus of control	$.21^{(*)}$	$.23^{(*)}$	$-.22^{(*)}$	$.15$	$.08$

$*p < .05$, two-tailed. $**p < .01$, two-tailed.

study and .16 in another. A generalized locus of control was measured by Delta scale, a Polish equivalent of Rotter's Internal–External Locus of Control scale. These correlations show, once again, that "to want" means something different than "can."

In the preliminary studies done so far, most attention has been paid to differential effects of control preferences. Table 10.3 presents selected effects found in five recent

TABLE 10.3

A Sample of Differential Effects of Control Preferences

	SELF-CONTROL	POWER	RESPECT	DEPENDENCE	COLLABORATION
Incentive needed to pass control to others (Klimpel, 1998)	High	High		Low	
Searching information about partner (in ill-defined interdependence) (Grzelak, 1982)	Passive	Active		Passive	Active
Variance of opinions about others morality (Ogórek 1998, Slupska 1998)			High (when participants make decisions)		Low (when altruistic other makes decision) and high (when individualistic other makes decision)
Satisfaction with negotiation outcomes (Kulicka 1997)		Satisfied with outcomes			Satisfied with utilities
Alcohol drinking initiation;	Late	Early	Late		
Alcohol use	Low	High		High	
Readiness to join alcohol prevention activities (Wolniewicz & Grzelak, 1997)				Low	High
Anxiety (Wolniewicz & Grzelak, 1997)		High		High	Low
Satisfaction with					
Life achievements		High[a]	Low		
Life in the past		High			
Friendships				Low	Low
Morale of society				Low	Low
Situation in the country (Ogórek 1998, Slupska, 1998)					

[a] There was also a significant main effect of power, and a significant Power × Respect interaction. The highest satisfaction with life achievements was observed for those with both high power and high respect preferences, the lowest satisfaction among those with low power and high respect preferences.

unpublished studies. It becomes clear that the effects of control preferences are strong and cover a wide range of variables, from judgments about others to behaviors (assessment based on self-reports). Those with high self-control preferences do not act, perceive, or make evaluations in the way that others do. The same statement refers to other types of preferences.

Factors Affecting Control Preferences

Following Zajonc's (1980) idea that affect and cognition are under the control of separate and partially independent systems influencing each other, it has been claimed that it is not only preferences that channel information processing. Preferences can also be shaped by perception of the world, and they can be temporarily induced by situational factors. They can also be affected by social and demographic factors.

Some preliminary studies have shown that both the strength and the type of control preferences are person and situation dependent. Table 10.4 summarizes the results of these studies.

The last two factors seem to imply that control preferences, like social orientations, are not only connected with personality traits. They may vary from one situation to another, from one interaction to another. Various preferences may be activated in the same person depending on situational cues. This thesis, however, awaits further research.

Conclusion

Throughout the chapter, I have noted some implications for understanding interdependence situations. The underlying idea I hoped to convey was to relate, for the first time, one's intentions for outcome allocations to one's preferences for control.

It can be expected that the behavior of prosocial (altruistic and cooperative) individuals will be different depending on their control preferences. On the one hand, individuals with high respect for others' self-determination should be sensitive and responsive to the needs of others, including the others' control preferences (respecting the others' right to define what is good for them). On the other hand, prosocial individuals with high need for power should be more aggressive in enforcing whatever they consider to be good for others. A mother who wants the best for her child and exercises her power to make the child happy develops a substantially different relationship than a mother who respects the child's need to control himself or herself. Each of the two relationships provides a different type of satisfaction for both the mother and the child. In the long run, the educational outcomes of the two relationships are likely to be different, too. This is an example of how important the particular configuration of the two types of intentions can be.

TABLE 10.4

Some Factors Affecting Control Preferences

	SELF-CONTROL	POWER CONTROL	RESPECT	DEPENDENCE	COLLABORATION
Partners trustworthiness (*Grzelak, Kuhlman, Joireman, Shelly, & Doi, 1995*)[i]	High when partner distrusted	Low when distrusted		Low when partner distrusted	(*not measured*)
Age (*Wolniewicz & Grzelak, 1998*)		Increasing			
Gender (*Wolniewicz & Grzelak, 1998*)		High in men			High in women
Class group climate (in grammar and high schools) (*Wolniewicz & Grzelak, 1998*)		High when climate bad	High when climate good, supportive		High when climate good, supportive

A consideration of control preferences may account for a better understanding of various social settings at both the interpersonal and the societal level. Preferences for joint control (i.e., collaboration) and for respect for others should promote building up and maintaining democratic types of settings. An example to consider here is an individual in a democratic state. There is a great asymmetry between what an individual can do to and for the state and what the state can do to and for the individual. Still, because democracy assumes coordination of various groups in achieving their interests, acceptance of others' (whether they are individuals, groups, local, or state government) right to participate in decision making facilitates maintenance of democracy. Power preferences, however, do not. It seems important to develop respect preferences as a lasting impetus to building up and maintaining democracy.

The process aspects of control are also worth considering. Negotiations between individuals or groups are all about influencing others. The manner in which this influence is exerted is crucial. On the one hand, in tough, positional negotiations it is important for one to use all of one's power to entice the other to make as many and as big concessions as possible. This type of negotiation rarely leads to a win-win solution satisfying both parties. Moreover, the power orientations of one negotiation party induces the need for exercising power in the other party. This will likely lead to a breakdown in negotiations.

On the other hand, showing a desire for collaboration and respect will induce and activate the same attitude on the other side of the table. Instead of fighting, there will likely be problem solving. This is why so much attention is paid by theorists and practitioners to procedures that will elicit a desire for collaboration and respect for the other's control on both sides of the table.

Finally, the concept of control preferences has implications for extant theories of self-control, which turns out to be much more affected by deficits than other control types. Various psychological phenomena can be illuminated by a consideration of control preferences. For instance, it would seem that self-control individuals should be less likely to develop learned helplessness than will dependence-oriented people, for whom loss of control might be a desired state of nature. In reactance situations, a similar effect should be observed. And people who have different social preferences will likely also have different susceptibility or resistance to various techniques of social influence. Generally speaking, an individual's control preferences will influence the domains in which the various phenomena and processes of social psychological theory will occur.

References

Adler, A. (1929). *The science of living.* New York: Greenberg.

Brehm, J. V. (1966). *Responses to loss of freedom: A theory of psychological reactance.* Morristown, TN: General Learning Press.

Burger, J. M. (1993). Individual differences in control motivation and social information processing. In G. Weary, F. Gleicher, & K. Marsh (Eds.), *Control motivation and social cognition* (pp. 203–219). New York: Springer-Verlag.

Caporael, L., Dawes, R. M., Orbell, J., & Van de Kragt, A. (1989). Selfishness examined: Cooperation in the absence of egoistic incentives. *Behavioral and Brain Sciences, 12,* 683–739.

Christie, R., & Geis, F. (1970). *Studies in Machiavellianism.* New York: Academic Press.

Dawes, R. M., McTavish, J., & Shaklee, H. (1977). Behavior, communication and assumptions about other people's behavior in a common dilemma situation. *Journal of Personality and Social Psychology, 35,* 1–11.

De Charms, R. (1968). *Personal causation: The internal affective determinants of behavior.* New York: Academic Press.

Grzelak, J. L. (1982). Preferences and cognitive processes in social interdependence situations. In V. Derlega & J. Grzelak (Eds.), *Cooperation and helping behavior: Theory and research* (pp. 97–127). New York: Academic Press.

Grzelak, J. L. (1991). The model of *homo economicus.* Should it be revisited? In M. Lerner & R. Vermont (Eds.), *Social justice in human relations* (pp. 211–238). New York: Plenum.

Grzelak, J. L., Kuhlman, D. M., Joireman, J., Shelly, G., & Doi, T. (1996). Power preferences and trust. Unpublished manuscript.

Grzelak, J. L., Poppe, M., Czwartosz, Z., & Nowak, A. (1988). "Numerical trap": A new look at outcome representation in studies on choice behaviour. *European Journal of Social Psychology, 18,* 143–159.

Iedema, J., & Poppe, M. (1994). Effects of social value orientation on expecting and learning others' orientation. *European Journal of Social Psychology, 24,* 565–579.

Kelley, H. H. (1997). Expanding the analysis of social orientations to the sequential-temporal structure of situations. *European Journal of Social Psychology, 27,* 373–404.

Kelley, H. H., & Stachelski, A. J. (1970a). The inference of intentions from moves in the prisoner's dilemma game. *Journal of Experimental Social Psychology, 6,* 401–419.

Kelley, H. H., & Stachelski, A. J. (1970b). Social interaction basis of cooperators' and competitors' beliefs about others. *Journal of Personality and Social Psychology, 16,* 66–91.

Kelley, H. H., & Thibaut, W. (1978). *Interpersonal relations: A theory of interdependence.* New York: Wiley.

Klimpel, K. (1998). Control preferences and passing control to another person. Unpublished master's thesis. Warsaw University.

Kuhlman, M. D., & Marshello, A. M. J. (1975). Individual differences in game motivation as moderators of preprogrammed strategy effects in prisoner's dilemma game. *Journal of Personality and Social Psychology, 32,* 912–931.

Kulicka, M. (1997). Control preferences and the meaning of integrative solution of conflict of interests. Unpublished manuscript. Warsaw University, Poland.

Lewin, K. (1947). Frontiers in group dynamics: concept, method and reality in social science: Social equilibria and social change. *Human Relations, 1,* 5–41.

Liebrand, W. B. G. (1984). The effect of social motives, communication and group size in an *n*-person multi-stage mixed-motive game. *European Journal of Social Psychology, 14,* 239–264.

Liebrand, W. B. G., Jansen, R., Rijken, V., & Suhre, C. (1986). Might over morality: Social values and perception of other players in experimental games. *Journal of Experimental Social Psychology, 22,* 203–215.

Liebrand, W. B. G., & van Run, C. J. (1985). The effects of social motives on behavior in social dilemmas in two cultures. *Journal of Experimental Social Psychology, 21,* 86–102.

Maki, J., & McClintock, C. G. (1983). The accuracy of social value prediction: Actor and observer influences. *Journal of Personality and Social Psychology, 45,* 829–838.

McClintock, C. G. (1972). Social motivation—A set of propositions. *Behavioral Science, 17,* 458–464.

Messick, D. M., & McClintock, C. G. (1968). Motivational basis of choice in experimental games. *Journal of Experimental Social Psychology, 4,* 1–25.

Nash, J. F. (1951). Non-cooperative games. *Annals of Mathematics, 54,* 286–295.

Ogórek, J. (1998). The role of control preferences in forming judgments on intellectual potentials. Unpublished master's thesis. Warsaw University, Poland.

Poppe, M., Croon, M., & Sluytman, A. (1986, May). *The implicit structure of social values and justice rules in a context of social relations.* Paper presented at European Association of Experimental Social Psychology, East-West Meeting, Graz, Austria.

Sattler, D. N., & Kerr, N. L. (1991). Might versus morality explored: Motivational and cognitive bases for social motives. *Journal of Personality and Social Psychology, 60,* 756–765.

Slupska, A. (1998). The role of control preferences in forming moral judgements. Unpublished master's thesis. Warsaw University, Poland.

van Lange, P. A. M., & Kuhlman, D. M. (1994). Social value orientations and impressions of partner's honesty and intelligence: A test of the might versus morality effect. *Journal of Personality and Social Psychology, 67,* 126–141.

von Neumann, J., & Morgenstern, O. (1944). *Theory of games and economic behavior.* Princeton, NJ: Princeton University Press.

White, R. W. (1959). Motivation reconsidered: The concept of competence. *Psychological Review, 66,* 297–323.

Wieczorkowska, G. (1982). A formal analysis of preferences. *Polish Psychological Bulletin, 13,* 73–77.

Winter, D. G. (1973). *The power motive*. New York: Free Press.

Winter, D. G. (1988). The power motive in women and men. *Journal of Personality and Social Psychology*, 54, 510–519.

Wolniewicz, B., & Grzelak, J. L. (1997). Measures of the effectiveness of drug prevention programs. Unpublished research report. Institute for Psychiatry and Neurology.

Zajonc, R. B. (1980). Feeling and thinking: Preferences need no inferences. *American Psychologist*, 35, 151–175.

Zajonc, R. B. (1982). Altruism, envy, competitiveness, and the common good. In V. Derlega & J. Grzelak (Eds.), *Cooperation and helping behavior: Theory and research* (pp. 420–436). New York: Academic Press.

CHAPTER 11

Monitoring Adaptation to Social Change: Research at the Institute for Social Studies

Grazyna Wieczorkowska

Eugene Burnstein

Few people are able to change the direction of a field, and Robert Zajonc is one such person. However, he has done more than reorient social psychology. Overlooked is his ability to father institutions. Among other things, he is responsible for the birth of the Institute for Social Studies (ISS), an independent interdisciplinary research organization at the University of Warsaw—to the best of our knowledge it is Zajonc's latest offspring—which has come to play a key role in the revitalization of social science in Poland.

What does ISS do? Because it is sister to the Institute for Social Research at the University of Michigan, many of the projects are similar in kind (if not in magnitude), albeit with an emphasis on Central and Eastern Europe. However, peculiar to ISS— and one of its main objectives—is the monitoring of social, political, and economic reforms associated with the transition from totalitarianism and central planning to democracy and a market economy. In this chapter, we attempt to illustrate this work by examining the problem of psychological adaptation. To do so, we begin with a general analysis of the stages of the transition in Poland and the adaptive problems each stage poses. (We owe our gratitude to Janusz Grzelak, Andrzej Nowak, and Stan Mika for their long inspiring discussion of stages of adaptation.) Following this is a discussion of research carried out at ISS to test some implications of the analysis.

Stages of the Transition and Problems of Adaptation

Although the reforms occurring in Central and Eastern Europe are fundamental, they are nonlinear over time. In the short term, their trajectories vacillate unpredictably and, hence, cause uncertainty. We presume the end-state is political freedom and a market economy. History, however, demonstrates no law saying that when authoritarian regimes dissolve, they reconstitute themselves as democracies. The

155

conditions leading to the fall of Robespierre—namely, inflation, declining standards of living, and general social disorganization—were not greatly different from those in Eastern Europe in the late 1980s. Nonetheless, revolutionary France turned to Napoleon instead of the moderate Girondists. Similarly, the civil war and hyperinflation in the Soviet Union accompanying Lenin's policies produced Stalinism, not a return of the Kerensky regime.

In fact, Huntington's (1991) analysis suggests at best a "two-step-forward, one-step-backward" process: Since World War II there have been a few waves of democratization, each of which was followed by a reverse wave. At the peaks of democratization, between 32% and 45% of the countries in the world were free societies, whereas at troughs, only between 20% and 25% were free. Equally telling is that in 1990, during a new, third wave of democratization, 45% of the countries in the world had achieved freedom, the same percentage as in 1922! Also, a recent report (cited in Huntington, 1991, p. 25) estimated that in 1973 32% of the people in the world lived in democracies; by 1990, despite a large number of changes in regime, this had risen only to 39%. Democracy, therefore, is by no means an absorbing or inevitable state.

In the Polish case, the transition also has not been without its vicissitudes, some of which are, on the face of it, a puzzle. On one hand, there is good evidence that the reform has succeeded in key areas. Not only has the rate of unemployment gone down in the past few years but the gross domestic product has also grown appreciably. On the other hand, there is increasing disaffection with the present system and nostalgia for the old politics. In Poland's 1989 election to the national political assembly, or Sejm, the rate of participation was more than 62%, but in the 1991 election participation fell to about 40%. Furthermore, in 1989 the Communists and their allies, the Peasants Party, received less than 5% of the free vote, whereas in 1993 they received more than 30%.

We know about these and many other facts about what is happening in Eastern Europe because of the numerous studies that have been carried out. Every year, for instance, in coordination with the National Opinion Research Center, ISS conducts a massive national survey of attitudes toward economic and political events, called the Polish General Social Survey. The results provide a series of snapshots of the year-to-year changes in sentiment. Among other things, they indicate that some communes—Poland is divided into more than 2,000 such local units—are much more involved in the reform than others and that the involvement can change markedly over a relatively short period of time. For example, Nowak, Zienkowski, and Urbaniak (1994) measured commune involvement in terms of two indices: (a) the number of private businesses established per capita in a commune between 1989 and 1992 and (b) the percentage vote given by a commune in the 1993 elections to parties favoring economic and political reform. They observed differences in involvement in reform, often between physically adjacent communes, that were large and that frequently reversed so that many of the involved communes in

1989 became uninvolved in 1992 and many of the uninvolved become involved. If anything is clear about the transition in Poland, it is that adaptation to the postcommunist system, as mirrored by engagement in entrepreneurial activity and support for reform politics, is highly dynamic. What if any regularities underlay such dynamism?

Reform in Poland has occurred in stages. The issues that define them, of course, are complex and ambiguous and, to a degree, continuous; hence, their demarcations are bound to be fuzzy. Nonetheless, comparable categories of social change have been found useful in various contexts (e.g., Stewart, 1989), and the problems characteristic of these stages have been observed in other Eastern European nations during the same period. In any event, we present them merely as reasonable, useful, and reflecting first-hand knowledge.

Pre-Reform: Security and Dependence

Under communism, Poles' concept of the social system was relatively simple: "we" versus "they," with little differentiation within each group. The main actors were "atomized" citizens and powerful, well-organized party institutions. Individuals could control their private lives to a modest extent, but only as long as they did not threaten a regime whose threshold for threat or resistance was low. The upshot was a perception of an asymmetrically interdependent and minimally differentiated society made up of a very small cluster of political dissidents, a pervasive and powerful party with its dedicated supporters, and a very large cluster of isolated and feckless citizens sharing a common fate that they feel powerless to change and, hence, compelled to accept. As a consequence, Poles interpreted their own and others' actions in terms of situational pressures rather than individual choice and agency.

Under these conditions, adaptation meant that in most significant domains of everyday life such as schooling, jobs, housing, medical care, consumption, and leisure activities, Poles had to be willing to accept a wide range of options, many of which they would have rejected in happier circumstances. Those who refused to accept, say, low-quality goods and services and persisted in searching for something better met with frustration and usually failed. It may be worth noting at this point, although we return to this issue in detail below, that with the end of central planning and the onset of a market economy it was no longer as costly to reject low-ranked options and search for more attractive ones, rather it was often to the person's advantage to do so.

In any event, the lack of autonomy and agency, and the need to accept undesirable outcomes, resulted in chronic anger and ambivalence and the perception of self (and of others who share one's fate, namely, most other Poles) as inefficacious and helpless, with low self-esteem and low collective esteem. To illustrate, consider what was a typical case in Poland 10 years ago of a worker at a large factory, say, the Lenin Steel Mill near Krakow. The initial decision to apply for work there rather than another factory that had more interesting jobs was largely predetermined; some years ago, while a youth, the person was probably assigned by the educational bureaucracy to the technical school run by the Lenin Steel Mill with the clear expectation of him or her working there after graduation. Certainly, the flat or apartment where the person now lives, the stores at which the family shops, the children's preschool, where and when the family vacations, and to whom they go for medical care are all predictable because they are all functions controlled by the factory bureaucracy. There is clinical evidence that this lack of decision-making experience and the constraints on choice and pressures to accept what others decide is good enough for people induce dependence and an aversion to planning. The purposive style that evolves in these circumstances, as was later discovered, is not adaptive in a market economy. Reports by psychologists who deal with the problems of privatizing large factories in Poland indicate that longtime employees have difficulties even thinking about which doctor to visit or when to do it and where to go on vacation, and that the multitude of decision they are now obliged to make has had a paralyzing effect, resulting in feelings of helplessness and inefficacy.

The First Stage of the Reform: Enthusiasms and Illusions

After years of drab stability, there is an exhilarating discontinuity in national life. "We" have power, "they" do not! Poles perceived the triumph of democracy as a skillful as well as magnificent revolution. It was natural to place great trust in those who brought it about. Accordingly, one of the defining features of this stage is the enormous credibility of the new government and the democratic leadership—during the year after he was elected as the first post-communist prime minister, surveys showed that Tadeusz Mazowiecki had the support of between 70% and 90% of adult Poles.

Not surprisingly, many beliefs about the new leadership were unrealistic. The most common and perhaps the most pernicious was a carryover from pre-reform conceptions of the regime as having power to determine one's fate in matters of employment, education, housing, consumption, health, and so on. This, plus a belief in the new regime's skillfulness and trustworthiness, led to the expectation that the new government would resolve economic problems smoothly and cause standards of living to improve quickly. There was little recognition that the market economy and democracy meant that Poles have to take more personal responsibility. Keep in mind that for nearly 50 years the concept of the regime as the prime agent and the citizen as inefficacious and unaccountable had been an essential feature of Polish society. We ought not be surprised, therefore, that well after the reforms were initiated many individuals were still inclined to see the state as *the* responsible actor and not as simply the "manager of the commons." At the same time, however, Poles did perceive the new leadership as different from the pre-reform regime. Early on it was considered by almost all as "our government," concerned with public opinion and subject to the will of the people. And while many did not yet recognize that the reform implied increased individual responsibility, they did believe that the citizenry as a whole had regained control over social life and that the era of party control was ended.

A second characteristic of this stage is the appearance of a new actor: the anti-Communist opposition. At this point Polish society had few other distinguishable groups—perhaps a small cluster of the apathetic and a still smaller cluster of old leaders along with their remaining supporters, but none was comparable in size, unity, energy, or single-mindedness. Hence, members of the anti-Communist group not only interacted frequently and felt a common fate but also perceived new opportunities, ends that until now were unattainable.

Social beliefs during this stage were informed by two distinct biases. One is an *illusion of efficacy*. At this point the nation's economic and political goals were fuzzy. Precisely what independence, democracy, or a market was and how to bring them about were unclear. Disagreements, however, were discounted so that to all appearances the anti-Communist majority seemed unified, powerful, and about to determine the shape of Polish society. It is this illusory belief, we think, that explains the extraordinarily large number of people who neglected their personal lives and private interests to devote themselves to antisystem activities. Perhaps as justification for the considerable investment in public affairs, there arose a second misconception, the *illusion of total victory*. Witnessing the collapse of the old system is a heady experience. It confirms the antisystem leadership's acumen, which, during the pre-transitional stage, most considered deficient to say the least. Following its victory, however, even its more farfetched predictions about democratization seemed credible. This state of mind generates overly optimistic expectations: Democracy has triumphed, authoritarian structures have been destroyed, and reform will go forward without opposition. The vast majority was now poised to enjoy the benefits of the reforms, unmindful of the costs.

The Second Stage of the Reform: Disillusionment and Skepticism

In our estimation, Poland is now at or near the end of the second stage, probably the most difficult one. It is during this period that there has been inflation, unemployment, and a worsening in the standard of living. People grow disillusioned with reform and start to think of it as the cause of the decline in well-being. They become uninterested in pro-reform activities and skeptical about the market and democracy. Once again there is fear of inefficacy and loss of control, along with renewed feelings of helplessness, low self-esteem, and low collective esteem (Grzelak, 1987, 1993; Grzelak & Czabala, 1996). Consequently, people focus more on their own personal affairs; self-interest comes to dominate. At the same time, there is widespread concern about the "pathologies" of inequality and corruption that most attribute to the reform.

Unsurprisingly, evaluations of the new government become less positive; as it happened, the decline was precipitous, producing a leadership crisis. Contrary to sentiment in the preceding stage, people now believe the new leadership has shown itself to be untrustworthy, incompetent, and heavy-handed, "bumblers" inclined to abuse power. For instance, between 1989 (i.e., before the first free election) and 1992, Polish political institutions underwent a profound democratic restructuring. However, according to data from the Center for Research on Public Opinion, Poland's largest private polling organization, there was no comparable shift in citizens' perceptions of their political efficacy: In 1989, 89% stated they had no control over governmental policies; and even if they themselves held public office, 12% still believed they would have no influence on government policy. In 1992, the comparable figures were 90% and 25%, respectively. The only significant change in opinion obtained in these polls that seemed to reflect institutional reform concerned the workplace; namely, in 1989, 70% felt they had no control over their work, and in 1992, feelings of lack of control in the workplace fell to 59%.

It is ironic that in the pre-reform period people were unhappy because the regime exercised inordinate control over society; now, during the early stages of reform, the malaise was due instead to the perception that those in political power were incapable of controlling society. In any case, the dashed hopes reactivated the old ways of thinking and feeling; external attributional styles and a willingness to accept less desirable options became more prevalent, and people began once again to feel inefficacious, helpless, low in self-esteem, and low in collective esteem.

The Third Stage of the Reform: Coping

During this stage, which we believe is about to begin in Poland, people adjust to their disappointment in reform, and their actions start to have constructive effects. To take an important example, the belief that the reform leadership was incompetent as well as untrustworthy caused people to become less involved in politics and devote themselves to private interests: cultural, business, or professional. One of the more significant (and unintentional) consequences of this shift in concerns was that by pursuing private interests individuals found it useful to form associations. At the same time, a belief that the regime was incompetent and untrustworthy fed people's anxiety about abuse of power that they recognized as threatening these private interests. To protect themselves at the institutional level, they began to exert pressure toward developing a modern legal system. Together, the growth of independent associations and the movement toward democratic legality were critical in bringing about the establishment during this stage of the reform of civil society.

Research on Adaptation to the Transition

In this section, we describe one of the projects at ISS on adaptation to the transition and the cognitive–behavioral strategies used to set goals in everyday life. Our analysis follows Pervin (1989) in that we conceive of goal setting as a process by which individuals form images of the end-states that they deem worth pursuing. However, whereas Pervin explained the vicissitudes of these images in terms of personality variables, we argue that goal setting is also a decision process, albeit one that is rooted in the personality of the actor, and that it can be usefully studied from the perspective of decision theory. Normally, however, decision theory concentrates almost exclusively on selection mechanisms, in which individuals are presented with a collection of options, called the *consideration set*, that they screen for inclusion in the choice set on the basis of its acceptability. Once the choice set is established, they then decide on its "best" member(s), which then becomes the individuals' actual goal(s) or the end-state(s) they intend to pursue (Beach, 1993). Personality theory, on the other hand, focuses on the generation of goals. Within this paradigm, people typically list and rate a series of end-states they are striving to achieve. The researcher then attempts to explain the organization of these strivings in terms of the characteristics of the respondents (e.g., Emmons, 1992).

The differences between the two approaches may cause some problems. Note that selection requires individuals to recognize whether a given option is "good enough" to belong in the choice set and, subsequently, whether it is one of the "best." Generation, on the other hand, requires individuals to reproduce from memory the options that correspond to their veritable strivings. Needless to say, because these two tasks involve rather dissimilar processes (e.g., selection depends on the discriminability of the goals in the consideration set whereas generation depends on their availability), they might well lead to different conclusions about goal setting. Be that as it may, our research depends on both approaches in that it makes use of decision theory variables but analyzes their relations primarily in terms of the characteristics of the actors.

We focus on probably the simplest property of the goal-setting process, namely, the number of end-states that have positive value and, hence, are deemed acceptable or worthwhile by the person. We call this feature the person's *goal-category range* (Wieczorkowska, 1990; Wieczorkowska & Burnstein, 1993; Wieczorkowska-Siarkiewicz, 1992). In decision theory terms, goal-category range reflects the size of the choice set. An analysis of the goals that individuals judge "good enough" assumes the existence of a preference structure. At its simplest, this implies that (a) individuals first decide whether an option is acceptable and, hence, belongs in the goal category before they choose which option is "best" to pursue, and (b) the ease of choosing the "best" course of action depends not only on the nature of the options in the goal category but also on their number. Indeed, we would argue that to understand purposive behavior in general—planning and achieving as well as goal setting—it is necessary to consider both what and how many options individuals identify as acceptable.

Note that the range of a goal category is empirically and conceptually quite different from Pettigrew's (1958) well-known concept of category width (CW).

The CW measure is simply a predicted maximum and minimum in respect to a unidimensional property that the person believes includes all objects or events within the category (e.g., the speeds of the fastest and slowest species of bird). The range of a goal category, however, refers to a set of multidimensional objects, often from different substantive categories, that have positive value to the person and, hence, are choice-set members (e.g., the goal category for pets may include various kinds of dogs, cats, birds, fish, snakes, and so forth, depending on what individuals find acceptable). However, this is not to say that CW judgments are necessarily unrelated to goal-category range. Suppose individuals possess a general strategy for representing options in decision tasks whereby some prefer to consider many possibilities prior to making a final choice and others, only a few. Then, for instance, the number of different animals they imagine to be acceptable as pets would be correlated with their CW predictions about maximum and minimum speeds of flight for birds. We believe that the existence of such a general strategy is the most reasonable explanation of the moderate correlation between CW and goal-category range found in our research (Wieczorkowska & Burnstein, 1999; Wieczorkowska-Siarkiewicz, 1992).

To illustrate the basic concepts of our theoretical model, imagine that several new professionals with PhDs in psychology are looking for a job. Examining the advertisements in a professional newsletter, they discover the following jobs are available: a lecturer at a small college, an analyst in a marketing agency, an educational counselor, a human-resource manager, and a psychotherapist. These jobs constitute their consideration set. Often people find the consideration set too large, that it is simply not worthwhile applying to every job advertised. Instead, they *satisfice*, meaning they form a goal category consisting only of those options in the consideration set that seem acceptable to them. Of course, some have stringent standards, whereas others are more lenient. Individuals who reject a relatively large number of options as unacceptable we call *point strategist* (Wieczorkowska, 1990; Wieczorkowska & Burnstein, 1993). They have a more constricted or fixed conception of their professional identity so that few jobs are "good enough" and, hence, form narrow goal categories. Others, called *interval strategists*, reject relatively few of the options in the consideration set. Their professional identity is more diffuse or malleable, allowing them to imagine themselves doing many different types of things; as a result, they form broad goal categories.

Our previous research has shown (Wieczorkowska-Nejtartdt, 1998, Wieczorkowska & Burnstein, 1999; Wieczorkowska-Siarkiewicz, 1992) that these two strategies operate over a variety of decision domains. Thus, we find substantial and statistically significant correlations between goal-category ranges over markedly different kinds of decisions. In our first study (Wieczorkowska & Burnstein, 1993, 1999), for example, individuals who formed a broad or a narrow goal category in deciding which carpets were acceptable for their apartment evidence a similar tendency not only in deciding which of a large number of jobs were acceptable but also whether various obscure and trivial events fall within a broad or narrow range of possibilities (Pettigrew's, 1958, CW task). To be more specific, the correlation coefficients between the goal-category ranges for carpets and jobs, carpets and CW, and jobs and CW were .62, .48, and .53, respectively. Other studies (Wieczorkowska & Burnstein, 1993; Wieczorkowska-Siarkiewicz, 1992) have analyzed goal-category range in respect to renting an apartment, deciding on a career, and choosing a vacation resort and have consistently found that individuals characteristically adopt either an interval or a point strategy.

Implications of Broad and Narrow Goal Categories

The concept of goal-category range has a number of important implications. It reveals a person's capacity to substitute among goals or to switch to a new pursuit when an old one is interrupted or frustrated (Atkinson & Birch, 1970; Lewin, 1938). Because the capacity to make substitutions increases with the number of options that individuals consider acceptable, it follows that when blocked from pursuing one goal, interval strategists are more likely to have a backup and, thus, suffer less frustration than point strategists. Interesting evidence along these lines is contained in a study by Caplan, Vinokur, Price, and van Ryn (1989) on job seeking. They observed that inducing unemployed individuals to recognize that their choice set for jobs is in fact larger than they previously thought, or in our terms, broadening their goal category for jobs, increased their success in gaining reemployment and reduced the stress they experienced while seeking a job. Needless to say, the ability to substitute among goals is handy in a social system that limits members' choice and provides them with few attractive courses of action.

Let us consider some other implications of individual differences in the range of goal categories. The first is straightforward. If the representation of interval strategists contains more options than that of point strategists, then, in order to actually decide ("Should I really buy this carpet?"), interval strategists have to make a larger number of comparisons and, hence, ought to need more time than point strategists. The second is almost equally direct. The scenarios that guide individuals in goal setting contain two kinds of information (namely, knowledge about means and knowledge about ends), as well as what goals are worthwhile and how to go about achieving them. Because there are limits to the amount of information decision makers are able to hold in mind at one time, they confront a dilemma: The more end-states that are represented in the choice set, the less detailed the representation of paths. In other words, we hypothesize a trade-off between elaborating on outcomes and elaborating on plans, so that the broader the goal category, the less precise and detailed the planning. This suggests that point strategists typically should have a greater capacity for planning, which is taken to mean that, compared with interval strategists, when making decisions, point strategists (a) are more avid planners, (b) plan with greater frequency, (c) are more concerned with completing a plan or evidence greater persistence, (d) pay more attention to details or are more meticulous, and (e) resist distractions more and are more engrossed in planning. We found reasonable support for these hypotheses: Compared with point strategists, interval strategists reported that they (a) planned infrequently, (b) paid little attention to details, and (c) were readily distracted (Wieczorkowska & Burnstein, 1999; Wieczor-kowska-Siarkiewicz, 1992).

In light of this analysis, it may be useful to think of two classes of planning scenarios, each of which reflects a distinct purposive style (also see Apter, 1989). One describes the quintessential interval strategist—an individual whose goal category is so broad that his or her scenarios lack detail but only suggest a general direction and vague paths, not a tangible end and specific means. The direction and paths, we assume, reflect the relatively abstract and indeterminate or mixed (in the multipro-totype case, see below) information contained in the category prototype of interval strategists. Because it is difficult to represent in other than pallid fashion, the person is inclined to be guided less by such knowledge and more by the stimulus or external information. In short, individuals with this style attend to the activities demanded by the task rather than to ends adumbrated in the scenario as long as the task activity is consistent with the general direction implied by the prototype.

Put differently, the style of goal setting associated with an interval strategy makes activity perceptually dominate outcome as in the figure-ground effect, to the degree that the activity may become an end in itself. The contrasting purposive style reflects a form of goal setting inherent to point strategies. It characterizes individuals whose goal category is so narrow that they have appreciable capacity to encode each scenario vividly and in detail. Once a goal category is activated—that is, when the person decides what ends he or she wants to pursue, and for point strategists only a small number are deemed worth pursuing—a scenario can be implemented with little effort, often automatically. Therefore, individuals inclined to this style pay attention to the goal rather than the activity. Here rationality is bounded by making the outcome figure and activity ground.

Differences in strategies are likely to lead to differences in communication and interpersonal understanding. Interval strategists, for instance, probably find it harder to explain their reasoning than do point strategists. This is because, compared with point strategists, the interval strategists' goal-category prototype describes the options imprecisely (e.g., "I want a job that pays a reasonably decent salary and is fairly interesting") or because there are a large number of options, albeit precisely described (e.g., "I want a job that pays at least $50,000 either in college teaching, clinical psychology, consulting, government, personnel, or marketing research; I don't want to go into drug counseling or school psychology"). In the first instance, the goal category is fuzzy; in the second, it is what we call *multiprototype*, that is, the person has more than one ideal goal.

Multiprototype preferences are particularly difficult to communicate to others. Suppose that somebody asked you about the kind of car you like. In research studies, the usual way of getting people to describe their preferences is by having them list or rate the important features, say, of a car. However, this procedure is inappropriate for fuzzy and multiprototype representations. In the fuzzy case the reason is obvious, namely, the person has only a vague notion of his or her preferences. The multiprototype or multipoint case is more interesting because individuals can have clear and precise preferences but cannot describe them in terms of noncompensatory trait dimensions. For example, a multipoint car buyer may have as ideal points "a small economy vehicle and a large expensive touring limousine." The latter is highly desirable because it allows the person who is planning to visit the great cities of Europe during vacation to drive in comfort; however, the person would not have enough money left to fly between the most distant cities. The former has the opposite costs and benefits; it allows the person to fly but does not provide much comfort when driving. Imagine a salesperson trying to understand a potential customer who upon being asked "A small or big car?" or "Economy or luxury?" replies "Either one." The difficulty in description can be overcome by eschewing trait ratings and presenting people with a sizable sample of exemplars from the consideration set and allowing them to accept or reject them. In short, our car buyer could more easily describe his or her preference function and would be more readily understood if he or she were asked to identify members of his or her goal category rather than to list or rate individual, isolated features.

Another example of interpersonal difficulties stemming from differences in purposive style has to do with time estimation. Our research has shown that there is a trade-off between ends and means; the broader the goal category, the less capacity to plan. Achieving a highly desirable goal usually requires careful preparation and meticulous planning, however. The cognitive resources of interval strategists, therefore, are smaller than those of point strategists, and they can spend relatively little time and effort preparing and planning. Indeed, interval strategists are likely to underestimate or even be unaware of the time and effort needed to obtain a particular end. This creates conflicts when dealing with point strategists who have a good idea of the time and effort needed to perform a task. For instance, a promise to meet at or to finish a job by 5 p.m. means 5 p.m. sharp to point strategists and 5 p.m. plus or minus several minutes to interval strategists. The major differences between these two purposive styles in respect to the kinds of interpersonal dynamics each gives rise to are summarized in Table 11.1.

Point and Interval Strategies in Adapting to Social Change

In a society of scarcity, choice is relatively simple, at least for interval strategists. This is most obvious in the domain of consumption. When there is only one brand of tea or coffee available in shops, interval strategists should be less bothered than point strategists because this brand is more likely to fall within the former's goal

TABLE 11.1

Distinguishing Features of Point and Interval Strategies

POINT STRATEGY	INTERVAL STRATEGY
In making choices, rejects a lot and forms narrow goal categories.	In making choices, accepts a lot and creates broad goal categories.
Standards of equivalence: EXACTLY the same.	Standards of equivalence: MORE OR LESS the same.
Pays attention to details and considers them very important.	Does not pay attention to details and considers them unimportant.
Behavior is oriented toward a particular goal.	Behavior is oriented in a general direction.
Carefully plans and prepares.	Does not plan or prepare.
Reluctant to shift or substitute goals when a goal is blocked.	Readily shifts or substitutes goals when a goal is blocked.
Tries to achieve one goal at a time.	Tries to achieve many goals at a time.
Rigidity: Persists in attempts to complete an activity before switching to another.	Flexibility: Readily gives up an activity before it is completed and switches to another.
Accurately estimates time needed to complete a task.	Underestimates time needed to complete a task.
Pleasure derived from the feeling of having completed a specific task.	Pleasure derived from the feeling of moving ahead in a desirable direction.
Irritated when something goes wrong.	Finds the good side of something gone wrong.

category than within that of the latter. Generally speaking, under the command economies in Eastern Europe, the availability of many goods and services was unpredictable and what was available was usually of low quality. This made for many everyday dilemmas. If you wanted to buy meat and you happened to see nice steak for sale when you are about to catch the bus to work, you know you better skip the bus and buy the meat then and there because the likelihood of finding it in the shop later is very low. At the same time, however, you are aware that there is no certainty the next bus will arrive as scheduled. Hence, purchasing the meat will probably cause you to be late for work. In short, decisions about the consumption of goods and services were often conflicted and difficult. This is especially true for point strategists who like to plan their course of action with precision and are disinclined to substitute one goal for another or switch courses of action, although compared with interval strategists they would incur fewer costs in environments where consumption is predictable. It follows then that during the period of the command economy point strategists experienced more daily frustrations and, as a result, felt less efficacious and less satisfied with conditions of life than did interval strategists. This hypothesis was confirmed in a survey conducted in Poland in 1987 (Wieczorkowska-Nejtardt, 1996).

In recent years, however, Eastern Europe as a whole and Poland in particular have been moving toward a market economy. One of the more benign consequences of the transition was a large increase in the availability and quality of goods and services. As a consequence, individuals who have a clear goal and know precisely how to achieve it incur smaller costs; that is, they function more efficiently and experience less daily frustration, compared with those who have only a vague idea of what they want or how to get it. According to our analysis, therefore, the relationship between decision strategies and self-efficacy as well as life satisfaction changed with the onset of a market economy. In fact, we predicted a reversal in this relationship, so that now point strategists feel more efficacious and more satisfied with conditions of life than do interval strategists.

To test these ideas, we constructed a scale to distinguish between interval and point strategies that could be readily administered in sample surveys. On the basis of the finding that there are reliable differences between the two strategies in the extent to which they encourage meticulous planning, a five-item inventory to measure such meticulousness called the MET scale was constructed and validated with Polish samples (Wieczorkowska-Siarkiewicz, 1992; Wieczorkowska & Burnstein, 1999). Each of five items ($\alpha = .61$) described two individuals who differ in the meticulousness with which they planned (e.g., "Person X typically works out all the details of what he or she is going to be doing" vs. "Person Y typically pays little or no attention to the details of what he or she is going to be doing"), and respondents rated which of the two they resembled more. We also asked about adaptation to systemic change (e.g., "Compared with 1989, how satisfied are you with your current objective life situation?"). The data were collected in 1995 on the subsample of a representative national sample of adult Poles who were in the labor market or were actively searching for a job. In the 1997 Polish General Social Survey, the identical questions were asked, this time of all respondents (Cichomski & Morawski, 1998). The larger sample size allowed us to compare Poles who were involved in the economy—that is, adults who were employed or actively seeking employment—with those who were not involved in the economy, the majority of whom were retired plus some unemployed who were not seeking work.

For those involved in the economy, the pattern was exactly the same as that observed in 1995: Point strategists were more likely than interval strategists to feel better off and to express greater self-efficacy since the transition. However, the relationship was reversed for people not involved in the economy: Point strategists were more likely than interval strategists to feel worse off and express less self-efficacy since the transition. Hence, point strategists benefited more from the transition to a market economy only if they were engaged in significant purposive activities as indicated by their participation in the labor market. Among those who did not become so engaged, as indicated by their lack of participation in the labor market, interval strategists benefited more (or suffered lower costs), as was the case prior to the transition.

Additional research along these lines was carried out in Job Clubs where individuals go in search of employment (Wieczorkowska-Nejtardt, 1998). We found a general tendency for point strategists, as measured by the MET scale, to be unemployed for a longer period ($M = 11.82$ months) than interval strategists ($M = 5.96$ months), and for women to be unemployed ($M = 15.22$ months) longer than men ($M = 7.24$ months). Moreover, there was a significant interaction between gender and strategy. Women who were point strategists remained unemployed twice as long ($M = 22.4$ months) as those who were interval strategists ($M = 9.74$ months).

The general effect of point versus interval strategies is consistent with research on reemployment intervention programs in the United States that has demonstrated that unemployed individuals who were persuaded to consider many different types of jobs (i.e., to use an interval rather than a point strategy) found reemployment more rapidly than those who were not so persuaded (Caplan et al., 1989). In addition, it seems that a point strategy is especially costly for women seeking reemployment, at least in Polish society that takes a much more traditional view of the role of women than in the United States or Western Europe.

Finally, we attempted to demonstrate that these goal-setting strategies are sensitive to search costs. This implies that people recognize that a particular purposive style is adaptive in some circumstances but not in others. We assume a point strategy is conducive to success in a market economy and an interval strategy is more successful in a command economy. Hence, if individuals understand this contingency between purposive style and type of economy, they should infer that entrepreneurs who failed prior to 1989 but have succeeded since are probably point strategists and entrepreneurs who were successful prior to 1989 but have failed since are probably interval strategists. To test these ideas, we presented respondents with either of two descriptions. One was about an entrepreneur who failed in business prior to the transition, that is, under central planning, but became quite successful under the market economy; the other was about an entrepreneur who succeeded in business under central planning but failed under the market economy. After reading the description, respondents indicated the kind of strategist the entrepreneur was by predicting his answers to the MET scale. The findings demonstrated that people are quite sensitive to which strategy is more adaptive under central planning and which is more adaptive under the market economy: They attributed an interval strategy to the entrepreneur who succeeded prior to the transition but failed after and a point strategy to the entrepreneur who failed prior to the transition but succeeded after.

Conclusion

Since 1989, Poland has gone from totalitarianism and a command economy, in which a willingness to accept less desirable outcomes was adaptive, to democracy and a market economy, in which settling for less is not adaptive. If our analysis of the comparative advantage of broad versus narrow goal categories is valid, it follows that in present-day Poland a point strategy should produce more positive returns than an interval strategy. Initial studies (Wieczorkowska-Nejtardt, 1995, 1998; Wieczorkowska- Siarkiewicz,1992) established that broad and narrow goal categories do in fact reflect different characteristic purposive styles.

First, we found interval strategists take longer than point strategists to decide on a purchase, supporting the idea that in making their final choice the former considers a larger number of options than the latter. Next, we reasoned that to the extent goal-category range is a characteristic of the person, it should inform a variety of decisions. This was demonstrated by the finding that individuals who were interval or point strategists in screening carpets use a similar strategy when screening occupations as well as when setting boundaries for the trivial categories that make up the CW task.

Finally, because search costs and goal-category range covary, we know that people are unlikely to include an outcome in their goal category if they cannot imagine feasible means of achieving it. At the same time, however, as an outcome's desirability increases, so does the effort to think of such means. Because the capacity of working memory is limited, planning and goal-category range inevitably compete for encoding resources. We speculated that the cognitive system has evolved a solution whereby a trade-off occurs between outcome information and procedural information: namely, the more that individuals elaborate goals, the less they elaborate plans.

As a consequence of this trade-off, individuals who are biased toward broad goal categories have a different purposive style from those biased toward narrow goal categories: Interval strategists elaborate many options but do little planning, and point strategists elaborate few options but do lots of planning. Evidence for these two purposive styles was found when individuals who were classified as interval or point strategists on the basis of their goal-category range for carpets responded to the MET items that asked them to describe their planning of everyday activities. Interval strategists said they plan infrequently, imprecisely, and with little attention to details, whereas point strategists said they plan frequently, precisely, and in detail.

As search gets cheaper (e.g., high-quality goods and services become regularly available), individuals who reject low-ranked options should benefit more than those willing to accept such options. Consistent with this hypothesis, we found that point strategists feel their conditions of life and self-efficacy have improved more since the transition than do interval strategists. Our last study tested an assumption underlying strategic flexibility, namely, individuals can recognize when broad or narrow goal categories are adaptive. We found that Poles infer that an entrepreneur who failed prior to 1989 but succeeded since the transition is a point strategist and an entrepreneur who was successful prior to 1989 but failed since is an interval strategist. In short, people are able to distinguish which decision strategy works best under different economic conditions.

Still, it may be misleading to conclude that an interval strategy lost its adaptive value the moment the transition to democracy and a market economy began or that a point strategy now leads to larger returns in all domains of everyday life. Recall that our 1995 survey found that among people uninvolved in the economy (e.g., retirees), those using an interval strategy felt better off than those using a point strategy. Let us briefly consider a few additional ideas that would seem to follow from the assumption that interval strategists have a larger range of acceptable options and, hence, are better able to substitute a less costly option for a more costly one.

One obvious implication is that conforming to social pressure creates fewer cognitive inconsistencies for interval strategists than for point strategists (Eagly, 1969; Eagly & Telaak, 1972). Research on divergent and convergent thinking makes a similar point: That is, in deciding how to construct a "democrat-even-before-1989" identity, interval strategists will tend to engage in divergent processing rather than convergent processing. As a consequence, they have a greater likelihood of hitting on an adaptive solution compared with point strategists (Anderson & Cropley, 1966; Ibrahim, 1972; Martindale, 1976). In brief, when it comes to adroit shifts in self-categorization and self-presentation, interval strategists have an advantage over point strategists. More generally, we might speculate that because they easily resolve (i.e., find substitutes for) inconsistent beliefs, interval strategists change their mind incrementally whereas point strategists do so "catastrophically."

Besides resolving inconsistencies, an interval strategy may, by promoting substitution among ends, lead to an expectation that there are always "other options." A meta-cognitive belief of this kind could produce in interval strategists a mood whereby they discount short-term failures and persist doing *something* in the face of adversity. Put differently, early in the transition social change was rapid and chaotic; those pursuing an education, a career, or simply attempting to make a living (not to mention doing research) had repeated disappointments. Evidence suggests that despite these conditions a society can continue to carry on purposively when members think positively or optimistically about the future (Scheier & Carver, 1992; Seligman, 1991; Taylor, 1989).

Optimists anticipate that when a course of action is blocked they can always find an alternative that allows them to go in the same general direction. And, as we have argued here, a sufficient condition linking optimism and persevering in the face of frustration is the ease with which a person can substitute one goal for another. We at ISS are greatly indebted to Robert Zajonc for precisely this reason (among others, of course): giving us an alternative model for doing social research—not to mention his help and encouragement in attaining that model—at a time when our usual path was blocked.

References

Anderson, C. C., & Cropley, A. J. (1966). Some correlates of originality. *Australian Journal of Psychology, 11,* 284–294.

Apter, M. (1989). *Reversal theory: Motivation, emotion, and personality.* London: Routledge.

Atkinson, J. W., & Birch, D. (1970). *The dynamics of action.* New York: Wiley.

Beach, L. R. (1993). Broadening the definition of decision making: The role of prechoice screening of options. *Psychological Science, 4,* 215–220.

Caplan, R. D., Vinokur, A. D., Price, R. H., & van Ryn, M. (1989). Job seeking, reemployment, and mental health: A randomized field experiment in coping with job loss. *Journal of Applied Psychology, 74,* 759–767.

Cichomski, B., & Morawski, P. (1998). *Polski Generalny Sondaz Spoleczny, Skumulowany komputerowy zbiór danych 1992–1997* [Polish General Social Survey]. Warsaw, Poland: Wydawnictwa Instytute Studiów Spoteunych [Institute for Social Studies Press].

Eagly, A. H. (1969). Responses to attitude-discrepant information as a function of intolerance of inconsistency and category width. *Journal of Personality, 37,* 601–617.

Eagly, A. E., & Telaak, K. (1972). Width of the latitude of acceptance as a determinant of attitude change. *Journal of Personality and Social Psychology, 23,* 388–397.

Emmons, R. A. (1992). Abstract versus concrete goals: Personal striving level, physical illness, and psychological well-being. *Journal of Personality and Social Psychology, 62,* 292–300.

Grzelak, J. L. (1987). O bezradnosci spolecznej [On social helplessness]. In M. Marody & A.Sulek (Eds.), *Rzeczywistosc polska i sposoby radzenia sobie z nia* [Social ways of coping with the Polish reality] (pp. 243–266). Warsaw, Poland: Wydawnictwa Instytute Studiów Spoteunych [Institute for Social Studies Press].

Grzelak, J. L. (1993). Bezradnosc Spoleczna. Szkic teoretyczny [Social helplessness. A theoretical framework]. In M. Kofta (Ed.), *Psychologia aktywnosci: Zaangazowanie, sprawstwo i bezradnosc* [Psychology of activity: Commitment, agency and helplessness] (pp. 225–247). Poznan, Poland: Nakom.

Grzelak, J. L., & Czabala, C. (1996). Psychological aspects of economic and political transformation. In K. Cichocki & P. Marer (Eds.), *Education for transition to market economy in countries of Central and Eastern Europe* (pp. 98–105). Warsaw: Polish–U.S. Fulbright Commission.

Huntington, S. (1991). The third wave: Democratization in the late twentieth century. Norman: University of Oklahoma.

Ibrahim, A. (1976). Sex differences, originality, and personality response styles. *Psychological Reports, 39,* 859–868.

Lewin, K. (1938). *The conceptual representation, and the measurement of psychological forces.* Durham, NC: Duke University Press.

Martindale, C. (1972). Anxiety, intelligence, and access to primitive modes of thought in high and low scorers on The Remote Associates Test. *Perceptual and Motor Skills, 35,* 375–381.

Nowak, A., Zienkowski, L., & Urbaniak, K. (1994). Clustering processes in economic transition. *Research Bulletin RECESS,* 3, 43–61.

Pervin, L. W. L. (1989). *Goal concepts in personality and social psychology.* Hillsdale, NJ: Erlbaum.

Pettigrew, T. F. (1958). The measurement and correlates of category width as a cognitive variable. *Journal of Personality, 26,* 532–544.

Scheier, M. F., & Carver, C. S. (1992). Effects of optimism on psychological and physical well-being: Theoretical overview and empirical update. *Cognitive Therapy and Research, 16,* 201–228.

Seligman, M. E. P. (1991). *Learned optimism.* New York: Knopf.

Stewart, A. J. (1989). Social intelligence and adaptation to life changes. In R. S. Wyer & T. K. Srull (Eds.), *Advances in social cognition* (Vol. 2, pp. 187–196). Hillsdale, NJ: Erlbaum.

Taylor, S. E. (1989). *Positive illusions: Creative self-deception and the healthy mind.* New York: Basic Books.

Wieczorkowska, G. (1990). The range of perceived variability of object and its representation in cognitive structure. *Polish Psychological Bulletin, 2,* 320–328.

Wieczorkowska-Nejtardt, G. (1995). An interval cognitive–behavioral strategy can decrease the stimulative value of events. *Polish Psychological Bulletin, 4,* 353–366.

Wieczorkowska-Nejtardt, G. (1996). Wartosc adaptacyjna szerokich i waskich kategorii celu w okresie zmiany systemowej [The adaptive value of point and interval strategies during systemic transformation]. In M. Marody & E. Gucwa-Lesny (Eds.), *Podstawy zycia spolecznego* [The basis of social life], (pp. 274–287). Warsaw, Poland: Wydawnictwa Instytute Studiów Spoteunych [Institute for Social Studies Press].

Wieczorkowska-Nejtardt, G. (1998). *Inteligencja motywacyjna: Skuteczne strategie wyboru celu i sposobu dzialania* [Motivational intelligence: Smart strategies for choosing goals and ways of action]. Warsaw, Poland: Wydawnictwa Instytute Studiów Spoteunych [Institute for Social Studies Press].

Wieczorkowska, G., & Burnstein, E. (1993). *Cross-national studies on decision strategies* (Grant proposal funded by NATO). Warsaw, Poland: Warsaw University and University of Michigan.

Wieczorkowska, G., & Burnstein, E. (1999). Adapting to the transition from socialism to capitalism in Poland: The role of screening strategies in social change. *Psychological Science, 10,* 98–105.

Wieczorkowska-Siarkiewicz, G. (1992). *Punktowe i przedzialowe reprezentacje celu: Uwarunkowania i konsekwencje* [Point and interval goal representations: Determinants and consequences]. Warsaw, Poland: Psychology Press.

Conclusions

CHAPTER 12

The Art of Bob Zajonc and the Communicative Basis of Prejudice

Claude M. Steele

I confess. I learned a lot about the philosophy of science from *Zen and the Art of Motorcycle Maintenance* by Robert Pirsig (1974), a book that was all the rage in the early 1970s. This fact surely pegs me as a product of my times. During those times, I was struggling to become a scientist, and this book gave me a metaphor about the nature of science that allowed me to better see its possibilities. It described science as a long train of boxcars. The cars represent all the knowledge and techniques a scientist has to know, in this case, the principles of research design, statistics, measurement, the empirical facts, and theories that make up the state of the art in a field. These things extend scientists' access to phenomena under study, and if they do not extend the investigation beyond scientists' biases, they at least extend it beyond their full control. One of the main points of the book is that these boxcars do not direct the train. They may constrain where it can go, but they cannot set its direction.

Pirsig (1974) made the point that once a scientist has a circumscribed question to research and is working back in the boxcars, so to speak, one's activity and thought are fairly well guided—by the techniques, theories, rules, norms, and so on, that make up the boxcars. But the process by which a scientist gets to that question from a vague interest, or some breakpoint in the progression of a research area, is painfully unguided, every bit as much art as science.

In this unguided space of problem selection and formation, no two scientists are likely to make the same decision. It is a kind of "free-for-all" moment during which everything that one is and everything about one's experience comes to bear on what decision is made. Here, biography, idiosyncrasies, social experience, culture, and perspective all count. At this unguided point in the process, a woman might well take the train of science in a different direction than a man. A younger person might take it in a different direction than an older person. In this way, science is situated.

I do not believe that people always know when they are in the midst of such a moment. Perhaps most often it comes and goes with a great sense of ordinariness. "We did that study because it seemed like the best thing to do."

But over a career, one can see that some people have been artists at this moment. All scientists have their heroes in this regard: people who showed them how great the science could be and people who made the enterprise seem at first possible and then important. There is a set of such heroes who formed the contours of modern social psychology, names including Kurt Lewin, Leon Festinger, Solomon Asch, and Bob Zajonc. And Zajonc's work, perhaps more than the others', gives me the awareness that the choice of where the train goes can be a freeing moment in the scientific process, and that science can address the seemingly unaddressable.

Those who know Bob are aware that they cannot ask him about his philosophy of science or how he goes about his work. For someone who is a psychologist, a social psychologist at that, he is not given to self-reflection about his science.

So it is without his help or authorization that I try, in this chapter, to describe a number of regularities that I see in the way he directs his science train. I should note first that he has more boxcars in his train—more skills, more knowledge—than most of us, and like good fundamentals in any domain, this gives him a unique degree of flexibility.

But one of his regularities, I can remember, noting back was when I was in graduate school in the late 1960s. I had just read Zajonc's (1968) monograph in the *Journal of Personality and Social Psychology* on mere exposure and had the sense that it was a brilliant idea that came *out of nowhere*.

As with others, I take this as a hallmark of Bob's science: ideas that seem to come out of nowhere. They seem to come from a perspective outside the main confluence of the field. They were not unrelated to that confluence; they often revealed what had not been seen about it or redirected it entirely, but they did not seem directly derivable from it. I return to mere exposure as a prime example. From the set of theories and understandings about attitudes that existed at the time, the idea that mere exposure to something could enhance attraction to it seemed to have no prior staging. Yes, once the idea was formulated, one could point to precedents, in the practice of advertising and in associationism. But the idea did not come from the dominant attitude paradigms of the day. Now I know of course that Bob Zajonc enjoys a certain oppositional relation to the mainstream of the field—working and thinking around the corner from what is generally understood and what can be derived from what is understood—as in mere exposure, the confluence model, and the primacy of affect in a time of cognitive domination.

Zajonc is also an aesthetic about ideas; he wants them to make music, as he says, to excite pleasure. He would hate, above all else, to bore. The idea itself has to please and attract. I remember reading that most great scientists all shared a particular strategy: Whether by luck or intention, they tended to start their work by picking important problems to work on. I would not say that Bob Zajonc works this way. He is not blind to the importance of the problems he works on, but I see him directed as much by the motive to have a beautiful idea, an idea that in its own right provokes and excites. If it is on something topically important, all the better. But his first interest is that it excites and pleases.

And then there is Zajonc's love of risk: predicting the level of SAT scores 25 years hence (Zajonc, 1986); claiming mere exposure is sufficient for attraction (Zajonc, 1968; Saegert, Swap, & Zajonc, 1973); that affect has primacy over cognition (Zajonc, 1984); that faces of married couples will grow more similar with time (Zajonc, Adelmann, Murphy, & Niedenthal, 1987). He does not let what is fundable drive his ideas. It seems to make the work of research more enjoyable. And as one who has had the good fortune of being a colleague of his in recent years, I can attest that it affects the culture around him. It puts one in the frame of mind of thinking more about where the train can go.

With the exception of one recent line of research that I describe later in the chapter, my own research cannot lay claim to direct lineage from Bob's. But beyond his being such a distinctive model of a scientist, I do feel several, substantive influences.

First is his interest in collective processes and their effect on the individual. I remember having a Group Dynamics retreat in Dick Nisbett's living room several years ago in which we were searching for a theme that would unify our research focus, give us a distinctive, not to mention lucrative, identity—the beast of funding prospects always sat quietly offstage. We floundered about. Eventually, Bob produced a galvanizing idea: That we should focus on the effect of the collective on the individual. His interest in this area went back to his dissertation on cognitive tuning and communication. And now, in that context, with a then beginning interest in culture, in stereotypes, and in the effect of stereotypes on people, with the role of social structure and race in mediating psychological outcomes, it gave us a cohering direction in which to take the train. Many of us in that room have been on that train ever since.

Another broad, stage-setting influence of Bob's from which I have greatly benefited is that he kept the field warm when it threatened to be too cold. He was among the first social cognitive psychologists. But as the field grew more exclusively cognitive, he embodied a compelling commitment to heat, to affect, to the unconscious. It gave the field depth and kept a variety of positions before us. If Bob Zajonc can afford affect and motivation such psychological status, then there is room for these things in this field.

But recently a student, Julio Garcia, and I got a direct idea from Bob's work. Bob had given a Katz–Newcomb talk on communication and circulated a paper on "Cognition, Communication, Consciousness: A Social Psychological Perspective" (Zajonc, 1992). Its roots, of course, went back to his dissertation on cognitive tuning, in which he manipulated whether people who heard a persuasive message were "tuned" to "transmit" the message to someone else or simply to "receive" it. He found that transmitters imposed greater organization on the material and were, accordingly, more resistant to persuasion.

This paper stressed the distinct role that communication itself plays in the construction of cognition and representations and that the process of constructing cognition through communication was often an "outside-the-head" process not rooted in, or even reflective of, internal beliefs and knowledge structures. Zajonc gave a memorable example of asking his roommate to describe a spoon that lay on the table between them. Here is how he described the incident:

> I don't know what possessed me to ask Joe how he liked that little ugly spoon. He said it was awful. So I asked him if he could tell me something specific about the teaspoon. . . . He started with some mundane features—shape, metal, design, function. It soon became apparent that he could go on and on. So we went to my room. I got a small writing pad and asked him to start all over again, writing down each thing on a separate piece of paper.
>
> He went on to put down minute details of the design, wrote how this spoon differed from all other spoons, about a bird called spoon bill, pointed at blemishes and scratches, invented incredible functions, explained why the spoon was not magnetic, wrote that the plural of spoon was spoons, and spelled backward it made snoops, said that the spoon was different from a bucket (a bucket could be seen in the kitchen), because you could eat a soft-boiled egg with a spoon but not with a bucket.
>
> He went on and on . . . until about 4:00 in the morning. He filled 3 writing pads, each having 200 sheets. . . .
>
> The session with Joe . . . made two conclusions inescapable. First it became obvious to me that nowhere in Joe's head was there an orderly LIST of characteristics sitting and waiting for access and retrieval. Joe was not retrieving anything from his head that was organized around some core category, THE SPOON. He was constructing a picture of the spoon, with a theory of a spoon, its probable history, ethnography, chemistry, atomic structure, commercial and industrial origin, aesthetic qualities, and so on and on and on. And he was doing it as he was going along. Of course, there was something in Joe's head. But that something was not a bunch of representations each standing for a different feature, all waiting their turn to be put down on the writing pad.
>
> A second conclusion was obvious: Joe was not just spewing these features of the spoon—he was giving them to me! I doubt very much that he would have given the same picture of that spoon to another person or even to me on another occasion. I, the experimenter, was an important modulator of what came out of Joe's head. (Zajonc, 1992)

In the act of communicating to Zajonc, using various theories about the spoon, Joe could construct things to say about it that went beyond what he knew about it. Communication—the act fundamental to collective functioning—had an agency of its own, an "outside the head" agency to construct cognitions, ideas, and representations, that were not in the heads of either participant. Like many of Zajonc's ideas, this one was tantalizing and had claimed a lot.

Julio and I wondered if it might have something to do with the unconscious and unintentional use of stereotypes. The idea is simple: Perhaps stereotypes influence a person's judgments of others because they get inadvertently used in the process of constructing communication—much like generating features of a spoon. Moreover, their use in this way may reflect nothing distinctive about the knowledge and belief structures of the individuals involved. People who are low in prejudice might be just as likely to generate and use stereotypes in the act of constructing communication as people who are higher in prejudice.

We designed a simple experiment (Garcia, Steele, & Sherman, 2000). Participants read a brief vignette about a fifth-grade boy that was filled with nondiagnostic information about this boy's life in his neighborhood, his love for riding his bike, that he had older married sisters and an uncle, and so forth. For half of the participants, a cue was implanted in the information that could prime the use of a racial stereotype. He was described as a member of the African Methodist church choir. For the other half of the participants, this cue was absent. In the second paragraph of the vignette, the boy was described as someone who, though a good student, sometimes got into conflict with another student, and the vignette ends with the two of them caught in a fracas at the back of the classroom.

Participants were then led to expect that they would either have to communicate with another subject about this vignette or that they would simply have to answer a few questions about it. Note that this manipulation is the "tuning" manipulation Bob used in his dissertation research—the project that came from his night-long conversation with Joe.

Julio and I reasoned that this tuning manipulation would help us get at the effect of communication, or at least the set to communicate, on stereotype usage. Expecting to communicate with another participant should induce participants to construct a narrative of the vignette and, in doing this, they should be more influenced by the stereotype cue in interpreting the vignette. This in turn should lead them to make harsher judgments of the boy in the vignette than would participants who did not expect to communicate, and thus did not have to form a narrative of the vignette's events.

The study took the form of a 2 × 2 design. Participants were either exposed or not exposed to a cue in the vignette that could prime stereotype usage, and they either expected or did not expect to communicate about the vignette. Our primary dependent measure was how culpable participants judged the protagonist to be for the classroom fracas described in the vignette. We expected participants exposed to the stereotype cue to make harsher judgments than those not exposed to this cue. But we also expected this effect to be significantly augmented among participants who were tuned to communicate about the vignette. Figure 12.1 reveals what happened.

Most of our expectations were born out. It was not the case that merely being exposed to the stereotype cue fostered harsher culpability judgments. Perhaps our participants, many of whom were relatively low in prejudice (as measured by the

FIGURE 12.1

Study 1: Mean Judgment of Target's Culpability by Condition (+ SE). Stereotype Communication (N= 15), Stereotype Non Communication (N= 14), Non Stereotype Communication (N= 15), Non Stereotype Non Communication (N= 16).

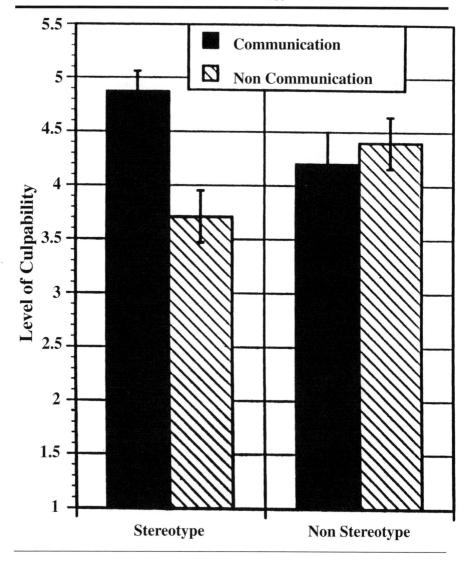

Modern Racism Scale), were able to somehow inhibit the effect of this cue. But in the communication-set condition, this cue did foster harsher culpability judgments.

However, there is an alternative interpretation of this effect. Perhaps the communication-set condition augmented stereotype usage not by fostering its incorporation in a narrative, but by providing an extra "cognitive load" or "busyness" that, by distracting participants, allowed the activated stereotype to have more effect.

In Study 2, we replicated Study 1 except for two things: (a) We included only participants who were below the subject pool median in prejudice (as measured by the Modern Racism Scale), and (b) we included an extra condition in which participants were told that they would be communicating with another participant, but this time about how well the vignette was written rather than about its content. This instruction, we felt, would impose on participants a cognitive load comparable with that experienced in the regular communication-set condition except that it would not lead, or even allow, participants to develop a narrative of the vignette story. If the communication-set condition of Study 1 fostered harsher judgments through the extra cognitive load it imposed, then this condition too should foster harsher judgments. But if the communication-set condition had its effect by fostering use of the stereotype in developing a narrative, then this writing-set condition should have no effect on culpability judgments. Figure 12.2 reveals the results.

It can be seen from Figure 12.2 that expecting to communicate about the content of the vignette fostered harsher culpability judgments. This establishes the reliability of this effect observed in Study 1 and shows that it can occur even in participants very low in prejudice. The figure also shows that expecting to communicate about the writing quality of the vignette had no effect on culpability judgments. These results, then, offer evidence that the communication-set manipulation did not have its effect through the cognitive load it imposed.

A third study pursued more direct evidence of the hypothesized mediating process. If the communication-set manipulation led to harsher culpability judgments by fostering a narrative that allowed the stereotype cue to have greater influence, then the stereotype should be more cognitively activated in this condition than in the condition that included the stereotype cue but not the communication set. To test this, we replicated the basic design and procedures used in Study 1, except that this time, just before participants expected to complete the culpability judgments, we asked them to complete a measure of stereotype activation. On this measure, participants completed 75 word fragments in which two letters were missing. Embedded in this list were 12 fragments that we knew from pretesting could be completed with words related to negative stereotypes about African Americans. We also used only participants low in prejudice. If the combination of being exposed to the stereotype cue and expecting to communicate about the vignette fostered greater use of negative African American stereotypes, then participants in this condition, more than in any of the others conditions, should show the greatest activation of the stereotype.

As the results in Figure 12.3 depict, this is precisely what happened. Although it is clear that merely being exposed to the stereotype cue in this vignette is enough to significantly activate racial stereotypes in low-prejudiced participants, it is also clear that merely preparing to communicate about the vignette is enough to signifi-

FIGURE 12.2

Study 2: Mean Judgment of Target's Culpability by Condition (+ SE). Stereotype Communication (N= 10), Stereotype Non Communication (N= 10), Non Stereotype Communication (N= 7), Non Stereotype Non Communication (N= 9), Stereotype Writing Communication (N= 12).

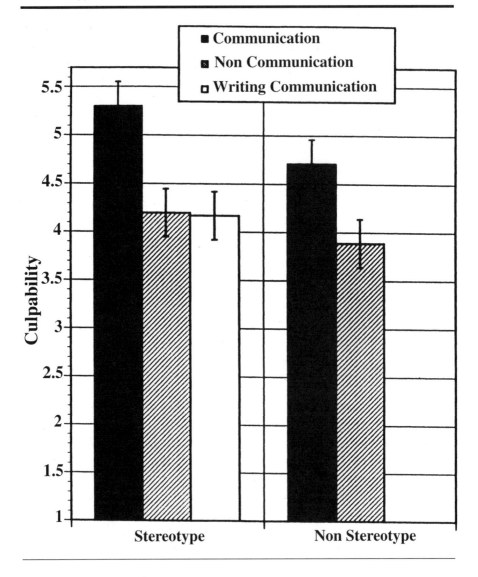

cantly augment this activation—an effect that clearly goes beyond anything implied by the internal attitudes, beliefs, and knowledge structures of these participants. It is an effect—anticipated by Zajonc's reasoning on communication—that arises from

FIGURE 12.3

Study 3: Mean Level of Stereotype Activation by Condition (+ SE). Stereotype Communication (N= 13), Stereotype Non Communication (N= 13), Non Stereotype Communication (N= 14), Non Stereotype Non Communication (N= 8).

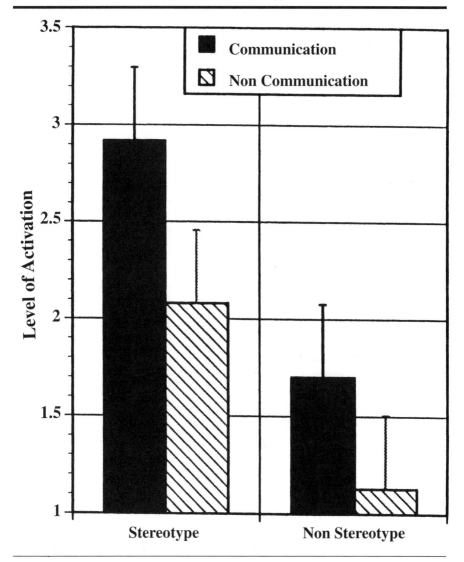

the first step in the communication process. It suggests that communication has a constructive agency that goes beyond the "inside-the-head" representations and beliefs of the individual. It is an agency that derives from the transaction of the person with his or her context. In these data, it is especially clear that the source or agency of the prejudice is not inside the person but derives from the communicative interaction of the person with his or her immediate context. That much seems to be true, and that much opens up new theoretical and practical directions for the understanding of prejudice and stereotyping.

I described this work and the chain of ideas that led to it in this chapter to bring to light a less emphasized theme in Zajonc's work, going back to his beginnings. I highly recommend his Katz–Newcomb paper (Zajonc, 1992). I have described only a small portion of its arguments, which extend to a reconceptualization of cognitive psychology and social psychology's relation to it. It is a corner of Zajonc's oeuvre that has received less attention but that I believe has important implications for social psychology.

I also describe this work to illustrate the unguided nature of the idea process, whether it is Zajonc's roommate never running out of communicative associations about a spoon or a graduate student seeing the implications of this for how prejudice can work. It shows how chance events, intellectual acumen, personal background and perspective, and capacity for insight—just like in art—combine in some unguided, if not random, way to drive the science train. The action at the front of the train is itself a collective force.

And among the careers that have formed this force in social psychology, Zajonc's career, to me, distinctively illustrates this artistic part of science and the courage it takes to do it well. He has been almost uniquely willing to take risks—a wise, brilliant, daredevil that we in the field have watched with a sense of anticipation about what will happen. And in defiance of the odds, his feats have paid off time and time again. If social psychology were popular music, Bob Zajonc would have more hits than anybody in its history.

One way of gauging a career is to do the *It's a Wonderful Life* test. Remember that the technique of that movie was to take Jimmy Stewart back through his life and show him what would have happened had he not been there. He finds a much sadder, corrupt, dispirited place than the one he knows. The town had fallen under the control of the evil Mr. Potter and had, without the counterinfluence of Jimmy Stewart's good-heartedness, become a ruthless place—a place in which neighbor turned against neighbor, the woman he married lived out her days as a lonely spinster, and the loving mother he knew was a bitter woman.

Now in fairness to the rest of us, I do not believe social psychology would have been quite this bad without Bob. But my point is clear. It would not be the place it is today. It would not have the prestige and value it has. It would lack major lines of thought that give the field depth, excitement, and promise. Many of the people who are important contributors to the field, lacking the modeling and inspiration of his work, would not be in the field. It would be a lesser place. As John Coltrane said once in answer to some complex question about his artistic vision, "Look man, I just want to be a good force." We of this *Festschrift* thank Bob for being that kind of force in our lives and in the life of this science.

References

Garcia, J., Steele, C. M., & Sherman, D. A. (2000). Social communication and stereotype use. Unpublished manuscript, Tufts University.

Pirsig, R. (1974). *Zen and the art of motorcycle maintenance.* New York: William Morrow.

Saegert, S., Swap, W., & Zajonc, R. B. (1973). Exposure, context, and interpersonal attraction. *Journal of Personality and Social Psychology, 25,* 234–242.

Zajonc, R. B. (1968). Attitudinal effects of mere exposure. *Journal of Personality and Social Psychology Monograph Supplement, 9,* 1–27.

Zajonc, R. B. (1984). On the primacy of affect. *American Psychologist, 39,* 117–123.

Zajonc, R. B. (1986). The decline and rise of scholastic aptitude scores: A prediction derived from the confluence model. *American Psychologist, 41,* 862–867.

Zajonc, R. B. (1992, April). *Cognition, communication, consciousness: A social psychological perspective.* Paper presented at the 20th Katz–Newcomb lecture, University of Michigan, Ann Arbor.

Zajonc, R. B., Adelmann, P. K., Murphy, S. T., & Niedenthal, P. M. (1987). Convergence in the physical appearance of spouses. *Motivation & Emotion, 11,* 335–346.

Appendix

The Publications of Robert B. Zajonc

Zajonc, R. B. (1952). Aggressive attitudes of the stranger as a function of conformity pressures. *Human Relations, 5,* 205–216.

Zajonc, R. B. (1954). Some effects of "space" serials. *Public Opinion Quarterly, 18,* 367–374.

Zajonc, R. B. (1956). Method in social science. *Contemporary Psychology, 5,* 137–139.

French, J. R. P. Jr., & Zajonc, R. B. (1957). An experimental study of cross-cultural norm conflict. *Journal of Abnormal Social Psychology, 54,* 218–224.

Zajonc, R. B. (1957). Psychology in Poland. *American Psychologist, 12,* 730–733.

Zajonc, R. B. (1959). Myriads of memory experiments. *Contemporary Psychology, 4,* 150–152.

Zajonc, R. B., & Burnstein, E. (1959). Apparatus for recording orienting responses. *American Journal of Psychology, 72,* 271–274.

Zajonc, R. B., & Smoke, W. (1959). Redundancy in task assignments and group performance. *Psychometrika, 24,* 361–370.

Zajonc, R. B. (1960). The concepts of balance, congruity, and dissonance. *Public Opinion Quarterly, 24,* 380–396.

Zajonc, R. B. (1960). The process of cognitive tuning in communication. *Journal of Abnormal Social Psychology, 61,* 159–168.

Zajonc, R. B., & Morrissette, J. (1960). Cognitive behavior under uncertainty and ambiguity. *Psychological Reports, 6,* 31–36.

Zajonc, R. B., & Morrissette, J. (1960). The role of uncertainty in cognitive change. *Journal of Abnormal Social Psychology, 61,* 168–176.

Zajonc, R. B., & Burnstein, E. (1961). The resolution of cognitive conflict under uncertainty. *Human Relations, 14,* 113–119.

Zajonc, R. B., & Wahi, K. (1961). Conformity and need achievement under cross-cultural norm conflict. *Human Relations, 14,* 241–250.

Smoke, W., & Zajonc, R. B. (1962). On the reliability of group judgments and decisions. In J. Criswell, H. Solomon, & P. Suppes (Eds.), *Mathematic methods in small group processes* (pp. 322–333). Stanford, CA: Stanford University Press.

Zajonc, R. B. (1962). The effects of feedback and probability of group success on individual performance. *Human Relations, 15,* 149–163.

Zajonc, R. B. (1962). *Methods in small group processes* (pp. 322–333). Stanford, CA: Stanford University Press.

Zajonc, R. B. (1962). A note on group judgments and group size. *Human Relations, 15,* 177–180.

Zajonc, R. B. (1962). A note on Mooney's "Perception as related to military problems." In F. A. Geldard (Ed.), *Defense psychology* (Vol. I, pp. 272–274). New York: Pergamon Press.

Zajonc, R. B. (1962). Response suppression in perceptual defense. *Journal of Experimental Psychology, 64,* 206–214.

Zajonc, R. B., & Burnstein, E. (1962). A reply to Dr. Jordan's comments. *Human Relations, 15,* 280.

Zajonc, R. B., & Smoke, W. (1962). Optimal task assignments for group performance. In N. F. Washburne (Ed.), *Decisions, values, and groups* (pp. 279–290). New York: Macmillan.

Zajonc, R. B., & Dorfman, D. D. (1963). Some effects of sound, background, brightness, and economic status on the perceived size of coins and discs. *Journal of Abnormal Social Psychology, 66,* 87–90.

Zajonc, R. B., & Taylor, J. (1963). The effects two methods of varying group task difficulty on individual and group performance. *Human Relations, 16,* 359–368.

Zajonc, R. B., & Dorfman, D. D. (1964). Perception, drive, and behavior theory. *Psychological Review, 71,* 273–290.

Zajonc, R. B., & Nieuwenhuyse, B. (1964). Relationship between word frequency and recognition: Perceptual process or response bias? *Journal of Experimental Psychology, 67,* 276–285.

Burnstein, E., & Zajonc, R. B. (1965). The effect of group success on the reduction of status incongruence in task-oriented groups. *Sociometry, 28,* 349–362.

Burnstein, E., & Zajonc, R. B. (1965). Individual task performance in a changing social structure. *Sociometry, 28,* 16–29.

French, J. R. P. Jr., & Zajonc, R. B. (1965). Eine experimentelle Studie des interkulturellen Normkonflikts. In H. Thomae (Ed.), *Die Motivation menschlichen Handelns.* Cologne: Kiepenheuer & Witsch.

Zajonc, R. B. (1965). The requirements and design of a standard group task. *Journal of Experimental Social Psychology, 1,* 71–88.

Zajonc, R. B. (1965). Social facilitation. *Science, 149,* 269–274.

Zajonc, R. B., & Burnstein, E. (1965). The learning of balanced and unbalanced social structures. *Journal of Personality, 33,* 153–163.

Zajonc, R. B., & Burnstein, E. (1965). Structural balance, reciprocity, and positivity as sources of cognitive bias. *Journal of Personality, 33,* 570–583.

Zajonc, R. B., & Cross, D. V. (1965). Stimulus generalization as a function of drive shift. *Journal of Experimental Psychology, 69,* 363–368.

Zajonc, R. B. (1966). *Social psychology: An experimental approach.* Belmont, CA: Wadsworth. Translated into French by Y. Noizet as *Psychologie sociale experimentale,* and published by Dunod, Paris, 1967. Translated into Spanish by I. Acarreta as *La psicologia social: Estudios experimentales,* and published by Marfil, S. A., Alcoy (Spain), 1967. Translated into Swedish by Monica Aberg-Johansson as *Experimentell Socialpsykologi,* and published by Wahlstrom Widstrant, Stockholm, 1968.

Zajonc, R. B., & Sales, S. (1966). Social facilitation of dominant and subordinate responses. *Journal of Experimental Social Psychology, 2,* 160–168.

Zajonc, R. B., & Wolfe, D. M. (1966). Cognitive consequences of a person's position in a formal organization. *Human Relations, 19,* 139–150.

van Kreveld, D., & Zajonc, R. B. (1966). The learning of influence structures. *Journal of Personality, 34,* 205–223.

Siegel, S., & Zajonc, R. B. (1967). Group risk-taking in professional decisions. *Sociometry, 30,* 339–349.

Zajonc, R. B., & Marin, I. C. (1967). Cooperation, competition, and interpersonal attitudes in small groups. *Psychonomic Science, 7,* 271–272.

Zajonc, R. B., & Sherman, S. J. (1967). Structural balance and the induction of relations. *Journal of Personality, 35,* 635–650.

Zajonc, R. B. (1968). Attitudinal effects of mere exposure. *Journal of Personality and Social Psychology, Monograph Supplement, 9,* 1–27.

Zajonc, R. B. (1968). Cognitive theories in social psychology. In G. Lindzey & E. Aronson (Eds.), *Handbook of social psychology* (319–411). New York: Random House.

Zajonc, R. B. (1968). Conformity. In *International encyclopedia of the social sciences* (pp. 253–260). New York: Crowell-Collier.

Zajonc, R. B. (1968). Social facilitation in the cockroach. In E. C. Simmel, R. A. Hoppe, & G. A. Milton (Eds.), *Social facilitation and imitative behavior* (pp. 73–87). Boston: Allyn & Bacon.

Zajonc, R. B. (1968). Thinking: II. Cognitive organization and process. In *International encyclopedia of the social sciences* (pp. 615–622). New York: Crowell-Collier.

Matlin, M., & Zajonc, R. B. (1968). Social facilitation of word associations. *Journal of Personality and Social Psychology, 10,* 455–460.

Rubin, Z., & Zajonc, R. B. (1969). Structural bias and generalization in the learning of social structures. *Journal of Personality, 37,* 310–324.

Zajonc, R. B. (1969). *Animal social psychology.* New York: Wiley.

Zajonc, R. B., & Brickman, P. (1969). Expectancy and feedback as independent factors in task performance. *Journal of Personality and Social Psychology, 11,* 148–156.

Zajonc, R. B., Heingartner, A., & Herman, E. M. (1969). Social enhancement and impairment of performance in the cockroach. *Journal of Personality and Social Psychology, 13,* 83–92.

Zajonc, R. B., & Rajecki, D. W. (1969). Exposure and affect: A field experiment. *Psychonomic Science, 17,* 216–217.

Zajonc, R. B., Wolosin, R. J., & Sherman, S. J. (1969). Group risk taking in a two-choice situation: Replication, extension, and a model. *Journal of Experimental Social Psychology, 5,* 127–140.

Harrison, A. A., & Zajonc, R. B. (1970). The effects of frequency and duration of exposure on response competition and affective ratings. *Journal of Psychology, 75,* 163–169.

Zajonc, R. B. (1970). Brainwash: Familiarity breeds comfort. *Psychology Today, 3,* 32–35, 60–62.

Zajonc, R. B., Wolosin, M. R. J., Wolosin, M. A., & Loh, W. D. (1970). Social facilitation and imitation in group risk-taking. *Journal of Experimental Social Psychology, 6,* 26–46.

Zajonc, R. B. (1971). *Animal social behavior*. Morristown, NJ: General Learning Press.

Zajonc, R. B. (1971). Attraction, affiliation, and attachment. In J. F. Eisenberg & W. Dillon (Eds.), *Man and beast: Comparative social behavior* (pp. 142–179). Washington, DC: Smithsonian Institution Press.

Zajonc, R. B., Swap, W. C., Harrison, A. A., & Roberts, P. (1971). Limiting conditions of the exposure effect: Satiation and relativity. *Journal of Personality and Social Psychology, 18*, 384–391.

Zajonc, R. B. (1972). Some empirical and theoretical continuities in the social behavior of animals and men. In R. Chauvin (Ed.), *Modeles animaux du comportement humain* (Colloques internationaux du C.N.R.S. 198, pp. 303–342). Paris: Editions Centre National de la Recherche Scientifique.

Zajonc, R. B., Shaver, P., Tavris, C., & van Kreveld, D. (1972). Exposure, satiation, and stimulus discriminability. *Journal of Personality and Social Psychology, 21*, 270–280.

Zajonc, R. B., Wolosin, R. J., & Wolosin, M. A. (1972). Group risk-taking under various group decision schemes. *Journal of Experimental Social Psychology, 8*, 16–30.

Saegert, S. C., Swap, W., & Zajonc, R. B. (1973). Exposure, context, and interpersonal attraction. *Journal of Personality and Social Psychology, 25*, 234–242.

Zajonc, R. B., Reimer, D. J., & Hausser, D. (1973). Imprinting and the development of object preference in chicks by mere repeated exposure. *Journal of Comparative Physiological Psychology, 83*, 434–440.

Zajonc, R. B., Crandall, R., Kail, R. V., Jr., & Swap, W. (1974). Effect of extreme exposure frequencies on different affective ratings of stimulus. *Perceptual and Motor Skills, 38*, 667–678.

Zajonc, R. B., Wilson, W. R., & Markus, H. (1974). Exposure, object preference, and distress in the domestic chick. *Journal of Comparative and Physiological Psychology*, 581–585.

Zajonc, R. B., Markus, H., & Wilson, W. R. (1974). Exposure effects and associative learning. *Journal of Experimental Social Psychology, 10*, 248–263.

Zajonc, R. B. (1975, January). Dumber by the dozen. *Psychology Today*, pp. 37–43.

Zajonc, R. B., & Markus, G. B. (1975). Birth order and intellectual development. *Psychological Review, 82*, 74–88.

Zajonc, R. B., Wilson, W. R., & Rajecki, D. W. (1975). Affiliation and social discrimination produced by brief exposure in day-old chicks. *Animal Behavior, 23,* 131–138.

Moreland, R. L., & Zajonc, R. B. (1976). A strong text of exposure effects. *Journal of Experimental Social Psychology, 12,* 170–179.

Zajonc, R. B. (1976). Falling SAT's and rising reading scores. *Economic Outlook USA, 3,* 62–63.

Zajonc, R. B. (1976). Family configuration and intelligence. *Science, 192,* 227–236.

Markus, G. B., & Zajonc, R. B. (1977). Family configuration and intellectual development: A simulation. *Behavioral Science, 22,* 137–142.

Moreland, R. L., & Zajonc, R. B. (1977). Is stimulus recognition a necessary condition for the occurrence of exposure effects? *Journal of Personality and Social Psychology, 35,* 191–199.

Moreland, R. L., & Zajonc, R. B. (1979). Exposure effects may not depend on stimulus recognition. *Journal of Personality and Social Psychology, 37,* 1085–1089.

Zajonc, R. B., Markus, H., & Markus, G. B. (1979). The birth order puzzle. *Journal of Personality and Social Psychology, 37,* 1325–1341.

Kunst-Wilson, W. R., & Zajonc, R. B. (1980). Affective discrimination of stimuli that cannot be recognized. *Science, 207,* 557–558.

Zajonc, R. B. (1980). Cognition and social cognition: A historical perspective. In L. Festinger (Ed.), *Four decades of social psychology* (pp. 180–204). New York: Oxford University Press.

Zajonc, R. B. (1980). Compresence. In P. P. Paulus (Ed.), *Psychology of group influence* (pp. 35–60). Hillsdale, NJ: Erlbaum.

Zajonc, R. B. (1980). Feeling and thinking: Preferences need no inferences. *American Psychologist, 35,* 151–175.

Zajonc, R. B., & Bargh, J. (1980). Birth order, family size, and decline of SAT scores. *American Psychologist, 35,* 662–668.

Zajonc, R. B., & Bargh, J. (1980). The confluence model: Parameter estimation for six different data sets on family factors and intelligence. *Intelligence, 4,* 349–361.

Zajonc, R. B., Berbaum, M., Hamill, R., Moreland, R. L., & Akeju, S. A. (1980). Family factors and the intellectual performance of Nigerian eleven-year olds. *The West African Journal of Educational and Vocational Measurement, 5,* 19–26.

Zajonc, R. B. (1981). A one-factor mind about mind and emotion. *American Psychologist, 36*, 102–103.

Zajonc, R. B. (1981). Soziale Aktivierung. In W. Stroebe (Ed.), *Sozialpsychogie* (Vol. 2, 227–246). Darmstadt: Wissenschaftliche Buchengesellschaft.

Berbaum, M., Markus, G. B., & Zajonc, R. B. (1982). A closer look at Galbraith's closer look. *Developmental Psychology, 18*, 174–180.

Moreland, R. L., & Zajonc, R. B. (1982). Exposure effects in person perception: Familiarity, similarity, and attraction. *Journal of Experimental Social Psychology, 18*, 395–415.

Zajonc, R. B. (1982). Altruism, envy, competitiveness, and the common good. In V. Derlega & J. Grzelak (Eds.), *Cooperation and helping behavior: Theories and research* (pp. 417–437). New York: Academic Press.

Zajonc, R. B., & Markus, H. (1982). Affective and cognitive factors in preferences. *Journal of Consumer Research, 9*, 123–131.

Zajonc, R. B., Pietromonaco, P., & Bargh, J. (1982). Independence and interaction of affect and cognition. In M. S. Clark & S. T. Fiske (Eds.), *Affect and cognition: The Seventeenth Annual Carnegie Symposium on Cognition* (pp. 211–227). Hillsdale, NJ: Erlbaum.

Bootzin, R. R., Loftus, E. F., & Zajonc, R. B. (1983). *Psychology today*. New York: Random House.

Zajonc, R. B. (1983). Validating the confluence model. *Psychological Bulletin, 93*, 457–480.

Izard, C. E., Kagan, J., & Zajonc, R. B. (Eds.). (1984). *Emotions, cognition, and behavior*. New York: Cambridge University Press.

Zajonc, R. B. (1984). On the primacy of affect. *American Psychologist, 39*, 117–124.

Zajonc, R. B., & Markus, H. (1984). Affect and cognition: The hard interface. In C. E. Izard, J. Kagan, & R. B. Zajonc (Eds.), *Emotions, cognition, and behavior* (pp. 73–102). New York: Cambridge University Press.

Markus, H., & Zajonc, R. B. (1985). The cognitive perspective in social psychology. In G. Lindzey & E. Aronson (Eds.), *Handbook of social psychology* (pp. 137–230). New York: Random House.

Zajonc, R. B. (1985). Emotion and facial efference: A theory reclaimed. *Science, 228*, 15–21.

Zajonc, R. B. (1985). Emotion and facial expression. *Science, 230*, 608–687.

Zajonc, R. B. (1985). Uczucia a myslenie: Nie trzeba sie domyslac, by wiedziec, co sie woli. *Przeglad Psychologiczny, 28*, 27–72.

Zajonc, R. B., & Markus, H. (1985). Must all affect be mediated by cognition? *Journal of Consumer Research, 12*, 363–364.

Berbaum, M. L., Moreland, R. L., & Zajonc, R. B. (1986). Contentions over the confluence model: A reply to Price Walsh and Vilburg. *Psychological Bulletin, 100*, 270–274.

Bootzin, R. R., Bower, G. H., Zajonc, R. B., & Hall, E. (1986). *Psychology today* (6th ed.). New York: Random House.

Zajonc, R. B. (1986). Basic mechanisms of preference formation. In R. A. Peterson, W. D. Hoyer, & W. R. Wilson (Eds.), *The role of affect in consumer behavior: Emerging theories and applications* (pp. 1–16). Lexington, MA: Lexington Books.

Zajonc, R. B. (1986). The decline and rise of scholastic aptitude scores. *American Psychologist, 41*, 862–867.

Zajonc, R. B. (1986). Family factors and intellectual test performance: A reply to Steelman. *Review of Educational Research, 56*, 365–371.

Zajonc, R. B. (1986). La confluence du development intellectuel dans la famille, et sa resonance nationale. *Bulletin de Psychologie, 39*, 259–266.

Bower, G. H., Bootzin, R. R., Zajonc, R. B., & Hall, E. (1987). *Principles of psychology today*. New York: Random House.

Zajonc, R. B., & Adelmann, P. K. (1987). Cognition and communication: A story of missed opportunities. *Social Science Information, 26*, 3–30.

Zajonc, R. B., Adelmann, P. K., Murphy, S. T., & Niedenthal, P. M. (1987). Convergence in the physical appearance of spouses. *Motivation and Emotion, 11*, 335–346.

Zajonc, R. B. (1988). Comment on interpersonal affiliation and the golden section. *Journal of Social and Biological Structures, 10*, 212–214.

Zajonc, R. B. (1988). Prologomena for the study of access to mental events: Notes on Singer's chapter. In M. J. Horowitz (Ed.), *Psychodynamics and cognition* (pp. 347–359). Chicago: University of Chicago Press.

Adelmann, P. K., & Zajonc, R. B. (1989). Facial efference and the experience of emotion. *Annual Review of Psychology, 40*, 249–280.

Zajonc, R. B. (1989). Bischofs gefühlvolle Verwirrungen über die Gefüble. *Psychologi-sche Rundschau, 40*, 218–221.

Zajonc, R. B. (1989). Styles of explanation in social psychology. *European Journal of Social Psychology, 19*, 345–368.

Zajonc, R. B., Murphy, S. T., & Inglehart, M. (1989). Feeling and facial efference: Implications of the vascular theory of emotion. *Psychological Review, 96*, 395–416.

Zajonc, R. B. (1990). Leon Festinger (1919–1989). *American Psychologist, 45*, 661–662.

Berridge, K. C., & Zajonc, R. B. (1991). Hypothalamic cooling elicits eating: Differen-tial effects on motivation and pleasure. *Psychological Science, 2*, 184–189.

Zajonc, R. B., Markus, G. B., Berbaum, M. L., Bargh, J. A., & Moreland, R. L. (1991). One justified criticism plus three flawed analyses equals two unwarranted con-clusions: A reply to Retherford and Sewell. *American Sociological Review, 56*, 159–165.

McIntosh, D. N., & Zajonc, R. B. (1992). Emotions research: Some promising questions and some questionable promises. *Psychological Science, 3*, 70–74.

Murphy, S. T., & Zajonc, R. B. (1993). Affect, cognition, and awareness: Affective priming with optimal and suboptimal stimulus exposures. *Journal of Personality and Social Psychology, 64*, 723–739.

Zajonc, R. B. (1993). The confluence model: Differential or difference equation. *European Journal of Psychology, 23*, 211–215.

Zajonc, R. B. (1993). Emotional expression and temperature modulation. In S. vanGoozen (Ed.), *Emotion: Essays on emotion theory* (pp. 3–27). Hillsdale, NJ: Erlbaum.

Zajonc, R. B., Murphy, S. T., & McIntosh, D. N. (1993). Brain temperature and subjective emotional experience. In M. Lewis & J. M. Haviland (Eds.), *Handbook of emotions* (pp. 209–220). New York: Guilford Press.

McIntosh, D. N., Druckman, D., & Zajonc, R. B. (1994). Socially-induced affect. In D. Druckman & R. A. Bjork (Eds.), *Learning, remembering, believing: Enhancing human performance* (pp. 251–276). Washington, DC: National Academy Press.

Murphy, S., & Zajonc, R. B. (1994). Afekt, poznanie i swiadomosc: rola afektywnych bodzcow poprzedzajacych przy optymalnych is suboptymalnych ekspozycjach. *Przeglad Psychologiczny, 36*, 261–299.

Zajonc, R. B. (1994). An early insight into the affect–perception interface. In P. M. Niedenthal & S. Kitayama (Eds.), *The heart's eye* (pp. 17–21). San Diego: Academic Press.

Zajonc, R. B. (1994). Evidence for nonconscious emotions. In P. Ekman & R. J. Davidson (Eds.), *The nature of emotions: Fundamental questions* (pp. 293–297). New York: Oxford University Press.

Murphy, S. T., Monahan, J. L., & Zajonc, R. B. (1995). Additivity of nonconscious affect: Combined effects of priming and exposure. *Journal of Personality and Social Psychology, 69*, 589–602.

McIntosh, D., Zajonc, R. B., Vig, P. S., & Emerick, S. W. (1997). Facial movement, breathing temperature and affect: Implications of the vascular theory of emotional efference. *Cognition and Emotion, 11*, 171–195.

Winkielman, P., Zajonc, R. B., & Schwarz, N. (1997). Subliminal affective priming is impervious to attributional manipulation. *Cognition and Emotion, 11*, 433–465.

Zajonc, R. B. (1997). Emotions. In D. Gilbert, S. T. Fiske, & G. Lindzey (Eds.), *Handbook of social psychology* (4th ed., Vol. 1, pp. 591–632). New York: McGraw-Hill.

Zajonc, R. B., & Mullally, P. R. (1997). Birth order: Reconciling conflicting effects. *American Psychologist, 52*, 685–699.

Zajonc, R. B. (1999). One hundred years of rationality assumptions in social psychology. In A. Rodrigues & R. V. Levine (Eds.), *Reflections on 100 years of experimental social psychology* (pp. 200–214). New York: Basic Books.

Zajonc, R. B. (2000). Feeling and thinking: Closing the debate over the independence of affect. In J. P. Forgas (Ed.), *Feeling and thinking: The role of affect in social cognition* (pp. 31–58). New York: Cambridge University Press.

Marie, A., Gabrielli, J. D. E., Vaidya, C., Brown, B. R., Pratto, F., Zajonc, R. B., & Shaw, R. J. (in press). The mere exposure effect in patients with schizophrenia. *Schizophrenia Bulletin*.

Monahan, J. L., Murphy, S. T., & Zajonc, R. B. (in press). Subliminal mere exposure: Specific, general and diffuse effects. *Psychological Science*.

Author Index

A

Adelmann, P. K., 31, 37, 42, 53, 56, 67, 177, 185
Adler, A., 145, 152
Alpert, M., 134, 138
Andersen, C. C., 170, 171
Andersen, S. M., 55, 66, 118, 126
Ansfield, M. E., 114, 127
Apter, M., 164, 171
Arbib, M. A., 32, 37
Archer, J., 89, 92
Ariés, P., 133, 138
Arnold, M. B., 72, 92
Ashmore, R. D., 55, 67
Astington, J. W., 135, 138
Atkinson, J. W., 163, 171

B

Baldwin, M. W., 55, 56, 57, 59, 60, 61, 62, 64, 66
Banaji, M. R., 114, 127
Bandura, A., 31, 34
Bargh, J. A., 27, 29, 30, 31, 33, 34, 34, 36, 58, 66, 114, 118, 126, 127, 130
Baron-Cohen, S., 136, 138
Bassok, M., 117, 129
Baumeister, R. F., 34, 35, 81, 83, 92
Beach, L. R., 161, 171
Beebe-Center, J. G., 89, 92
Bem , B. J., 28, 35
Berkowitz, L., 31, 35
Berlyne, D. E., 80, 92
Bernieri, F. J., 31, 35
Berntson, G. G., 87, 92, 96, 97, 98, 99, 102, 103, 104, 108
Berridge, K. C., 77, 78, 91, 92
Birch, D., 163, 171
Birnbaum, M. H., 5, 9
Blass, E. M., 79, 92
Bodenhausen, G. V., 114, 127, 128
Bogart, L. M., 56, 67
Boiten, F. A., 77, 92
Bond, R. N., 29, 34

Bordern, R. J., 127
Bornstein, R. F., 50, 52, 87, 92
Boysen, S. T., 96, 103, 104, 108
Bradley, M. M., 102, 109
Brakke, K. E., 139
Bratslavsky, E., 34, 35
Brehm, J. V., 145, 152
Brekke, N., 113, 130
Brewer, M. B., 27, 35
Brown, J. D., 112, 113, 127, 129
Bruner, J. S., 111, 127, 134, 135, 138, 139
Bühler, C., 82, 92
Bühler, K., 72, 92
Burger, J. M., 145, 152
Burnstein, E., 161, 162, 163, 164, 167, 172
Burrows, L., 33, 35
Buss, A. H., 63, 66
Byrne, R. W., 136, 138

C

Cacioppo, J. T., 87, 92, 96, 97, 98, 99, 103, 104, 108, 109
Campbell, J. D., 112, 127
Cantor, N., 17, 20
Caplan, R. D., 163, 168, 171
Caporael, L., 142, 152
Capps, L., 136, 139
Carrell, S. E., 59, 60, 66
Carver, C. S., 31, 35, 87, 92, 116, 127, 170, 172
Chaiken, S., 29, 30, 34, 35, 36, 123, 128
Chambers, W., 31, 35
Chartrand, T. L., 29, 30, 31, 34, 35
Chen, M., 30, 33, 35
Christensen, S. M., 114, 127
Christie, R., 145, 152
Cialdini, R. B., 113, 127
Cicchetti, P., 105, 109
Cichomski, B., 167, 171
Clark, D. M., 63, 67
Clark, R. E., 106, 108
Clore, G. L., 50, 53
Cole, S. W., 55, 66
Coles, M. G. H., 96, 108

Collins, B. E., 13, *20*
Cook, M., 103, *108*
Cottrell, N. B., 25, *35*
Crites, S. L., Jr., 96, 97, *108*
Croon, M., 143, *153*
Cropley, A. J., 170, *171*
Csikszentmuhalyi, I. S., 75, *92*
Csikszentmuhalyi, M., 75, *92*
Cuthbert, B. N., 102, *109*
Czabala, C., 159, *171*
Czwartosz, Z., 143, *152*

D

Damasio, A. R., 96, 101, *109*
Darley, J. M., 32, *35*
Davis, M., 96, *109*
Dawes, R. M., 142, 144, *152*
De Charms, R., 145, *152*
Dennett, D. C., 137, *138*
Devine, P. G., 27, *35,* 114, *127*
Diener, E., 96, *109*
Dijksterhuis, A., 33, *35, 36*
Ditto, P. H., 124, *127*
Doi, T., 146, *152*
Dovidio, J. F., 106, *109*
Duckworth, K., 30, *36*
Dunham, P. J., 135, *139*
Dunton, B. C., 114, *127*

E

Eagly, A. H., 170, *171*
Ekman, P., 47, *52*
Emmons, R. A., 161, *171*
Erdelyi, H. M., 112, *127*
Erdelyi, M. H., 40, *53*

F

Fazio, R. H., 27, 28, 29, 32, *35, 36,* 114, *127*
Feldman, C. F., 135, *138*
Fenigstein, A., 63, *66*
Ferguson, M. J., 30, *36*
Fiske, A. P., 55, *66*
Fiske, S. T., 12, 17, *20,* 27, *36,* 112, *127*
Fong, G., 124, *129*
Frederick, S. L., 97, *110*
Freeman, S., *127*
French, J. R. P., Jr., 19, *20*
Frey, D., 123, *130*
Friedrich, J., 122, *127*
Frijda, N. H., 73, 77, 84, 87, 90, 91, *92, 93*
Froming, W. J., 31, *35*

G

Gaertner, S. L., 106, *109*
Ganellen, R. J., 31, *35*
Garcia, J., 179, *185*
Garcia, M., 30, *36*
Gardner, W. L., 87, *92,* 96, 97, *108*
Gaver, W. W., 84, 88, *93*
Gazzaniga, M., 105, *109*
Geis, F., 145, *152*
Gibbs, B. J., 50, *53*
Gilbert, D. T., 4, *9*
Giuliano, T., 57, *67*
Gopnik, A., 135, 136, *138, 139*
Govender, R., 29, *34*
Greenberg, J., 112, 116, 123, *128, 129*
Greenwald, A. G., 112, *127*
Gregory, J. C., 80, *93*
Griffin, D. W., 115, *129*
Grzelak, J. L., 143, 146, 148, 150, *152, 154,*
159, *171*

H

Ha, Y., 117, *128*
Haidt, J., 79, *94*
Hamm, A., 103, *110*
Hannan, M. B., 103, *108*
Happé, F., 136, *138*
Hardin, C., 114, *127*
Harrison, A. A., 50, *53*
Hearst, E., 118, *128*
Heingartner, A., 26, *37*
Herman, E. M., 26, *37*
Higgins, E. T., 27, *36,* 56, *67,* 112, 117, 118,
119, *128*
Higgins, T., 4, *9*
Hodgins, H. S., 117, *130*
Holland, J. H., 34, *36*
Holmes, J. G., 56, 57, *66*
Holt, K., 123, *129*
Hommel, B., 31, *36*
Horowitz, M. J., 55, *67*
Hugdahl, K., 103, *110*
Hume, D., 73, *93*
Huntington, S., 156, *171*
Hymes, C., 29, *34*

I

Ibrahim, A., 170, *172*
Iedema, J., 144, *152*
Inglehart, M., 18, *21,* 44, 45, *53*
Ito, T. A., 97, *109*
Ivins, B., 26, *36*
Iwata, J., 105, *109*

J

Jackson, J. R., 114, *127*
James, W., 31, *36*
Jansen, R., 144, *153*
Jetten, J., 114, *128*
Joireman, J., 146, 150, *152*
Jones, C. R., 117, *128*
Jones, E. E., 13, *20*, 32, *36*

K

Kahneman, D., 80, 87, *93*, 96, *109*, 118, *129*
Kalnins, I., 134, *138*
Kaplan, M. F., 106, *109*
Kardes, F. R., 28, *36*
Kelley, H. H., 142, 143, 145, 146, *152*
Kerr, N. L., 144, *153*
Kessen, W., 133, *138*
Kidd, R. F., 26, *36*
Kiesler, C. A., 13, *20*
King, G. A., 117, *128*
Kitayama, S., 83, *93*
Klayman, J., 117, *128*
Klimpel, K., 146, 148, *152*
Knee, C. R., 117, *130*
Koehler, D. J., 118, *128*
Kouvumaki, J. H., 113, *129*
Kruglanski, A. W., 112, 116, *128*
Kubovy, M., 79, 83, 88, *93*
Kuhlman, D. M., 144, 146, 150, *152*, *153*
Kuhlman, M. D., 143, 144, *152*
Kulicka, M., 148, *153*
Kunda, Z., 112, 116, 123, 124, *128*, *129*
Kunst-Wilson, W. R., 5, *9*, 27, *36*

L

Landman, J., 87, *93*
Lang, P. J., 102, 103, *109*, *110*
Langer, E. J., 113, *128*
Latz, E., 137, *139*
Lazarus, R. S., 48, *53*
Leary, M. R., 63, *67*
Leary, R. M., 83, *92*
LeDoux, J. E., 48, *53*, 95, 96, 99, 105, *109*
Lehmann, A., 90, *93*
Lerner, M., 27, *37*
Leslie, A., 136, *138*
Levine, L. M., 56, *67*
Levine, S., 134, *138*
Lewin, K., 73, *93*, 142, *153*, 163, *172*
Liberman, A., 115, 116, 117, 123, *128*, *129*
Liebrand, W. B. G., 144, *153*
Lin, S., 115, *129*

Lombardi, W. J., 29, *34*
Lopez, D. F., 59, 60, *66*, 124, *127*

M

McIntosh, D. N., 43, *53*
Mackie, D. M., 106, *110*
Maclean, P., 88, *93*
Macrae, C. N., 114, *127*, *128*
Main, K., 62, 64, *66*
Maki, J., 144, *153*
Mandler, G., 84, 88, *93*
Marcel, A., 73, 91, *93*
Marin, I. C., 19, *21*
Markus, G. B., 5, 6, 7, *9*, *10*
Markus, H. R., 83, *93*, 112, *128*
Marshall-Goodell, B. S., 104, *108*
Marshello, A. M. J., 143, 144, *152*
Martindale, C., 170, *172*
Mavin, G. H., 117, *128*
McCauley, C. R., 79, *94*
McClintock, C. G., 142, 144, *153*
McTavish, J., 144, *152*
Meertens, R. W., 106, *110*
Mellers, B. A., 5, *9*
Meltzoff, A. N., 135, 136, 137, *138*, *139*
Menzel, E., 136, *139*
Messick, D. M., 142, *153*
Meyer, L. B., 88, *93*
Miedema, J., 33, *35*
Millar, M., 113, *129*
Miller, D. T., 80, *93*, 112, 113, *128*
Miller, N., 14, *20*
Milne, A. B., 114, *128*
Mineka, S., 103, *108*
Mitchell, S. A., 55, *67*
Miyake, K., 117, *130*
Monahan, J. L., 49, 51, *53*
Moore, C., 135, *139*
Moore, J., 113, *129*
Morawski, P., 167, *171*
Moreland, R. L., 5, *9*, 26, *36*, 40, 50, *53*
Morganstern, O., 141, *153*
Muesseler, J., 31, *36*
Mullally, P. R., 6, *10*, 19, *21*
Murphy, J., *139*
Murphy, S. T., 18, *20*, *21*, 27, 31, *36*, 37, 42, 43, 44, 45, 46, 48, 50, 51, *53*, 58, *67*, 91, *93*, 177, *185*
Murraven, M., 34, *35*

N

Nafe, J. P., 73, *93*
Narmour, E., 88, *93*

Nash, J. F., 141, *153*
Neely, J. H., 28, *36*
Nelson, K., 135, *139*
Neuberg, S. E., 27, *36*
Newman, J. P., 118, *128*
Niedenthal, P. M., 31, *37*, 42, *53*, 177, *185*
Nisbett, R. E., 105, *110*, 112, 114, *128*
Nowak, A., 143, *152*, 156, *172*
Nurius, P., 112, *128*

O

Oatley, K., 80, *93*
Ogilvie, D. M., 55, *67*
Ogórek, J., 146, 148, *153*
Ohman, A., 103, *110*
Orbell, J., 142, *152*

P

Panskepp, J., 81, *94*
Papousek, H., 134, *139*
Perner, J., 135, *139*
Pervin, L. W. L., 161, *172*
Pettigrew, T. F., 106, *110*, 161, 163, *172*
Petty, R. E., 104, *108*, 116, *129*, *130*
Pfaffmann, C., 89, *94*
Pietromonaco, P., 58, *66*
Pirsig, R., 175, *185*
Pittman, T. S., 17, *20*
Planalp, S., 55, *67*
Polanyi, M., 57, *67*
Poppe, M., 143, 144, *152*, *153*
Postman, L., 111, *127*
Powell, M. C., 28, *36*
Pratto, F., 29, *34*
Premack, D., 136, *139*
Prentice-Dunn, S., 106, *110*
Pribram, K. H., 85, *94*
Price, R. H., 163, *171*
Prinz, W., 114, *128*
Pyszczynski, T. A., 112, 116, 123, *128*, *129*

Q

Quattrone, G. A., 124, *129*

R

Rajecki, D. W., 26, *36*
Raymond, P., 29, *34*
Reis, D. J., 105, *109*
Reisenzein, R., 91, *94*
Rholes, W. S., 56, *67*, 117, *128*
Rijken, V., 144, *153*
Rimé, B., 83, *94*

Rizzolatti, G., 32, *37*
Rogers, R. W., 106, *110*
Romanski, L., 105, *109*
Rosenzweig, M., 134, *139*
Ross, L., 112, 113, 115, *128*, *129*
Ross, M., 112, *128*, *129*
Rothman, A. J., 114, *127*
Rozin, P., 78, 79, 80, 83, *94*
Rumbaugh, D. L., *139*
Russell, J. A., 91, *94*

S

Saegert, S., 177, *185*
Safran, J. D., 55, *67*
Sanbonmatsu, D. M., 28, *36*
Sanders, G. S., 25, 26, *37*
Sanitoso, R., 124, *129*
Sartre, J. P., 74, *94*
Sattler, D. N., 144, *153*
Savage-Rumbaugh, E. S., 136, 137, *139*
Scaife, M., 135, *139*
Scheier, M. F., 63, *66*, 87, *92*, 116, *127*, 170, *172*
Scherer, K. R., 76, *94*
Schlenker, B. R., 63, *67*
Schooler, J., 114, *130*
Schopenhauer, W., 79, *94*
Schwarz, N., 50, *53*, 96, *109*, 111, *130*
Seligman, M. E. P., 170, *172*
Sevcik, R. A., *139*
Shah, A., 79, *92*
Shaklee, H., 144, *152*
Shelly, G., 146, 150, *152*
Sherman, D. A., 179, *185*
Shizgal, P., 91, *94*, 96, *110*
Showers, C., 17, *20*
Sicoly, F., 112, *129*
Sigman, M., 136, *139*
Slone, L. R., *127*
Slupska, A., 146, 148, *153*
Sluytman, A., 143, *153*
Smith, E. R., 27, *37*
Smith, S. M., 116, *130*
Snell, A., 50, *53*
Snyder, M., 17, *20*, 118, *129*
Spence, E. L., 102, *110*
Spielman, L. A., 118, *126*
Squire, L. R., 106, *108*
Srull, T. K., 27, *37*, 117, *129*
Stachelski, A. J., 143, *152*
Stechler, G., 137, *139*
Steele, C. M., 179, *185*
Stern, D. N., 55, *67*
Stewart, A. J., 157, *172*

Stopa, L., 63, *67*
Stroessner, S. J., 106, *110*
Suhre, C., 144, *153*
Swap, W., 177, *185*

T

Tajifel, H., 113, *129*
Tan, E. S. H., 84, *94*
Tassinary, L. G., 104, *108*
Taylor, S. E., 12, 13, 17, *20*, 112, 113, *127*, *129*, 170, *172*
Telaak, K., 170, *171*
Tesser, A., 113, *129*
Thibaut, W., 142, 145, *152*
Thorne, A., *127*
Tice, D. M., 34, *35*
Titchener, E. B., 72, *94*
Tota, M. E., 29, *34*
Trope, Y., 115, 116, 117, *129*
Tucker, D. M., 97, *110*
Turner, D. R., 114, *127*
Turner, J. C., 113, *129*
Tversky, A., 80, 87, *93*, 118, 124, *129*

U

Uranowitz, S. W., 118, *129*
Urbaniak, K., 156, *172*

V

Vallone, R. P., 115, *129*
Van de Kragt, A., 142, *152*
van Knippenberg, A., 33, *36*
Van Lange, P. A. M., 144, *153*
van Run, C. J., 144, *153*
van Ryn, M., 163, *171*
Varey, C., 50, *53*
Vinokur, A. D., 163, *171*
von Neumann, J., 141, *153*
Vrana, S. R., 102, *110*

W

Wahi, N. K., 19, *21*
Walker, M. R., *127*
Wanshula, L. T., 106, *109*
Waynbaum, I., 43, *53*

Webster's Ninth New Collegiate Dictionary, 41, *53*
Wegner, D. M., 57, *67*, 114, 116, *127*, *129*, *130*
Weinstein, N. D., 112, *130*
Wellman, H., 135, *139*
Wheatley, T., 114, *130*
White, R. W., 81, *94*, 145, *153*
Whiten, A., 136, *138*
Wieczorkowska, G., 142, *153*, 161, 162, 163, 164, 167, *172*
Wieczorkowska-Nejtardt, G., 162, 167, 168, 169, *172*
Wieczorkowska-Siarkiewicz, G., 161, 162, 163, 164, 167, 169, *172*
Wientjes, C. J. E., 77, *92*
Williams, C. J., 114, *127*
Williams, S. L., *139*
Wilson, T, D., 105, *110*, 113, 114, *128*, *130*
Wilson, W. R., 26, *37*
Winkielman, P., 111, 126, *130*
Winter, D. G., 145, *153*
Wolff, W. T., 118, *128*
Wolniewicz, B., 148, 150, *154*
Woodruff, G., 136, *139*
Wundt, W., 72, 89, *94*
Wyer, R. S., 117, 123, *129*, *130*
Wyer, R. S., Jr., 27, *37*

X

Xagorasis, A., 105, *109*

Y

Young, P. T., 79, 89, *94*

Z

Zajonc, R. B., 3, 4, 5, 6, 7, *9*, *10*, 11, 12, 14, 16, 18, 19, *20*, *21*, 25, 26, 27, 30, 31, 32, *36*, *37*, 39, 40, 41, 42, 43, 44, 45, 46, 48, 50, 51, *53*, 56, 58, 59, *67*, 79, 87, 91, *93*, *94*, 95, 99, *110*, 111, 126, *130*, 141–142, 143, 149, *154*, 176, 177, 178, 184, *185*
Zanna, M. P., 106, *109*
Zdanuik, B., 56, *67*
Zeigarnik, B., 82
Zienkowski, L., 156, *172*
Zuckerman, M., 112, 117, 118, *130*

Subject Index

A

Adaptation
  goal-setting style and, 165–168
  group processes, 7–8
  in sociopolitical change in Poland, 155,
    156–160
Aesthetic experience, 83–84, 88–89
Affective functioning, 95
  action disposition and, 90–91
  additivity of nonconscious affect, 48–50
  in approach–withdraw behaviors, 97–100
  automatic evaluation effects and, 30–31,
    40–41
  cognitive functioning and, 5, 7, 17–18,
    39–41, 96
  evaluative component, 74
  experience of pleasure, 73–74
  extreme emotional experience, 88
  information-processing in, 97, 99
  mastery and, 80
  mimicry effects, 31
  in motivational system, 103
  neuropsychology, 5, 7, 47–48, 96–97, 105
  nonconscious influences, 5–6, 7, 18, 50–52
  nonverbal processes in, 41–44
  priming effects, 46–47
  as primitive evaluative mechanism, 101–105
  role of, 95–96
  social psychology conceptualization, 12–13,
    177
  vascular theory of emotional efference,
    43–44
Agency, 7–8
  in authoritarian regimes, 157, 158
  control preferences in social
    interdependence, 145–149
  infant capacity, 134
  self-perceived, 113–115
Altruism, 142, 144–145
  control preferences and, 149
Amygdala, 48, 99
Attentional processes, 28
  experience of pleasure, 72
  in infants, 133–134

Attitudes and beliefs
  in aesthetic experience, 84
  automatic evaluation effects, 28–31
  control preferences in social
    interdependence, 146–149, 151
  goal setting as decision process, 161–163
  latent inhibition, 104–105
  mere-exposure effects, 5, 6, 17, 26–27
  nonconscious influences, 5, 17–18
  nonverbal expression, 41
  perception and, 111–112
  post-communist Poland, 158–160
  pre-reform Poland, 157–158
  See also Preferential believing
Autism, 135, 136
Automatic process
  automatic evaluation effect, 28–31, 40–41
  conditional automaticity, 27–28
  experimental research, 27

B

Birth order, 4–5, 18–19

C

Chameleon effect, 32
Cognitive balance, 14
Cognitive dissonance, 13–14
Cognitive functioning
  affective functioning and, 5, 7, 17–18, 39,
    96
  biased information search, 124–125
  confabulation, 105
  decision-making in post-authoritarian
    regimes, 158
  decision theory, 161
  deviation from rational choice, 141
  in experience of pleasure, 73–74
  formation and maintenance of prejudice,
    106–107
  goal setting as decision process, 161–165,
    169, 170
  in mere-exposure effect, 26–27
  multiple-level model of evaluative
    mechanisms, 102–105

role of communications in, 178
self-perceived control over, 113–115
social motivation effects, 17
social outcome orientations, 142–145
social psychology conceptualization, 3,
  12–16
See also Goal-setting; Hypothesis-testing
Cognitive tuning, 14–16, 25, 56, 177, 179
Communication game, 4
Communications, 4
  activation of stereotypes in, 178–184
  cognitive tuning in, 56, 177, 179
  in construction of cognition, 178
  goal-setting style and, 164–165
  interaction patterns, 56
  noverbal communication of affect, 41–44
Competitive social orientation, 142, 143–145
Confabulation, 105
Conscious and nonconscious processing
  additivity of nonconscious affect, 48–50
  in affective processes, 5–6, 18, 50–52
  automatic evaluation effect, 28–31, 46–47
  conditional automaticity, 27–28
  evidential bias in hypothesis-testing, 118
  experience of pleasure, 75, 77, 78, 91
  experimental testing, 34
  nature of feelings, 72
  preference formation, 5, 6–7, 17–18
  relational schema effects in self-construal,
    57–61
Cooperative social orientation, 142, 143–145
  control preferences and, 149
  as rational choice, 142–143

D

Decision theory, 161
  goal selection in, 161–162
Drive theory of social facilitation, 4–5

E

Epilepsy, 88
Event-related brain potential, 96–97
Evolutionary biology
  adaptive value of pleasure, 78, 83
  role of affect, 95–96, 97–99
  sexual attractiveness, 85–86
Expectancies
  acquiescence bias in hypothesis-testing, 117
  in experience of pleasure, 88–89
  social orientation, 143–144

F

Facial expression
  mimicry, 31–32

priming effects of exposure to authority
  figure, 58–61
spousal resemblance, 32, 42–43
vascular physiology, 43–44
Family factors in academic performance, 5–6,
  18–19
Fear response, 103, 105

G

Goal setting
  activity orientation *vs.* outcome orientation,
    164
  adaptation to social change and style of,
    165–168, 169–170
  assessment of style of, 167
  category width, 161–162
  communication style and, 164–165
  consideration set, 161
  as decision process, 161
  decision theory, 161
  flexibility, 163
  goal-category range, 161–165
  interval strategists, 162, 163–164, 165–168,
    169–170
  personality theory, 161
  planning and, 163–164
  point strategists, 162, 163–164, 165–168,
    169–170
  search costs, 169
Group processes, 177
  adaptation, 7–8
  control preferences, 151
  goal conflicts, 7, 19
  hostility, 19
  preferential believing, 113

H

Head Start program, 137–138
Health behaviors, 123–124
Hostile behavior
  group processes, 19
  stereotype effects, 33–34
Hypothesis-testing
  acceptance and rejection thresholds in, 122
  asymmetric error costs in, 116, 119–125,
    126
  confidence thresholds, 119–121
  evaluative bias in, 116
  evidential bias in, 117–119
  information search for, 124–125
  mechanisms for confirming preferred
    hypothesis, 117, 122–123
  memory processes in, 117–118

motivation, 115
of non-preferred hypothesis, 125
possible decision outcomes, 119
propensity for testing preferred hypothesis, 116–117, 126
pseudodiagnostic testing, 117
termination of testing upon confirmation, 123–124

I

Imitative behavior, 31–32
spousal facial resemblance, 32, 42–43
Immersed experience, 74, 75
Individualist social orientation, 142, 144–145
Infants
agentic behavior, 7, 134
attentional processes in, 133–134
competence, 135
conceptualizations of mentality in, 133–137
enculturation processes, 136–137
intersubjectivity research, 135–136
perception of intentionality by, 137
sociocultural context of research, 133, 137–138
stimulation effects on development, 134
Institute for Social Studies, 8, 155
Intentionality, 27–28
automatic evaluation effects and, 29–30
in enculturation process, 136
in experience of pleasure, 73, 86
in infant development, 137
social interaction and, 141–142, 149
Interpersonal relations
attributions of social motivation, 143–144
contextual factors, 143, 149
control preferences in, 145–149, 151
cued activation of anxiety, 61–65
effects of social orientation, 143–145
goal-setting style and, 164–165
goal valuation in, 142
individual intentionality and, 141–142
infant intersubjectivity research, 135–136
noverbal communication of affect, 41–44
perceptual effects, 31, 32–34
private audience effects, 56–57
rational compromise, 141
relational schemas, 55–56
as source of pleasure, 83, 85, 87
stereotype effects, 33–34
subjective matrix transformation, 142–143
types of social orientation, 142
Intoxication, 88
Irreflexive experience, 74, 75

L

Latent inhibition, 104–105
Learned helplessness, 151

M

Mastery
self-perceived, 113–115
as source of pleasure, 80–81, 84
Maxi-min rule, 141
Memory, in hypothesis-testing, 117–118
Mere-exposure effects, 5, 6, 17, 26–27, 50, 51, 176
affective primacy theory and, 40
Mere-presence theory, 4–5, 6, 16–17, 25, 27, 34
Mimicry. See Imitative behavior
Motivated social cognition, 17
Motivated tactician, 17
Motivation
affective system in, 103
attributions of social orientation, 143, 144
control preferences in social interdependence, 145–149, 151
goal setting as decision process, 161
Hullian drive theory, 4
for hypothesis-testing, 115
mere-exposure effects, 26–27
outcome orientation in social interdependence, 142
pleasure and, 72, 77
positivity–negativity model, 103
social psychology research and theory, 3, 16–17

N

Narcissistic pleasure, 87
Neurophysiology, 5, 7, 18
of affective learning, 105
of approach–withdraw behaviors, 99–101
evaluative functions, 99–102
event-related brain potentials, 96–97
evidence of primacy of affect, 47–48
in imitative behavior, 31, 32
response to aversive stimulus, 100
structure and function of affect system, 96–97
vascular theory of emotional efference, 43–44
New Look, 111–112

O

Optimism, 112–113, 170

P

Pain, 72
as feeling, 73–74
pleasure as absence of, 79–80
process conceptualization, 76
sensation and, 72–73
as subjective experience, 74
Perception
effect on behavior, 31, 32
effects on social interaction, 31, 32–34
preferences and, 111–112
Performance
birth order and, 4–5
family factors, 5–6, 18–19
pleasure of achievement, 80–81, 84
preferential believing about self, 112
presence of others and, 4–5, 6, 17, 25–26
relational schemas in self-evaluation, 57
Pleasure, 7
as achievement and mastery, 80–81, 84
as action phenomenon, 90–91
activity as source of, 81–82
aesthetic, 83–84, 88–89
approach and avoidance model, 78
awareness and, 75, 77, 78, 91
as being able to do things, 84–85
definition and meaning, 71
desire and, 78
engagement and, 75
evaluative component, 74
evanescence of, 72, 73
experience of, 72
as feeling, 72, 73–74
intentionality and, 73, 86
kinds of, 78–79
as monitoring of well-functioning, 85–87, 90
as motivation, 72
motivational qualities, 77
narcissistic, 87
object of, 91
post hoc nature, 75, 76
process conceptualization, 71, 76–78, 90, 91
as relief from pain, 79–80, 86
role of familiarity in, 87–88
sensation and, 72–73
sensory, 79, 89–90
social sources of, 83, 85, 87
as subjective experience, 74
without pleasant feeling, 75–76
Poland
goal-setting style and adaptation to reform, 167–168, 169

pre-reform experience, 157–158
sociopolitical reform experience, 155, 156–157, 158–160
Power relations
control preferences in social interdependence, 145–149, 151
democratic functioning and, 151
Preferenda, 30
Preferential believing
about cognitive control, 113–115
about in-group, 113
capacity for accepting non-preferred believing, 115
evidence for, 112–115
hypothesis-testing process, 116–125, 126
inferences and, 126
self-concept, 112
social psychology conceptualizations, 111–112
Prejudice, 106–107, 114
communicative use of stereotypes and, 179–184
Priming effects, 27, 28–29
additive effects, 48–50
in affective evaluative mechanism, 103
exposure to authority figure, 58–60
primacy of affect and, 46–47
private audience effects, 56–57
Prisoner's Dilemma, 142–143, 144

R

Racial prejudice, 106–107, 114, 179–182
Relational schemas, 55–56
cued activation, 61–65
private audience effects, 56–57
reactions to failure and, 57
as unconscious process, 57–61
Research Center for Group Dynamics, 3, 8

S

SAT scores, 5–6, 177
Schema theory, 55–56
experience of pleasure, 88–89
Scientific method, 175, 184
Self-concept
preferential believing, 112–113
relational schemas in self-evaluation, 57
self-perceived agency, 113–115
Self-fulfilling prophecies, 32–34
Sexual attractiveness, 85–86
Social facilitation theory, 4–5, 6, 8–9, 16–17
Social psychology research and theory
on affect, 12–13, 177

on cognition, 3, 12–16
on motivation, 16–17
Socialization
   development of racial prejudice, 106, 107
   enculturation of infants, 136–137
Sociopolitical change, 7–8
   conception of humanity and, 138
   control preferences in social interaction, 151
   disillusionment with reform, 159–160
   goal-setting style and adaptation to,
      165–168, 169–170
   historical experience, 155–156
   Polish experience, 155, 156–160
   post-authoritarian attitudes, 158–159
Startle reflex, 102–103
Stereotyping, 27
   activation of, in communication, 178–184
   prejudice and, 106–107, 179, 181
   social interaction effects, 33–34
Subliminal presentations, 5, 27
   authority figure, 58–61

T

Thalamus, 48, 99

U

Unconscious processing. *See* Conscious and
   unconscious processing

V

Vascular Theory of Emotional Efference, 43

Z

Zajonc, Robert
   affect research and theory, 17–18, 39–41,
      95, 107
   birth order research, 5–6
   communications theory, 4
   contributions and influence of, 8, 9, 13, 19,
      34, 52, 95, 155, 177, 184, xv–xvi
   education and training of, 3–4, xv
   group process research, 19
   intellectual style, 8–9, 11–12, 26, 176–177,
      184
   nonconscious preference research, 5
   social cognitive theories, 14–16, 25
   social facilitation research, 4–5, 8–9, 16–17

About the Editors

John A. Bargh is professor of psychology and director of the graduate program in social psychology at New York University, where he has been on the faculty since 1981. He graduated summa cum laude in psychology from the University of Illinois in 1977 and received his PhD in psychology from the University of Michigan in 1981. His dissertation that year, under the supervision of his advisor, Robert B. Zajonc, received the annual Dissertation Award from the Society for Experimental Social Psychology. Dr. Bargh is the coeditor of three other books: *Unintended Thought* (with J. Uleman), *The Psychology of Action* (with P. Gollwitzer), and *The Use and Abuse of Power* (with A. Lee-Chai). He is the author of more than 100 research and theoretical publications centering on unintended, nonconscious influences on a person's judgments, emotions, motivations, and behavior. In 1989, Dr. Bargh received the Distinguished Early Career Contribution in Psychology award from the American Psychological Association, and in 1990 he and Peter Gollwitzer were awarded the Max Planck Society (Germany) Research Prize for their collaborative research.

Deborah K. Apsley has been with the University of Michigan since 1985. Currently she is an administrative associate in the School of Information, where she is in charge of human resources and personnel services. She worked formerly for the Department of Psychology, from 1994 to 1999. From 1985 to 1994, she worked for Robert B. Zajonc, first while he was director of the Research Center for Group Dynamics at the Institute for Social Research (ISR), University of Michigan, and then while he was director of the ISR. Most recently, she served as managing editor of the journal *Peers and Preventions: A Journal of Undergraduate Peer Helping Research* (Sherry L. Hatcher, Ed.). In 1998 she received support staff recognition for Outstanding Leadership from the University of Michigan. She received her BS degree from Eastern Michigan University in 1991.